ENTREPRENEURSHIP: NEW PERSPECTIVES IN A GLOBAL AGE

Entrepreneurship:
New Perspectives in a Global Age

Edited by
ANNE DE BRUIN and ANN DUPUIS
Massey University

LONDON AND NEW YORK

Contents

List of Contributors

Rolf D. Cremer, PhD, is Professor of Economics and Pro Vice-Chancellor of the College of Business, Massey University, New Zealand. Concurrently, he is President of Netbig International University, in Nanchang, China. From January 2003, Professor Cremer will join the China Europe International Business School, in Shanghai, China. His research interests cover a wide range of issues, including labour market and employment, international economic relations, and linguistics and economics.

Anne de Bruin, PhD, is Professor of Economics in the Department of Commerce, Massey University at Albany, Auckland, and the Director of the Academy of Business Research, Massey University, New Zealand. Her research areas include labour market dynamics, community solutions to unemployment, new entrepreneurship concepts, and rethinking the welfare state. She is a strong advocate of the benefits of inter-disciplinary research. Several of her recent international journal articles and other publications are in collaboration with colleagues in Sociology, Marketing and Finance.

Ann Dupuis, PhD, is a Senior Lecturer in Sociology in the School of Social and Cultural Studies at Massey University, Auckland, New Zealand. Her current research interests include the changing nature of labour market, especially with respect to non-standard work, women entrepreneurs, urban governance, urban sustainability, urban development and new forms of urban housing patterns.

Patrick Firkin is a Massey University Scholar and researcher with the Labour Market Dynamics Research Project at Massey University, New Zealand. The chapters he has contributed to emerged from the combining of his post-graduate research interests in the sociology of ageing and economic sociology, particularly in relation to the experiences of self-employed people and families.

Kate Lewis is a researcher at the New Zealand Centre for SME Research at Massey University. She has a particular interest in the phenomenon of youth entrepreneurship, and her thesis (an evaluation of the New Zealand Young Enterprise Scheme) formed the basis for chapter 12.

Claire Massey, PhD, is the Director of the New Zealand Centre for SME Research at Massey University. Her research focus is 'enterprise development', i.e. on the processes and systems that can be put in place to help individuals and enterprises become more successful.

Peter Mataira, PhD, was a visiting fellow to the University of Hawaii's School of Social Work when his contribution was written and has now taken up a full time position at the school. He is New Zealand Maori of Ngatiporou and Ngati Kahungunu descent. His research interests include comparative analyses of indigenous entrepreneurship, the politics of tribal development, integrated models of social work practice and community development.

Chris Moore, PhD, is Professor of Finance and Banking and Head of the Department of Finance, Banking and Property at Massey University, New Zealand. His research areas include the banking environment in New Zealand, strategic issues related to banking and banking technology, and sustainability and ethics.

Acknowledgements

One of the joys of completing a project like *Entrepreneurship: New Perspectives in a Global Age*, is the opportunity it affords us to publicly convey our gratitude to those who have helped along the way.

We thank colleague and fellow researcher Patrick Firkin for his assistance to us over the period of writing and editing this book. We benefited greatly from his insightful comments and the excellence of his scholarship. We are sincerely grateful to him.

Important thanks are also due to those who were part of the refereeing process for this book. These include Paul Spoonley, Professor of Sociology and Regional Director, Auckland, of the College of Humanities and Social Sciences, Massey University, Professor Brian Murphy, Department of Commerce, Massey University and the anonymous referees whose comments were most instructive.

We especially thank Dr Ruth Taplin, editor of *The Journal of Interdisciplinary Economics*, who over the years has been supportive of our interdisciplinary research approach, Dr Hedva Sarfati for her support, Jordan Dupuis for his research assistance and Allen Bartley for his technical help.

Several chapters in this book draw on research from the Labour Market Dynamics Project, funded by the New Zealand Foundation for Research, Science and Technology. We acknowledge with gratitude that support. We also acknowledge the funding from the Academy of Business Research Fund, College of Business, Massey University, for the 'Entrepreneurship and Local Communities' project. We are indebted to Massey University, our academic home, whose strong research culture encouraged our efforts. The support throughout the process of the publishers, Ashgate, has been much appreciated.

We also wish to thank the other people in our lives who have helped us through this endeavour – Jan, Anne-Marie, Phillip, Roseanne, Chris, Tim and Jordan.

Chapter 1

Introduction: Concepts and Themes

Anne de Bruin and Ann Dupuis

Inspiration and Rationale

There is almost universal recognition today that entrepreneurial spirit and activity is vital for a market oriented, globally competitive economy. Accompanying this recognition has been a rise in the research and study of entrepreneurship, particularly in the last two decades. Yet despite the burgeoning literature it still appears that 'entrepreneurship research is in its adolescence' (Low, 2001: 17). We agree with Low and believe that insufficient attention has been paid, at both the theoretical and empirical levels, to the vital aspect that Thornton points to, that entrepreneurship occurs 'as a context-dependent, social and economic process' (1991: 20). Our desire to give prominence to the question of context and emphasis to the social aspects of entrepreneurship has thus been an important motivator for this book.

Context is a multi-layered concept, taking in a range of forms and levels. It implies geographical localities: neighbourhoods, communities, cities, regions, nations and the global setting. It also implies social milieu. We are, all of us, part of various social networks based on family, friendships, workplaces, common interests and pursuits and so on. Entrepreneurial activity can occur in a range of other contexts too, that can overlap with those already mentioned. Thus, there are the economic and political contexts, both of which can be seen in local, national or global terms. Of course we acknowledge the connection between context and entrepreneurship is not new. The context, or environment of entrepreneurial operation has been explicitly incorporated by others into entrepreneurship research and analysis. For example, in his small business analysis framework, Julien (1998a) draws attention to the internal and external environment that influences small business activity and decision-making when he notes that, 'small businesses exist in symbiosis with their *environment*, in a system of complex interrelations formed by networks of all kinds and all levels that develop within and outside the region' (Julien, 1998a: 18). Our approach, however, emphasizes entrepreneurship as an embedded activity. We take up the concept of 'embeddedness' later in this chapter and make it an underlying theme of the text.

Embeddedness has become a fundamental platform within the burgeoning field of economic sociology. Focusing on the importance of social networks in economic activity, this theme has been prominent in related work already published by the editors. Additionally, for the last seven years, the editors have been involved in exploring innovative approaches to entrepreneurship. For example, together we have researched and written on entrepreneurship in relation to the informal sector, women entrepreneurs and disadvantaged ethnic minority groups, and at the community and local government levels (de Bruin and Dupuis, 1995a, 1995b, 1999, 2000a, 2000b; Cremer *et al.*, 2001). Independently, and with others, we have produced work theoretically informed by the notions of embeddedness and networks (Dupuis, 1997; de Bruin, 1998; de Bruin and de Bruin, 2002). The book therefore, builds extensively on our research on networks and entrepreneurship.

An important element of our collaboration over the years, has been our overt intention to bridge traditional academic boundaries. Hence, the adoption of an unambiguous interdisciplinary, heterodox approach. The reader will discern strong sociological influences, interwoven through strands derived from feminist, development, and new institutional economics, as well as from management, finance, marketing and social policy. This interdisciplinary approach we see as a major strength in the advancement of entrepreneurship scholarship from adolescence to maturity.

A further aim of the book is to bring closer together the practice of entrepreneurship with the theory of entrepreneurship. We concur with Swedberg when he recommends that, '[i]t would also be good if it was possible to develop more of a direct overlap between practical entrepreneurship, as taught in business schools, and social science research at universities. Both parties would no doubt benefit from this' (Swedberg, 2000: 43). We hope that this text will go some way to bridging the theory/practice divide that Swedberg has observed.

A perceived lacuna in the entrepreneurship literature is the noticeable gap in the theorization of entrepreneurship to meet more local, regional and group-specific needs. This is of particular concern in the context of the new global age, characterized by fragmentation and plurality. Part of our task for this book therefore, is to bring to the attention of readers, new perspectives on entrepreneurship that fit the global age, thus mitigating gaps within the theorization of entrepreneurship and highlighting hitherto overlooked aspects of entrepreneurship which have assumed greater significance in a global age.

Entrepreneurship: An Activity Continuum

As the opening lines of a 1980s article in the Harvard Business Review commented:

> Suddenly entrepreneurship is in vogue. If only our nation's businesses – large and small – could become more entrepreneurial, the thinking goes, we would improve our

productivity and compete more effectively in the world market place. ... But what does entrepreneurial mean? (Stevenson and Gumpert, 1985: 85).

Clarification of this question is vital in any book on entrepreneurship. The literature clearly shows that as the terms entrepreneur and entrepreneurship are frequently applied within a range of settings and widely use with marked variations, so this is no easy task. In fact much attention has been paid in the literature to the nature and sources of these differences (e.g. Long, 1983; Gartner, 1988; Hébert and Link, 1988, 1989; Ripsas, 1998; Bygrave and Hofer, 1991).[1] For instance, Gartner (1988) surveying 32 pieces of significant literature identified 23 definitions of the entrepreneur, though some shared features or agreed on themes. Given these definitional complexities, a shift in emphasis from the entrepreneur to the entrepreneurial process (Bygrave and Hofer, 1991; Shaver and Scott, 1991) or what entrepreneurs do (Gartner, 1988), has been advocated. Of course, this focus simply transfers conceptual difficulties to determining what characterizes any particular business activity as entrepreneurial.

Four key strands of thinking may be identified in relation to entrepreneurship (e.g. Ripsas, 1998; Birkinshaw, 2000). These approaches may be employed singly, or in combination, to define what entrepreneurship involves. Two of these strands link entrepreneurial activity to risk or uncertainty, and innovation. In these terms the entrepreneur is seen as the innovator and as the risk bearer. The second set of approaches portrays the entrepreneur as an intermediary, or opportunity-discoverer and as a co-ordinator.

Notions of risk and uncertainly are not new in the economic tradition. Through the work of Cantillon, ideas of risk were being incorporated into formal economic thinking regarding entrepreneurship early in the 18th century and the work of Knight further developed the relationship between risk and entrepreneurial activity (Hébert and Link, 1989; Ripsas, 1998). Innovation was a key feature of Schumpeter's (1934) highly influential work on entrepreneurship. In his terms, innovation could take various forms: the introduction of a new good, quality of a good, or a new untried method of production; the opening of a new market; the utilization of some new source of supply for raw materials or intermediate goods; or the carrying out of some new organizational form. Thus, the entrepreneur was not the risk bearer, unless he or she owned the resources as well, but rather was the driving force or key agent of change.

Another perspective within the second set of approaches, is that entrepreneurs are those who are alert to previously unnoticed profit opportunities. Distinguishing between interest and entrepreneurial profit, Schumpeter argued, in an essay written as early as 1918, that interest was the return from the ownership of assets, whereas profit is created by entrepreneurial activity, albeit for Schumpeter, activity associated with innovation:

> Entrepreneurial profit proper ... arises in the capitalist economy wherever a new method of production, a new commercial combination, or a new form or organisation is

successfully introduced. It is the premium which capitalism attaches to innovation (Schumpeter, 1991:113).

Yet another view from this second broad approach, emphasizes the entrepreneur as an organizer of factors of production, as first raised by economist J. B. Say early in the 19th century (Glancey and McQuaid, 2000). In a similar vein, Casson (1990) sees the entrepreneur as responsible for determining the best allocation and use of resources and for co-ordinating scarce resources. Into this he incorporates elements of Schumpeter's dynamism, Knight's bearing of economic uncertainty and the alertness to profit opportunity.

A fifth concept which identifies entrepreneurial activity with business founding, may also be delineated. Here entrepreneurship is about the creation of new businesses or organizations (Gartner, 1988; Thornton, 1999). Following on from this view, Gartner (1988) suggests that entrepreneurship ends when this creation stage is over.

Despite the prominence of these various ideas, alongside a wide array of subsidiary positions, there is no single definition of entrepreneurship that is commonly accepted. Though some definitions or themes are employed more often or widely, reservations are usually attached to each one when used outside their context of development, or when the choice of particular criteria would mean excluding those who would, in any terms, be considered entrepreneurial. For example, relying on entrepreneurs to be business founders would exclude Ray Kroc and Thomas Watson who are respectively recognized as responsible for the McDonalds and IBM success stories (Stevenson, 1999). Further difficulties can be illustrated by the problems created in limiting entrepreneurship to business creation. Not only might it be difficult to determine this end point, but questions can be raised about organizations that might undertake periodic 're-creation'. Similarly, owners or operators of even very settled businesses might have to engage in activities similar to those who founded the organization in order to respond to changes in market or economic conditions. That is, they need to be alert to opportunities and might have to take risks, or be innovative, in order to manage a period of change or uncertainty, or organizational restructuring.

A preference for a narrower view, emphasizing the entrepreneur-owner/manager dichotomy with a focus on risk and/or innovation, is similarly problematic. As Aldrich and Waldinger (1990: 112) argue:

> Many writers have suggested making a distinction between entrepreneurs and owner/managers on the basis of innovativeness and risk, but few have done a convincing job. Neither economists ... nor sociologists ... have been able to operationalise this distinction so that "entrepreneurs" are clearly differentiated from "owners" or even the self-employed.

Further, they suggest that risk is likely to be present in most businesses, even the mundane. We agree that there is some degree of risk even in these sorts of activities and add that not considering them entrepreneurial would create a situation, where many small business founders, owners and operators – who contribute an enormous amount to economies such as New Zealand's – might be eliminated from consideration. As to innovation, by observing that 'rather than breaking new ground in products, process or administrative form, most businesses simply replicate and reproduce old forms', Aldrich and Waldinger (1990: 112) seem to imply that a large proportion of the economy would similarly not be considered entrepreneurial using too narrow an interpretation. As Stewart (1991) notes, to some degree risk and innovation are likely to have been present – though, we would add, particularly in relation to the latter, the degree may be minor – in most fledgling enterprises, even if they are no longer apparent once the business is established and settled.

The reverse of a more inclusive approach is, of course, to assert that too broad a definition includes activities that dilute the concept of entrepreneurship of any special meaning, as Long (1983) is at pains to point out. By adding the caveat that a local innovation that copied competitors – and in doing so averted rather than undertook risk – is an example neither of entrepreneurial activity nor of an entrepreneurial firm, Miller (cited in Brazeal, 1999) clearly wants to establish some reduced parameters. Similarly, Sharma's (1999) view that the creation of a new organization need not be associated with any innovative activity, is clearly at odds with the observations regarding innovation presented earlier.

Such debates well illustrate the very different positions adopted by researchers and academics. They also demonstrate the problems in establishing thresholds for ideas such as innovation and risk. Further difficulties can arise when multiple criteria are used for evaluating the entrepreneurial nature of an enterprise. Sharma (1999) illustrates this in relation to using both innovativeness and business founding as markers of entrepreneurship. The argument here is that launching an innovative product or process need not necessitate creating a new organization. More generally, Cameron and Massey (1999: 39) suggest that definitional variations may, in part, be culturally based. They observe that:

> The view that all people in small business are entrepreneurs is commonly found in America and Canada whereas in New Zealand, Australia and Britain entrepreneurs are regarded as the innovative, opportunistic and risk-taking subset of the SME [small and medium enterprise] sector.

Clearly one way to manage the definitional difficulties is to establish at the outset of any discussion of entrepreneurship, what is meant by the use of this concept and its related terminology. As part of this, the requirements of any research or discussion might demand that a particular stance be adopted or prove most useful. What follows is our effort to define what we mean by the term entrepreneurship. Our use of this concept is based on a desire to include in many of the following chapters, work on entrepreneurship that focuses on a broad range of business activity.

As a first step we turn to Long's (1983) synthesis of prominent thinking on entrepreneurship. This isolates three key characteristics that need to be present for the activity to qualify as entrepreneurial. Though they mirror some of the discussion above, there are subtle and important differences. These factors are uncertainty and risk; complementary management competence; and creative opportunism. While his terms are still open to some debate, they give broad but defined and acceptable parameters to the idea of entrepreneurship. Uncertainty and risk, as has been argued, is likely to be present in most ventures, even if only to a small degree or briefly. As will be seen shortly, the introduction of the second factor regarding management competence is interesting for our purposes. Finally, the notion of creative opportunism, rather than innovation *per se*, allows for a much broader range of entrepreneurial activity since we would contend that many people enter business on this basis. It allows some counter to Miller's caveat noted earlier, since we feel that even those replicating businesses are trying to differentiate themselves in some albeit small way, a view that we feel is compatible with creative opportunism.

With these characteristics in mind, we then suggest a model based on the view that entrepreneurship might be more usefully conceived of as a continuum of activity. This possibility is inferred by the very fact that entrepreneurship means so many things to different people and that, as a concept, it is used to imply a range of activities (Hyrsky, 1999). It is further raised by work, such as that of Hébert and Link (1989), in which various theories of entrepreneurship are categorized as either static or dynamic. Both approaches offer possible outer poles for any continuum. Additionally, our continuum approach is supported by models that propose a behavioural spectrum, from entrepreneurial to a more administrative focus (Stevenson and Gumpert, 1985; Stevenson, 1999) and the overlap of the domains of entrepreneurship and management (Davidsson, 2001).

As has already been suggested as a useful distinction (de Bruin, 1998), we employ Leibenstein's (1968) approach, as the basis for our model. Leibenstein identifies two broad forms of entrepreneurship, namely 'routine entrepreneurship' and 'new type' or 'N-entrepreneurship'. Routine entrepreneurship encompasses:

> The activities involved in co-ordinating and carrying on a well-established, going concern in which parts of the production function in use (and likely alternatives to current use) are well known and which operates in well-established and clearly defined markets (1968: 73).

This has some resonance with Hébert and Link's (1989: 41) static forms of entrepreneurship, where the entrepreneur is 'a passive element because his actions merely constitute repetitions of past procedures and techniques already learned and implemented'. The second form, N-entrepreneurship, which Leibenstein acknowledges as Schumpeterian, includes:

The activities necessary to create or carry on an enterprise where not all the markets are well established or clearly defined and/or in which the relevant parts of the production function are not clearly known (Leibenstein, 1968:73).

We feel that using an activity continuum approach overcomes many of the definitional problems outlined above. Though it broadens the meaning of entrepreneurship to take in a range of business activities, it also better evaluates these in terms of their entrepreneurial make up. Such a continuum captures activities such as 'running a business' (Jones, 1998; de Bruin and Dupuis, 2000a), self-employment (Aldrich and Waldinger, 1990; Reynolds, 1991; Blanchflower and Oswald, 1998), and family business (Dyer and Handler, 1994), through to the Schumpeterian innovator or 'swashbuckling' entrepreneur (Casson, 1982). Importantly, however, any enterprise fitting one of these categories need not be identical, in entrepreneurial terms, with another of the same type, but can be evaluated on its own merits.

While some enterprises may match one or another type, the continuum approach allows for the many organizations that might not easily fit into specific categorizations. Thus some sets of activities within particular organizations might be seen as routine, while others could still be characterized in terms of N-entrepreneurship. Additionally, it also allows for this mix to change across time. Though we might be able to easily characterize organizations from cross-sectional snapshots, viewing them longitudinally reveals a more complex and dynamic nature (Stewart, 1991) that this type of continuum might more usefully capture. As well as being able to include the founding of an enterprise, this model incorporates other activities that could be considered entrepreneurial. Importantly, the question no longer has to be: when does entrepreneurship end? Rather it can become: how does it change?

If this model of entrepreneurial activity is adopted, then some compatible notion of the entrepreneur is obviously necessary. Morris (1998) portrays entrepreneurship from an input-output perspective. While the output side emphasizes the variable nature of entrepreneurship and the variety of possible outcomes and consequences that can occur, it is the input side that focuses on the entrepreneurial process. What Morris' model clearly shows is that resources are a vital input to this process and a key role of the entrepreneur is to determine, access and employ the necessary and appropriate resources. This is implicit in Leibenstein's model of entrepreneurial activity. The idea of resources is taken to include the vast array of tangible (e.g. finance, labour, raw materials) and intangible (e.g. ideas, enthusiasm, relationships) inputs that go into a business. In synthesizing a range of thinking in relation to entrepreneurship, Hébert and Link (1989: 47) provide a definition of the entrepreneur that is in keeping with the argument thus far. For them the entrepreneur is 'someone who specializes in taking responsibility for and making judgmental decisions that affect the location, form and the use of goods, resources and institutions'. This could be likened to Long's (1983) compatible management competence. As these authors point out, it covers entrepreneurship in a range of settings and contexts, and, we would add, can include both routine and N-entrepreneurial activity.

The conceptualization of entrepreneurship as a continuum of activity can also fit not only individual, but more collective forms of entrepreneurship. While it is still quite common to associate entrepreneurship with the entrepreneurial activities of individuals and for efforts to stimulate entrepreneurship to focus on building and strengthening the entrepreneurial capacity of the individual, entrepreneurialism is increasingly becoming evident, as well as vital, at more encompassing levels than that of the individual. More recently, however, there has been growing attention to collective entrepreneurship involving shared community outcomes and collective action (see for example Connell, 1999; Mourdoukoutas, 1999). The notions of 'community entrepreneurship', 'municipal-community entrepreneurship' and 'state entrepreneurship' that are discussed in Chapters 7, 8 and 9 respectively in this book, advances this recent awareness of collective entrepreneurship and hinge more on the creation, availing and/or enabling of opportunity and thus opportunity related strategic behaviour. As to the issue of risk taking, it is also more appropriate in the context of public entrepreneurship, to highlight opportunity, for 'after all, who wants bureaucrats taking risks with their hard-earned tax dollars? ... entrepreneurs do not seek risks, they seek opportunities' (Osborne and Gaebler, 1993: xx).

Despite the periodic pleas for conceptual coherence to the study of entrepreneurship (e.g. Davidsson, 2001), as Gartner (2001) eloquently illustrates with his elephant analogy, there is as yet no consensus. He uses the anecdote of the six young blind men to demonstrate that analysis of different parts of a phenomenon do not necessarily provide an understanding of the whole. Determined to discover what the elephant was like, each young man, in his haste, touched different parts of the animal and conveyed their partial perception of what they had touched as the description of the elephant. On so doing they managed to acquire followers to their beliefs. It was the old blind man who took the time and trouble to discover the truth for himself. The relevant question then becomes:

> Can the study of the parts of current entrepreneurship scholarship lead to a comprehensive theory in entrepreneurship? ... The conundrum, as I see it, is that the totality of current academic entrepreneurship research does not espouse (nor can it espouse) an entrepreneurship theory, per se; rather entrepreneurship research espouses a diverse range of theories applied to various kinds of phenomena. ... There is no elephant in entrepreneurship. The various topics in the entrepreneurship field do not constitute a congruous whole (Gartner, 2001: 34).

Our perspective, which presents entrepreneurship as a continuum of activities, overcomes the need to settle on an appropriate definition, or work toward a comprehensive theory in entrepreneurship. The continuum approach allows for the evolving nature of entrepreneurial behaviour and movement along the continuum from more routine to N-entrepreneurial activities; it takes into account different entrepreneurial contexts and is in accord with a range of entrepreneurship notions from more individualistic to collaborative and collective ones.

Entrepreneurship: An Embedded Activity

An analytical strand running throughout this text is that of the embedded nature of economic activity. The embedded perspective locates ongoing social relations as central to any analysis of economic activity, with that activity actually embedded in those relations (Granovetter, 1985). We contend that much entrepreneurial activity is also embedded. Indeed, the particular approaches to entrepreneurship developed in the following chapters highlight the embedded nature of entrepreneurship, either implicitly or explicitly.

The concept of embeddedness serves to counter a major assumption of neoclassical economics observable at two levels: the view of *homo economicus*, or the rational, independent, self-serving actor; and the view of firms behaving in the same rational and calculating way to promote their self-interest. These interests centre on the desire to maximize utility or profit, in accordance with their fixed preferences, and within the limits of scarce resources. Each party is considered to have reasonably full information and act in an individual or atomistic manner. This view of economic activity has been critiqued on a number of counts, one of which is that people simply do not act in the way the neoclassical model depicts. Underpinning this critique is a view of agency that repudiates the atomistic individual and argues that attempts by actors at 'purposive action are instead embedded in concrete, ongoing systems of social relations' (Granovetter, 1985: 487). Further, Granovetter argues that even in the work of such theorists as Becker (1976), who do attempt to take social relationships seriously, the result is little more than a recognition of roles. Roles, however, are not social relationships and do not recognize the 'history of relations and their position with respect to other relations – what might be called the historical and structural embeddedness of relations (Granovetter, 1985: 486). We follow a similar theme in Chapter 2 of this book, in which we base a critique of the rationality assumption of the neoclassical orthodoxy, in part, on a version of the embeddedness perspective, which offers further elaboration on, and an extension of Granovetter's views. The concept also guides the discussion in a number of ensuing chapters including Chapters 5 and 6.

The notion of embeddedness was introduced into the social sciences by the Austrian-born, economic historian, Karl Polanyi, by way of his comparison of economic activity in pre-market societies, with that in modern market societies (Polanyi, 1992). Polanyi argued that economic activity was deeply embedded in the social relations of pre-market, but not market societies, where transactions are characterized 'by rational calculations of individual gain' (Granovetter, 1985: 482). For decades now this view has been dominant in sociology, anthropology, political science and history. Economists, on the other hand, have tended to maintain instead that low levels of embeddedness characterize both types of societies and see social relationships as playing a frictional, or disruptive role in economic activity. The novel aspect of Granovetter's approach is the way he has managed to navigate a pathway through these opposing positions by arguing that the level of embeddedness in non-market societies was lower than claimed by some and in market economies has always been higher than allowed for by others (Granovetter, 1993).

Granovetter's particular take on the concept of embeddedness owes much to his Weberian and social constructionist orientation in that he posits economic action as both socially orientated and socially situated (Swedberg and Granovetter, 1992). Thus economic action must take account of 'the role of concrete personal relations and structures (or "networks")' (Granovetter, 1985: 490) in shaping such action, particularly as they are built up over time. Granovetter distinguishes between two forms of embeddedness; structural and relational. By structural embeddedness he means that 'economic action, outcomes, and institutions are affected by ... the structure of the overall network of relations', whereas relational embeddedness refers to these factors being affected by 'actors' personal relations' (Granovetter, 1990: 98). Hence, Granovetter adds, these networks are contingent and dynamic, they exist at the level of interaction and not as some sort of impersonal force and they affect us to varying degrees and at different points in our daily lives. In this way he is able to maintain some degree of independence for the actor. Embeddedness depicted in this way overcomes the undersocialized view of economic activity dominant in the neo-classical model and the oversocialized version that some sociologists posit, which places undue emphasis on co-operation, conformity and solidarity (Waldinger, 1995: 558).

Evidence in support of the nature, role and importance of embedded social relations in economic activity is being increasingly gathered. Granovetter's own research, for example, highlights the role of embeddedness in influencing the behaviour of employees in firms which, in turn, has implications for organizational activity (Granovetter, 1985). Because embeddedness operates at both the individual and structural levels, its value as a concept is markedly increased. This is evident in the work of Romo and Swartz (1995) who use an embeddedness perspective to help explain company migration. They find that the reluctance of many companies to relocate to areas that might offer better economic incentives is best understood by identifying the nature and strength of their relationships with other businesses that likewise do not relocate. Similarly, Uzzi (1997) examines the functioning of embedded relations within the garment industry in New York and creates a picture of highly developed and important networks that significantly affect the operation of business.

Zukin and DiMaggio (1990) advance the concept by proposing three further dimensions of embeddedness: cognitive, political and cultural. It is their third dimension, cultural embeddedness, which we feel offers interesting and wide-ranging possibilities in developing and exploring the notion of embeddedness and its relationship to entrepreneurship. Cultural embeddedness refers to the role that 'shared cognitions, values, norms, and expressive symbols' have in influencing and shaping economic activity, relationships and institutions (DiMaggio, 1994: 27). Although Granovetter too acknowledges culture, he tends to conflate cultural aspects of embeddedness into his structural schema but, as DiMaggio (1990, 1994) shows, cultural embeddedness may be influential in a wide range of ways and clearly needs to be considered separately from the structural. Indeed, he argues that 'economic processes have an irreducible "cultural" component' (DiMaggio, 1994: 27).

So far embeddedness has been presented somewhat uncritically, but as Portes points out in numerous places, it is all too easy to be seduced by the benefits of a particular concept (Portes, 1995, 1998, 2000a, 2000b; and with Sensenbrenner, 1993). Waldinger (1995), for instance, illustrates the 'other side of embeddedness' in his examination of how the intersection of ethnicity and entrepreneurship can impede access to outsiders. As well as exclusion, Portes (1998) identifies three other negative outcomes from recent studies: excessive claims might be made on group members, individual freedom can be restricted as a result of group membership, and there is the possibility of downward levelling pressure on group members. In his examination of inter-firm relations, Uzzi (1997) identifies what he calls the paradoxes of embeddedness. Some examples of these include embeddedness changing from an asset to a liability with the unexpected loss of a network's core member. Alternatively, over-embeddedness can stifle economic action if the social aspects come to outweigh other aspects of the relationship. Similarly, if relationships that are over-embedded sour, then the firm can be derailed into all sorts of unproductive negative activity, such as spite and revenge.

The idea of atrophied embeddedness has been offered as a means to conceptualizing some of the negative aspects of embeddedness (de Bruin and de Bruin, 2002). As part of a complementary and supplementary explanation for the slowdown in economic growth in Japan in the 1990s, this concept captures the process whereby embedded ties become too entrenched, hindering competitiveness and compromising economic growth. Consequently, embedded ties can become an impediment to growth, flexibility and adaptability to change. The potential that embeddedness offers is lost; it withers or is stifled. We see this concept as a useful means to capture the other side of embeddedness. Examples of atrophied embeddedness are offered, for example, in the discussion of familial entrepreneurship in Chapter 6 and virtual networking is presented as an option for mitigating this danger in Chapter 5.

The Global Age

The sub-title of this book clearly locates entrepreneurship in a global context. However, this is not meant to situate the discussion of entrepreneurship mainly as a global activity. Rather, the purpose is to highlight the possibilities and opportunities for entrepreneurship that the global age creates. Though our focus is on such possibilities, we simultaneously draw attention to the constraints that a global age might impose on entrepreneurship. This point comes through especially strongly in Chapters 2 and 3.

Our choice of the 'global age' terminology is deliberate. It is used to denote a transition to a new era, thus taking into account the importance of historical progression and passing stages. It recognizes epochal change. The global age epithet also overcomes the perception often associated with globalization accounts, which give centrality to the drive toward liberalization of trade and capital markets and/or changes in the world economy that focus on the economic activities of production, distribution and consumption. We concur with the view of Albrow (1997) where:

> Fundamentally the Global Age involves the supplanting of modernity with globality and this means an overall change on the basis of action and social organization for individuals and groups (1997: 4).

Importantly, the term globality rather than globalization, brings 'no connotation of necessary outcome', while the global age hypothesis conveys the significant dimensions of the contemporary transformation that globalization accounts tend to minimize (Albrow, 1997: 5).

Our preference for the global age phraseology, however, cannot absolve the need to make comment on what we understand by 'globalization', since globalization is a contested concept, with varying shades of meaning attached to it, signifying many things to many people. Over a relatively short space of time globalization has not only come into common usage, but has also engendered polarized and often emotive responses. In discussion and evaluation it is seen in positive or negative terms and is often greeted with varying degrees of unease, uncertainty or fascination.

At the outset therefore, it is useful to clarify what we mean by globalization. Guillén (2001: 2), in integrating the work of others, defines it as: 'a process leading to greater interdependence and mutual awareness (reflexivity) among economic, political, and social units in the world, and among actors in general'. Held *et al.* (1999: 16) offer a much more precise definition:

> A process (or set of processes) which embodies a transformation in the spatial organisation of social relations and transactions – assessed in terms of their extensity [stretching across geographical boundaries], intensity, velocity and impact – generating intercontinental or interregional flows and networks of activity, interaction and exercise of power.

Interestingly, given our focus, they situate globalization at one end of a continuum of relations and activities, with local and national and regional at the other end. Thus globalization does not replace or necessarily oppose these others, but rather it stands in a 'complex and dynamic relationship with them' (ibid). This idea of globalization as part of a continuum has resonance with our use of the same concept to capture entrepreneurial activity. Waters (2001) too, provides a similar, if slightly less turgid definition:

> A social process in which the constraints of geography on economic, political, social and cultural arrangements recede, in which people become increasingly aware that they are receding and in which people act accordingly.

Both definitions emphasize the embedded nature of globalization, at various levels, a perspective that we argue also applies to entrepreneurship. Globalization cannot be seen purely in economic terms, but is a social, political, technological and cultural phenomenon as well. These dimensions provide a schema by which we will work through the implications for entrepreneurship. Nevertheless, what globalization means for entrepreneurship essentially is that enterprises need not be geographically restrained, be that in terms of customers, suppliers and other connections or networks that provide ideas, support, knowledge and capital. The implications of the global age for entrepreneurship, however, are more comprehensive. The evolving configurations of the new era that has replaced the modern age, necessitates new thinking and perspectives on entrepreneurship. This is what our book attempts to provide or alert to.

Aspects of the Global Age: Chapter Threads

In this section, we draw attention to some underlying aspects of the global age that are of greater significance, relative to the previous age of modernity. Each chapter of the book therefore, specifically or in general, deals with one or some of these aspects and their implications for entrepreneurial activity.

New Technology

While it is easy to over-emphasize, it cannot be denied, as neo-Schumpeterians stress, that an interrelated set of basic and secondary innovations or 'new technology systems' (Freeman *et al.*, 1982) are crucial dimensions of the global age:

> ... The 'clusters' of innovations are associated with a technological web, with the growth of new industries and services involving distinct new groupings of firms with their own 'subculture' and distinct technology, and with new patterns of consumer behaviour (Freeman et al., 1982: 67-8).

The new age is marked by what Perez (1983, 1985, 1986) termed, a 'new technology style' which is:

... Grounded on the introduction of a cluster or constellation of interrelated innovations both technical and managerial which lead to the attainment of a general level of total factor or physical productivity clearly superior to what was 'normal' with the previous technological style (Perez, 1986: 32).

The low prices of the key factors of production – steel, electricity and petroleum, provided the prerequisite of 'substantial change in the relative cost structure' for the 'Fordist' style which dominated the modern age. Today, however, developments in microelectronics, fibre optics, software engineering, communications, computer and laser technology, collectively referred to as Information and Communication Technology (ICT) all characterize a new technology style. Tylecote (1991) adds new biotechnological developments to talk of a 'microelectronics and biotechnology style', compared with the 'steel and electricity style' of the previous phase. A key feature of the technology style of the old Fordist system was that it was energy intensive. By contrast, the new style is information and knowledge intensive.

The intensification and expansion of global communications and the role of technology are important aspects of the revolutionary face of globalization that we are currently experiencing (Giddens and Hutton, 2000). This has clear implications for entrepreneurship, where new opportunities are opened up for activities and relationships that people can engage in. For individuals or groups, electronic technology offers both entrepreneurial possibilities and tools that can be employed more broadly in the entrepreneurial process. Thus the potential of e-technology, e-commerce and virtual networking in opening up and generating opportunities for specific groups in self-employment is canvassed. Given that they have often grown up surrounded by, and actively engaged with the technology, it fits easily within the entrepreneurial activities of many young people. Alternatively, though older people might be considered outside the ICT world, the success of groups such as SeniorNet demonstrates that this is not necessarily the case. As younger cohorts age they are likely to be more comfortable and familiar with this technology. Certainly, ICT offers forms of work and ways of working that can overcome some of the limitations imposed by the physical aspects of ageing. These themes are extended in both Chapters 11 and 12. While the rise of software development companies, dot.com entrepreneurs and the like, are the most visible forms of entrepreneurship associated with new electronic technology, we signal more broadly, the range of new opportunities in terms of the resource-based perspective of entrepreneurial activity, offered by this medium, in a dedicated chapter – Chapter 5, 'Electronic Entrepreneurship'. Many instances of the facilitative role of technology in entrepreneurship are, however, also provided throughout the book.

The Importance of Ethics

The global age is marked by a rising 'voice of society' which demands concern for sustainable development, including consideration of the global environment – such as the increase in the concentration of green-house and ozone depleting gases and corporate social responsibility. Critical environmental disasters and human rights incidents have recently heightened such societal concern and the imperative for corporate citizenship (Warhurst, 2001). Chapter 3 – 'Ethical Entrepreneurship', specifically addresses this ethical conduct and social responsibility dimension within a framework of opportunity and commercial success, as well as inherent constraint. Although not a dedicated strand of the discussion, Chapters 8 and 10 – 'Municipal-community Entrepreneurship' and 'Indigenous Entrepreneurship', also make mention of the ethical core to entrepreneurship.

The Impacts of Demographic Changes

Changing demographic conditions characterize the transformation to the new age. The rapid ageing of the population is a significant feature of the developed world. This demographic phenomenon, however, has been recently acknowledged as a global trend – at the Second Assembly on Ageing held in Madrid in 2002 and not just an issue for the developed world (Annan, 2002). A 'longevity revolution' is well under way. 'A century ago just 1 per cent of the world's population was aged 65 and over. By the middle of the 21st century this will rise to 20 per cent' (Kirkwood, 2001). Thus Chapter 11 – 'Elder Entrepreneurship', investigates what entrepreneurship might offer 'old age' in the new global age. Ageing is no longer seen as merely a period of decline and withdrawal. Entrepreneurship opens up options for the elderly and the older demographic itself offers entrepreneurial opportunity.

While full employment characterized the 'golden age' of the previous modern age, the current global age is marked by a new international division of labour and high/growing unemployment among certain groups and within particular regions (Thorns, 1992; Littek and Charles, 1995; Cox, 1997; Hodson, 1997; de Bruin, 1999; Munck and Waterman, 1999; OECD, 1999). Older workers are often seen as a vulnerable group in contemporary labour markets. They are susceptible to job losses arising from the restructuring of economies and organizations necessitated by a globally competitive environment, and subsequently often experience difficulties getting re-employed. Chapter 11, 'Elder Entrepreneurship', examines the implications of this trend for entrepreneurial behaviour. Similarly, relatively high youth unemployment also characterizes contemporary labour markets. Moreover, despite a general ageing of the population, some groups, chiefly ethnic minorities and indigenous peoples, are increasingly a young population. Self-employment and community enterprises can open up opportunities for such labour market disadvantaged groups as well as regions. Several chapters, especially

Chapters 7, 8 and 10 on community, municipal-community and indigenous entrepreneurship respectively discuss these entrepreneurial opportunities.

The Role of the Nation State

Of great interest in the globalization debate is whether this process has eroded the power and identity[2] of, or even replaced, the nation-state. Held (2000) explicitly confirms a belief in the retention of the nation state and suggests the idea of a continuum of 'territories'. In his wide-ranging review of the literature and empirical evidence on globalization, Guillén (2001: 16) finds that the process does not undermine the nation-state. Others agree, with Waters (2001: 221) arguing that 'the nation-state will not only continue but proliferate'. However, Waters does feel that its sovereignty and potency have been weakened and, like Held (2000), he also situates the nation-state within a more diffuse political power hierarchy or continuum, that incorporates local, community, civic and regional (by this we mean within states) entities, through to supranational organizations. Rather than becoming entirely powerless, however, Waters (2001) feels that the powers of the nation-state and the way it acts are changing. The global age is thus distinguished by a reconfiguration of the role of the state, a theme taken up in Chapter 9, 'State Entrepreneurship'. The chapter looks at entrepreneurship at the central government and State Owned Enterprise (SOE) level, exploring this as a new dimension of entrepreneurship in the global age. Highlighting the need to re-conceptualize the role and responsibilities of the state in the global age, this chapter provides the new concept of the 'strategic state' to substitute for the welfare state, as the defining role for the state in the global era. The strategic state is strategic in its policy-making and support for entrepreneurship, particularly at the local and regional levels and is itself entrepreneurial.

Although seemingly paradoxical at a superficial level, the growing importance of the local scale and 'locality' is an important aspect of the global age.[3] As Giddens (2000) puts it, globalization is a force that 'pulls away' power and influence from the national and local arenas into the global. As well, it 'pushes downwards' creating pressures for local autonomy. This gives rise to the complex and dynamic relationship between the nation-state and the other entities that Held *et al.* (1999) spoke of. Giddens (2000) draws attention to the variety of possible outcomes that can occur when globalization also 'squeezes sideways' to create new economic and cultural zones, not only across nations but within them as well. Beck (2000) is keen to see what this means for these entities in managing their own affairs. As is apparent in Chapters 7 and 8, we believe that these sub-national entities can act in an entrepreneurial fashion.

For example, the idea of 'community entrepreneurship' is developed in Chapter 7. Community entrepreneurship envisages the community supplying initiative and enterprise for the creation, transformation and expansion of employment creating ventures. It is seen as a possible answer to both a lack of individual entrepreneurial skills and employment opportunities in labour market disadvantaged communities and among ethnic minority groups deficient in conventionally defined human capital. Innovative community efforts are a catalyst in this process. Community entrepreneurship also often involves partnerships with a range of stakeholders. Accordingly, building on the notion of community entrepreneurship, Chapter 8 seeks to capture the entrepreneurial spirit and lead role of local government bodies and organizations, and the various ways they stimulate and promote business activity in their regions, through the concept of 'municipal-community entrepreneurship'.

Culture and Identity

Of course, people need not be bound together by geographical boundaries (such as local municipalities or regions and the like). This is Amin's (1998: 9) point in advocating a relational rather than purely territorial perspective, thereby highlighting the role and importance of 'locally embedded social, cultural and institutional arrangements'. Similarly, in emphasizing the link between the global and the local, Meyer and Geschiere (1999) are keen not to imprison the local in bounded units or nameable groups. Consequently they prefer to talk of cultural closure, arguing as well that globalization reinforces the notion of cultural difference. Thus culture can no longer be treated as a residual category in economic development.

'Identity is people's source of meaning and experience' and identity is an important shaping force in the network society of the global age (Castells, 1997: 6). DiMaggio highlights the role of cultural embeddedness – 'shared cognitions, values, norms, and expressive symbols', in influencing and shaping economic activity, relationships and institutions (1994: 27). Thus cultural embeddedness and identity increasingly matters in the global age, where acculturation as a means to development is flawed. Policies of assimilation and integration, and the need for indigenous groups to lose their identity is no longer a predominant view. Thus for example, Native American Indians do not need to divest their culture of 'Indianness' to develop and the 'Aboriginality' of Aboriginal Australians is accepted as part of Australia's multicultural identity. Indigenous culture and heritage are increasingly being utilized as resources for economic development. Extracting entrepreneurial value from these and other resources, and entrepreneurship as the exercise of capital, becomes the main theoretical conceptualization contained in Chapter 4, 'Entrepreneurial Capital'. Chapter 5, 'Electronic Entrepreneurship' further operationalizes this concept and extends it by articulating the notion of the entrepreneurial value chain.

Since the global age opens up many more possibilities for belonging, there is likely to be a proliferation of 'multiple cross-cutting identities and hybrid or syncretic, cultural forms' (Holton, 2000: 148). This means that it need no longer be membership of the dominant group or culture, and possession of their knowledge and attributes, that necessarily lead to greater entrepreneurial opportunities and success. Instead, two forms of entrepreneurial possibilities can be seen to arise from what Giddens has described as the squeezing sideways and pushing downwards effects of globalization. One centres on the potential for cultural groupings to provide goods and services for themselves in ways that better satisfy the members of that group. The second extends this to providing these goods and services outside of the group since, as Beck (2000: 144) puts it, the 'world market rewards difference'. According to Beck (2000), however, these possibilities require new combinations of economics, culture and politics, a challenge which leads to our interest in indigenous entrepreneurship, evident in Chapter 10. The potential for marginalization of certain groups in the global age is also highlighted in this chapter, with the relatively low socioeconomic status of indigenous peoples being the case in point here.

Chapter 10 contends that entrepreneurial activity, at multiple levels, is a crucial element of any action package to enhance the economic development of indigenous peoples. At the more overarching level, the novel notion of 'heritage entrepreneurship' is put forward and argued to be necessary to acquire and secure cultural heritage resources. At the next more macro level, effective tribal entrepreneurship is proposed as a prerequisite for deriving commercial value from tribally owned resources. Tribal entrepreneurship includes indigenous enterprises at the larger community, reservation based or regional levels. Finally at the micro level of the individual and family, entrepreneurship, normally equated with self-employment, is also necessary to provide greater employment opportunities.

Identity is an important element of globalization at the individual level, since it provides a means whereby people try to '"fix the flow" and mark boundaries in the ongoing flux of globalization processes' (Meyer and Geschiere, 1999: 7). However, identity is no longer a necessarily closed, narrow, fixed and trajectory-like notion. While acknowledging the contradictory impact of globalization on identity, Hall (1992) recognizes that the global age is characterized by plural identities, bringing with them a variety of new possibilities and new positions of identification, thereby making identities 'more positional, more political, more plural and diverse; less fixed, unified and trans-historical' (1992: 309). Thus, the identity of the entrepreneur need not be fixed to a particular person or personality and, for example, people may no longer feel restrained by their age from engaging in entrepreneurial activity. Hence our interest in such activity at the two ends of the age spectrum as covered in Chapters 11 and 12, 'Elder Entrepreneurship' and 'Youth Entrepreneurship' respectively. As discussed in Chapter 12, it would appear, for instance, that the youth of today possess far more entrepreneurial potential than previous generations and many of them are selecting self-employment as an expression of this characteristic. Clearly the environment in which individuals exist can exert great influence over their perceptions about work and enterprise. Aspects of the environment that seem to have encouraged an increase in self-employment activity by the young are unlikely to dissipate. Alternatively, it is also being suggested that self-employment is an emerging trend for older people for a range of reasons, both positive and negative.

Concluding Comment

Our intent for this book has been to provide a fresh and innovative approach to an issue of great consequence in today's world. Its interdisciplinary objective is achieved, most obviously, through the melding of economics and sociology. However, the work of scholars from a number of other disciplines, including management, marketing, finance and social policy, augments and enhances the core concepts of the book. A flexible and expansive perspective on entrepreneurship is adopted which conceptualizes entrepreneurial behaviour and activity as a continuum. As the title indicates, a major concern of this book is the location of entrepreneurship in the new global age. A number of themes and threads drawing on this concern provide coherence throughout the text. The theme of the embedded nature of economic activity and relations is fundamental in a number of chapters. Other themes of major significance include the importance of new technology, ethics, and culture and identity. Of consequence too, is the insight that entrepreneurship can be located at various institutional levels, and promoted within wider social groupings. Together these perspectives and themes provide the agenda for our interpretation of entrepreneurship in a global age.

Notes

1. This represents just a small sample of literature in this area. The myriad of typologies of entrepreneurs and small businesses (see e.g. Garand, 1998; Julien, 1998a, for a discussion and summary), also adds to conceptualization complexities.
2. The question of identity and the construction and plurality of identity in the global age is a complex one (see e.g. Castells, 1997: 5-67). Confounding the issue are interpretations of 'ethnicity in the global age' (Albrow, 1997: 197-200). We take up the dimensions of identity later in this section as well.
3. The meaning of the words 'local', 'locality', 'localism' and the related word 'community', together with their associated approach to economic development, is by no means clear-cut. For a discussion see Julien (1998b).

Acknowledgement

We wish to thank colleague and fellow researcher Patrick Firkin for his assistance to us over the period of writing and editing this book. With much generosity he provided perceptive and thoughtful commentaries at critical points in the process. We are sincerely grateful to him.

References

Albrow, M. (1997), *The Global Age: State and Society Beyond Modernity*, Stanford University Press, Stanford, CA.

Aldrich, H. and Waldinger, R. (1990), 'Ethnicity and Entrepreneurship', *Annual Review of Sociology*, No. 16, pp. 111-135.

Amin, A. (1998), 'Globalization and Regional Development: A Relational Perspective', *Competition and Change*, Vol. 3(1/2), pp. 145-164.

Annan, K. (2002), *The Challenge of Building a Society Fit for All Ages*, Opening Address of the Secretary-General of the United Nations to the Second World Assembly on Ageing, Madrid, Spain, April 2002. http://www.un.org/ageing/coverage/pr/socm3.htm (accessed 15 April, 2002).

Beck, U. (2000), *What is Globalization?* (trans. by P. Camiller), Polity Press/Blackwell Publishers, Cambridge.

Becker, G. (1976), *The Economic Approach to Human Behavior*, University of Chicago Press, Chicago.

Birkinshaw, J. (2000), *Entrepreneurship in the Global Firm*, Sage, London.

Blanchflower, D. and Oswald, A. (1998), 'What Makes an Entrepreneur?', *Journal of Labour Economics*, Vol. 16(1), pp. 26-60.

Brazeal, D. (1999), 'The Genesis of Entrepreneurship', *Entrepreneurship: Theory and Practice*, Vol. 23(3), pp. 29-46.

Bygrave, W. and Hofer, C. (1991), 'Theorising about Entrepreneurship', *Entrepreneurship: Theory and Practice*, Vol. 16(2), pp. 13-22.

Cameron, A. and Massey, C. (1999), *Small and Medium-sized Enterprises: A New Zealand Perspective*, Longman, Auckland.

Casson, M. (1982), *The Entrepreneur: An Economic Theory*, Martin Robertson, Oxford.

Casson, M. (1990), *Entrepreneurship*, Edward Elgar, Aldershot.

Castells, M. (1997), *The Power of Identity*, Blackwell, Malden.

Connell, D. (1999), 'Collective Entrepreneurship: In Search of Meaning', http://www.djconnell.ca/articles/CollEntrep.pdf (accessed 11th August, 2002).

Cox, C. (ed.) (1997), *Spaces of Globalization: Reasserting the Power of the Local*, Guilford Press, New York.

Cremer, R., de Bruin, A. and Dupuis, A. (2001), 'International Sister-Cities: Bridging the Global-Local Divide', *American Journal of Economics and Sociology (Special Invited Issue: City and Country: An Interdisciplinary Collection of Original Articles and Case Studies)*, Vol. 60(1) (January), pp. 377-402,

Davidsson, P. (2001), 'Towards a Paradigm for Entrepreneurship Research', *RENT XV Research in Entrepreneurship and Small Business 15th Workshop, November 22-23, 2001 Turku, Finland Conference Proceedings*, Small Business Institute, Turku School of Economics and Business Administration.

de Bruin, A. (1998), 'Entrepreneurship in a New Phase of Capitalist Development', *The Journal of Interdisciplinary Economics*, Vol. 9(3), pp. 185-200.

de Bruin, A. (1999), *Escaping the Constraints of the New International Division of Labour: A Culture Based Approach*, Department of Commerce, College of Business Working Paper series (No. 99.07), Massey University at Albany, Auckland.

de Bruin, A. and de Bruin J. (2002) 'Atrophied Embeddedness: Towards Extending Explanation of Japan's Growth Slowdown', *The Journal of Interdisciplinary Economics*, Vol. 13(4), pp. 401-427.

de Bruin, A. and Dupuis, A. (1995a), 'A Closer Look at New Zealand's Superior Economic Performance: Ethnic Employment Issues', *British Review of New Zealand Studies (BRONZS)*, No. 8, pp. 85-98.

de Bruin, A. and Dupuis, A. (1995b), *An Examination of Ethnic Group Differential Employment Growth in New Zealand*, School of Applied and International Economics, Discussion Paper, No. 95-2, Massey University at Albany, Auckland.

de Bruin, A. and Dupuis, A. (1999), 'Towards a Synthesis of Transaction Cost Economics and a Feminist Oriented Network Analysis: An Application of Women's Street Commerce', *American Journal of Economics and Sociology*, Vol. 58(4), October, pp. 1-21.

de Bruin, A. and Dupuis, A. (2000a), 'Constrained Entrepreneurship: An Interdisciplinary Extension to Bounded Rationality', *The Journal of Interdisciplinary Economics*, Vol. 12(1), pp. 71-86.

de Bruin, A. and Dupuis, A. (2000b), 'The Dynamics of New Zealand's Largest Street Market: The Otara Flea Market', *International Journal of Sociology and Social Policy*, Vol. 20(1/2), pp. 52-73.

DiMaggio, P. (1990), 'Cultural Aspects of Economic Action and Organisation', in R. Friedland and A. Robertson (eds), *Beyond the Marketplace: Rethinking Economy and Society*, Aldine de Gruyter, New York.

DiMaggio P. (1994), 'Culture and Economy', in N. Smelser and R. Swedberg (eds), *The Handbook of Economic Sociology*, Princeton University Press, Princeton, NJ.

Dupuis, A. (1997), *Housing Wealth and Inheritance: A Theoretical and Empirical Exploration*, unpublished Doctoral Thesis, University of Canterbury, Christchurch.

Dyer, W. and Handler, W. (1994), 'Entrepreneurship and Family Business: Exploring the Connections', *Entrepreneurship: Theory and Practice*, Vol. 19(1), pp. 71-83.

Freeman, C., Clark, J. and Soete, L. (1982), *Unemployment and Technical Innovation*, Frances Pinter, London.

Garand, D. (1998), 'Entrepreneurship: Entrepreneurs and Small Business Owner-Managers' in P. Julien (ed.), *The State of the Art in Small Business and Entrepreneurship*, Ashgate, Aldershot and Brookfield, pp. 117-149.

Gartner, W. (1988), '"Who is an Entrepreneur?" Is the Wrong Question', *American Journal of Small Business*, Vol. 12(4), pp. 11-32.

Gartner, W. (2001), 'Is There an Elephant in Entrepreneurship? Blind Assumptions in Theory Development', *Entrepreneurship: Theory and Practice*, Vol. 25 (Summer), pp. 27-37.

Giddens, A. (2000), *Runaway World: How Globalization is Shaping our Lives*, Routledge, New York.

Giddens, A. and Hutton, W. (2000), 'In Conversation', in W. Hutton and A. Giddens (eds), *On the Edge – Living with Global Capitalism*, Jonathon Cape, London.

Glancey, K. and McQuaid, R. (2000), *Entrepreneurial Economics*, Macmillan Press, London.

Granovetter, M. (1985), 'Economic Action and Social Structure: The Problem of Embeddedness', *American Journal of Sociology*, Vol. 91(3), pp. 481-510.

Granovetter, M. (1990), 'The Old and the New Economic Sociology: A History and an Agenda', in R. Friedland and A. Robertson (eds), *Beyond the Marketplace: Rethinking Economy and Society*, Aldine de Gruyter, New York, pp. 89-112.

Granovetter, M. (1993) 'The Nature of Economic Relationships', in R. Swedberg (ed.), *Explorations in Economic Sociology*, Russell Sage Foundation, New York.

Guillén, M. (2001), 'Is Globalization Civilizing, Destructive or Feeble? A Critique of Five Key Debates in the Social Science Literature', *Annual Review of Sociology*, Vol. 27, pp. 235-260.

Hall, S. (1992), 'The Question of Cultural Identity', in S. Hall, D. Held and T. McGrew (eds), *Modernity and its Futures*, Polity Press/Open University Press, Cambridge.

Hébert, R. and Link, R. (1988), *The Entrepreneur: Mainstream Views and Radical Critiques*, Praegar, New York.

Hébert, R. and Link, R. (1989), 'In Search of the Meaning of Entrepreneurship', *Small Business Economics*, No. 1, pp. 39-49.

Held, D. (ed.) (2000), *A Globalizing World?: Culture, Economics, Politics*, Routledge, London.

Held, D., McGrew, A., Goldblatt, D. and Perraton, J. (eds) (1999), *Global Transformations: Politics, Economics and Culture*, Polity Press and Stanford University Press, Cambridge and Stanford, CA.

Hodson, R. (ed.) (1997), *The Globalization of Work*, JAI Press, Greenwich, CT.

Holton, R. (2000), 'Globalization's Cultural Consequences', *Annals, AAPSS*, Vol. 570, Special Edition, pp. 140-152.

Hyrsky, K. (1999), 'Entrepreneurial Metaphors and Concepts: An Exploratory Study', *International Small Business Journal*, Vol. 18(1), pp. 13-34.

Jones, G. (1998), *Don't Throw the Baby Out with the Bath Water: A Positive Interpretation of Transaction Cost Theory*, Working Paper, Department of Management, Texas A&M University, June.

Julien, P. (1998a), 'Introduction', in P. Julien (ed.), *The State of the Art in Small Business and Entrepreneurship*, Ashgate, Aldershot, pp. 1-20.

Julien, P. (1998b), 'Small Business and Local Development', in P. Julien (ed.), *The State of the Art in Small Business and Entrepreneurship*, Ashgate, Aldershot, pp. 46-75.

Kirkwood, T. (2001), Reith Lectures 2001 on Ageing, www.bbc.co.uk/radio4/reith2001/ (accessed 1 April, 2002).

Leibenstein, H. (1968), 'Entrepreneurship and Development', *American Economic Review*, Vol. 58(2) pp. 72-83.

Littek, W. and Charles, T. (1995), *The New Division of Labour: Emerging Forms of Work Organisation in International Perspective*, Walter de Gruyter, New York.

Long, W. (1983), 'The Meaning of Entrepreneurship', *American Journal of Small Business*, Vol. 8(2), pp. 47-56.

Low, M. (2001), 'The Adolescence of Entrepreneurship Research: Specification of Purpose', *Entrepreneurship: Theory and Practice*, Vol. 19(1), pp.17-25.

Meyer, B. and Geschiere, P. (1999), 'Introduction', in B. Meyer and P. Geschiere (eds), *Globalization and Identity: Dialectics of Flow and Closure*, Blackwell, Oxford and Malden, MA.

Morris, M. (1998), *Entrepreneurial Intensity: Sustainable Advantages for Individuals, Organisations, and Societies*, Quorum Books, Westport, CT.

Mourdoukoutas, P. (1999), *Collective Entrepreneurship in a Globalizing Economy*, Quorum Books, Westport, CT.

Munck, R. and Waterman, P. (1999), *Labour Worldwide in the Era of Globalization: Alternative Union Models in the New World Order*, St. Martin's Press, New York.

OECD (1999), '*Labour and Employment Practices in Today's Global Economy: Implications for the OECD Guidelines on Multinational Enterprises*', report on a meeting of management experts held under the OECD Labour/Management Programme, Paris, 10 March, 1999.

Osborne, D. and Gaebler, T. (1993), *Reinventing Government: How the Entrepreneurial Spirit is Transforming the Public Sector*, Plume, New York.

Perez, C. (1983), 'Structural Change and Assimilation of New Technologies in the Economic and Social Systems', *Futures* (October), pp. 357-75.

Perez, C. (1985), 'Microelectronics, Long Waves and World Structural Change: New Perspectives for Developing Countries', *World Development*, Vol. 13(3), pp. 441-463.

Perez, C. (1986), 'Structural Change and Assimilation of New Technologies in the Economic and Social System', in C. Freeman (ed.), *Design, Innovation and Long Cycles in Economic Development*, Frances Pinter, London.

Polanyi, K. (1992), 'The Economy as Instituted Process', in M. Granovetter and R. Swedberg (eds), *The Sociology of Economic Life*, Waterview Press, Boulder, CO, pp. 29-51.

Portes, A. (1995) 'Economic Sociology and the Sociology of Immigration: A Conceptual Overview', in A. Portes (ed.), *The Economic Sociology of Immigration: Essays on Networks, Ethnicity and Entrepreneurship*, Russell Sage Foundation, New York, pp. 1-41.

Portes, A. (1998), 'Social Capital: Its Origins and Applications in Modern Sociology', *Annual Review of Sociology*, Vol. 24, pp. 1-24.

Portes, A. (2000a), 'The Two Meanings of Social Capital', *Sociological Forum*, Vol. 15(1), pp. 1-12.

Portes, A. (2000b), 'Social Capital: Promises and Pitfalls of its Role in Development', *Journal of Latin American Studies*, Vol. 32, pp. 529-547.

Portes, A. and Sesenbrenner, J. (1993), 'Embeddedness and Immigration: Notes on the Social Determinants of Economic Action', *American Journal of Sociology*, Vol. 98(6), pp. 1320-1350.

Reynolds, P. (1991), 'Sociology and Entrepreneurship: Concepts and Contributions', *Entrepreneurship: Theory and Practice*, Vol. 16(2), pp. 47-70.

Ripsas, S. (1998), 'Towards an Interdisciplinary Theory of Entrepreneurship', *Small Business Economics*, Vol. 10, pp. 103-115.

Romo, F. and Schwartz, M. (1995), 'The Structural Embeddedness of Business Decisions: The Migration of Manufacturing Plants in New York State, 1960 to 1985', *American Sociological Review*, Vol. 60, December, pp. 874-907.

Schumpeter, J. (1934), *The Theory of Economic Development*, Harvard University Press, Cambridge, MA.

Schumpeter, J. (1991), R. Swedberg (ed.), *The Economics and Sociology of Capitalism/ Joseph A. Schumpeter*, Princeton University Press, Princeton, NJ.

Sharma, P. (1999), 'Towards a Reconciliation of the Definitional Issues in the Field of Corporate Entrepreneurship', *Entrepreneurship: Theory and Practice*, Vol. 23(3), pp. 11-28.

Shaver, K. and Scott, L. (1991), 'Person, Process, Choice: The Psychology of New Venture Creation', *Entrepreneurship: Theory and Practice*, Vol. 16(2), pp. 23-45.

Stevenson, H. (1999), 'A Perspective on Entrepreneurship', in W. Sahlman, H. Stevenson, M. Roberts and A. Bhidé (eds), *The Entrepreneurial Venture*, Harvard Business School Press, Boston, MA.

Stevenson, H. and Gumpert, D. (1985), 'The Heart of Entrepreneurship', *Harvard Business Review*, March-April, pp. 85-94.

Stewart, A, (1991), 'A Prospectus on the Anthropology of Entrepreneurship', *Entrepreneurship: Theory and Practice*, Vol. 16(2), pp. 71-91.

Swedberg, R. (2000), *Entrepreneurship: The Social Science View*, Oxford University Press, New York.

Swedberg, R. and Granovetter, M. (1992), 'Introduction', in M. Granovetter and R. Swedberg (eds), *The Sociology of Economic Life*, Westview Press, Boulder, CO, pp. 1-28.

Thorns, D. (1992), *Fragmenting Societies? A Comparative Analysis of Regional and Urban Development*, Routledge, London.

Thornton, P. (1999), 'The Sociology of Entrepreneurship', *Annual Review of Sociology*, Vol. 25, pp. 19-46.

Tylecote, A. (1991), *The Long Wave in the World Economy*, Routledge, London and New York.

Uzzi, B. (1997), 'Social Structure and Competition in Interfirm Networks: The Paradox of Embeddedness', *Administrative Science Quarterly*, Vol. 42, pp. 35-67.

Waldinger, R. (1995), 'The "Other Side" of Embeddedness: A Case Study of the Interplay of Economy and Ethnicity', *Ethnic and Racial Studies*, Vol. 18(3), pp. 555-580.

Warhurst, A. (2001), 'Corporate Citizenship and Corporate Social Investment: Drivers of Tri-Sector Partnerships', *The Journal of Corporate Citizenship*, 1, Spring, pp. 57- 73.

Waters, M. (2001), *Globalization* (2nd edition), Routledge, London and New York.

Zukin, S. and DiMaggio, P. (1990), 'Introduction', in S. Zukin and P. DiMaggio (eds), *Structures of Capital: The Social Organisation of the Economy*, Cambridge University Press, New York, pp. 1-36.

Chapter 2

Constrained Entrepreneurship

Anne de Bruin and Ann Dupuis

Introduction

This chapter presents and extends the concept of 'constrained entrepreneurship' as developed earlier by the authors (de Bruin and Dupuis, 2000; Dupuis and de Bruin, 2000), to provide an alternative to the view of entrepreneurship as an atomized, profit driven activity, which proceeds in an unfettered manner. The main purpose of this chapter is to heighten awareness of the entire context in which entrepreneurial activity is located. We put forward the constrained entrepreneurship construct, not as a model, but rather as a broad framework for contextual studies of entrepreneurship, noting that all entrepreneurship occurs within constraints: of social processes including institutional restraints at the macro level, and of cognitive limitations at the micro level of the individual. The concept is also hypothesized as a means of advancing an interdisciplinary synthesis, which is so necessary for a holistic perspective for understanding not only entrepreneurship, but all economic activity.

Our journey toward the development of the notion of constrained entrepreneurship commences with a critique of the neoclassical, orthodox view of rationality. From this critique, we take as the starting point for our conceptual development the notion of 'bounded rationality', which has become the basis of a well-developed alternative to the neoclassical hypothesis of the rational economic actor.

The concept of bounded rationality, introduced by Herbert Simon, differentiates between 'the perfect human rationality that is assumed in classical and neoclassical economic theory and the reality of human behaviour as it is observed in economic life' (Simon, 1992: 3). While the mainstream neoclassical economics condition of 'perfect human rationality' locates constraints in the external environment, the bounded rationality perspective has constraints mainly emanating from human cognitive limitations. Given their incomplete knowledge and limited processing capabilities, individuals substitute 'satisficing' behaviour for the maximizing behaviour of pure rationality (Simon, 1957). Satisficing behaviour is conceptualized in terms of satisfactory outcomes and '[A] decision-maker who chooses the best available alternative according to some criterion is said to optimize; one who chooses an alternative that meets or exceeds specified criteria, but that is not guaranteed to be either unique or in any sense the best, is said to satisfice' (Simon, 1987: 243). Thus for example, the objective of a satisfactory level of profits can be substituted for the profit maximization motive of the firm.

We argue that bounded rationality, to some extent, erodes the atomistic model of rational economic action central to the economic orthodoxy, where individuals make economic (and other) decisions as if they were doing so independently of the social settings in which they operate. Thus bounded rationality may be seen as an improvement on orthodox rationality and its recognition of constraints provides a starting point for developing our own concept of constrained entrepreneurship. The springboard of inspiration for the concept, however, comes from transaction cost economics (TCE), where bounded rationality is a key behavioural assumption. Our constrained entrepreneurship construct is therefore posited, not only as a necessary complement to the behavioural hypothesis of bounded rationality, but also an inclusive framework from which to extend the TCE[1] perspective.

Constrained entrepreneurship provides a means of extending TCE through incorporation of the Coasian insight that the development of TCE has tended to lose sight of the raison d'être of the firm, that of 'running a business' (Coase, 1988a). We assert that entrepreneurship usually goes hand in hand with running a business, which necessarily must take account of the significance of transaction cost economizing. The narrow focus of TCE, however, tends to underplay both entrepreneurial qualities at an individual level as well as entrepreneurial activity at a broader contextual level. The constrained entrepreneurship framework, by contrast, enables the incorporation of entrepreneurial elements which are integral to the successful running of a business.

Behavioural Underpinnings

In navigating towards our conceptualization of constrained entrepreneurship we use as our intellectual compass, the core behavioural assumption of rationality. In this section, we commence with outlining the neoclassical approach to rationality and point to major strands in the critique of this approach. By delineating and highlighting the shortcomings of rationality, this section serves to set the stage for the transition to our new concept.

One of the foundations of neoclassical economics is the core assumption of maximizing rational economic behaviour (Dequech, 1999). When definitions of economics emphasize this rationality perspective, the dominance of the conventional behavioural model in economic analysis is confirmed. Illustrative is Richard Posner's definition:

> Economics is the science of human choice in a world in which resources are limited in relation to human wants. It explores and tests the implications of the assumption that man is a rational maximizer of his ends in life, his satisfactions – what we shall call his 'self interest' (1972: 1).

The above definition captures the essence of the economics orthodoxy – that of egotistic 'economic man' driven solely by utility maximization. This standard '...assumption of the 'economic man' relentlessly pursuing self-interest in a fairly narrowly defined form has played a major part in the characterization of individual behaviour in economics for a very long time' (Sen, 1987a: 69). It also typifies the masculinist approach of the neoclassical economics standpoint.

It is no surprise, given the obvious plurality of motivations that characterize human behaviour, such as other-centredness, sentiments and emotions, that the self-interest pillar of rationality would be the subject of strong criticism equally from economists and non-economists. Nobel Prize winning economist Amartya Sen for instance has been among the harsh critics of the self-interest thesis (Sen, 1977, 1987b). Even Adam Smith, often cited as the originator of the self-interest behavioural hypothesis in economics, recognized the general importance of other motivations in human behaviour (see for example Winch, 1978; Brennan and Lomasky, 1985; Sen, 1987b; Coase, 1994). Nevertheless, the maximization-self interest characterization of rational behaviour is a simple, convenient, assumption that makes possible the specification of complex economic models, such as general equilibrium models, which can then used to derive significant theoretical predictions. Less easy to incorporate in modelling, however, is the behaviour of agents who do not act in a self-interested manner.

The unrealistic focus of the perfect rationality assumption of a large body of economic models has come in for heavy criticism. Many economists contend, however, that the validity and usefulness of economic models is not the realism of their assumptions but rather the testability of their predictions on the basis of actual economic data. As Langlois and Csontos remark, '...one of the most widespread, and most naïve, complaints about neo-classical economic models is that the behavioural assumptions they incorporate are "unrealistic"' (1993: 114). Nevertheless in this connection we firmly subscribe to the view of Sen who protests that '...the entire enterprise of getting to actual behaviour via models of rationality may itself be seen as methodologically quite dubious' (Sen, 1987a: 71).

Powerful critiques of the conventional model of rationality have come from both within and outside the economics discipline. The new institutional economics, mounts an effective challenge to the mainstream notion of the maximizing rational economic actor. Rationality 'in a true sense' is a common thread running through this approach (Langlois, 1986a, 1986b). A true sense of rationality exemplifies rejection of rationality based on perfect knowledge. This flawed neoclassical perspective of economic behaviour is captured in the caustic words of Simon as:

> The dream of thinking out everything before we act, of making certain we have the facts and know all the consequences, is a sick Hamlet's dream. It is a dream of someone with no appreciation of the seamless web of causation, the limits of human thinking, or the scarcity of human attention (Simon, cited in Loasby, 1989: 140-141).

The new institutional economics by contrast, recognizes the limited ability of individuals to 'take account of all the available information, compile exhaustive lists of alternative courses of action, and ascertain the value and probability of each of the possible outcomes' (Hindess, 1988: 69).

New institutional economics is chiefly associated with two key proponents, Douglas C. North and Oliver Williamson. North argues that although maximization behavioural assumptions may be of use for finding solutions to some economic problems, 'they are the stumbling block preventing an understanding of the existence, formation and evolution of institutions (North, 1990: 24). North's institutional focus adopts 'procedural rationality', which considers 'whether the procedures or rules that agents apply in order to reach decisions are sensible or rational' (Knudsen, 1993: 268). This approach is distinct from Williamson's, TCE focus on bounded rationality.

The popularity of the bounded rationality rubric has grown among economists dissatisfied with the '"perfect rational man" paradigm' (Rubinstein, 1998: 2). It has recently come to prominence in the field of experimental economics and attempts have been made to model bounded rationality especially through strategic games (Radner, 1996; Friedman, 1998; Rubinstein, 1998; Selten, 1998; Baak, 1999). The concept has also been embraced in disciplines outside economics. For example, additional experimental data and observations on deviation from optimal rational economic behaviour have been collected by psychologists who have then elaborated on other factors that contribute to bounded rationality, mainly human passions (see for example Oatley, 1992; MacLeod, 1996; Kaufman, 1999). Most recently (Wolozin, 2002), has signalled the need to incorporate the role of the unconscious and psychoanalytic theory in the analysis of economic behaviour.

An alternative to the rational individual of neoclassical economics who is both maximizing and consistent, is presented by socio-economist Amitai Etzioni when he puts forward the ideas of 'instrumental rationality' (1988: 144-165) and 'collective (macro) rationality' (1988: 185-198). Instrumental rationality relates to decision-making based on the collection and processing of information and evidence and reaching conclusions through this process. 'The term *instrumental* rationality is used because the definition views the actor as pursuing goals ... the definition focus is on the selection of means. The information amassed and utilized is used in finding efficient, "suitable", means' (1988: 144). It is thus argued that '...people are to be viewed as commanding varying degrees of instrumental rationality, rather than as being either rational or non-rational' (1988: 151). Through extending instrumental rationality of decision-making to social collectivities, macro-rationality is introduced. Etzioni emphasizes here that not only are social collectivities major decision-making units but they also often provide the context within which individual decisions are made (1988: 186).

Important challenges to the economic orthodoxy also arise outside the discipline of economics. For example, the embeddedness thesis has provided sociologists with a strong theoretical framework from which to critique neoclassical assumptions of rationality (see Chapter 1 for an extended discussion of the concept). The concept of embeddedness originated in the work of Karl Polanyi and others within the substantivist school in anthropology (Polanyi 1944; Polanyi *et al.*, 1957), but was incorporated into contemporary sociology by the economic sociologist Mark Granovetter (1985, 1992a). Polanyi (and other modernists) argued that during the modernization process the economy, which was socially embedded in traditional societies, became increasingly differentiated or separated. This view contrasted strongly with the dominant view in neoclassical economics and within the formalist school of anthropology, which saw individual utility maximizing behaviour as characterizing economic behaviour across both traditional and modern societies.

The key contribution Granovetter made to this debate was to effectively critique both the substantivist and formalist positions. His argument was that:

> The level of embeddedness of economic behavior is lower in nonmarket societies than is claimed by substantivists and development theorists, and it has changed less with "modernization" than they believe; but ... this level has always been and continues to be more substantial than is allowed for by formalists and economists (Granovetter, 1985: 482-483).

Granovetter's reworking of the embeddedness concept is his attempt to address the major sociological debate over the extent to which either agency or structure predominantly shapes behaviour, including economic behaviour. Drawing on the work of sociologist Dennis Wrong, Granovetter has critiqued both the oversocialized view of human action that has prevailed in functionalist and Marxist sociology and privileged structure, and the undersocialized view that characterizes classical and neoclassical economics, whereby:

> ... [T]he theoretical arguments disallow by hypothesis any impact of social structure and social relations on production, distribution, or consumption (Granovetter, 1985: 483).

Granovetter's path through this debate was to point to a major similarity between the undersocialized and oversocialized views of action, in that they both shared:

> A conception of action and decision carried out by atomized actors. In the undersocialized account , atomization results from narrow utilitarian pursuit of self-interest; in the oversocialized one, from the fact that behavioral patterns have been internalized and ongoing social relations thus have only peripheral effects on behavior (Granovetter, 1985: 485).

Granovetter's view was that the atomization evident in both these extreme positions should be avoided. He argued that people do not behave as atoms, outside a social context, but nor do they 'adhere slavishly to a script written for them' (Granovetter, 1985: 487). Instead it should be recognized that all behaviour is embedded in concrete, ongoing systems of social relations, which should then become the theoretical and empirical foundation for debates on economic activity and decision making.

Granovetter's development of the embeddedness concept is underpinned by two major sociological ideas: first, the pursuit of economic goals is normally accompanied by the pursuit of non-economic goals, such as sociability, and second, as already outlined, that economic action, like all action, is socially situated and must therefore be explained not solely by a focus on individual motivations, but also by an analysis of ongoing networks of personal relations in the form of social networks (Granovetter, 1992a).

The benefits (and costs) that can be derived from social networks have been well traversed (see Chapter 1). For example, Burt (1992: 78) delineates both informational and control benefits which accrue from privileged positions within the network. Informational benefits can come from both relational and structural embeddedness (Granovetter, 1990, 1992b), where relational embeddedness refers to the affect of personal relations on economic action, outcomes, and institutions, and structural embeddedness refers to these factors being shaped by 'the structure of the overall network of relations' (Granovetter, 1990: 98). Gulati (1998: 296) takes up Granovetter's point on relational embeddedness to show how fine-grained information can be gained directly from strong personal ties.

The embeddedness critique is fundamental to the development of the concept of constrained entrepreneurship we develop in this chapter. Constrained entrepreneurship focuses on the broader social context in which entrepreneurship (as a form of economic action) develops, thus embracing notions of structural embeddedness. Relational embeddedness is incorporated in the feminist perspective we adopt (see also de Bruin and Dupuis, 1999a).

A further critique of the model of rationality underpinning the economic orthodoxy is provided by feminist writers, both outside of and within economics. This body of work has also been influential in shaping our concept of constrained entrepreneurship. In particular, we draw on feminist critiques of the philosophy of science that focus on the masculinization of scientific thought and the specific type of rationality that has consequently come to dominate the contemporary world. We also incorporate work that demonstrates the connection between these feminist views and feminist critiques of the model of the rational economic man (REM), who is such a strong pillar within the economic orthodoxy.

Nelson (1993: 23) claims that the narrow definition of economics that is 'currently dominant in the most highly regarded research and in the core of graduate study', focuses on mathematical models that assume individual choice. Such a definition is far removed from Adam Smith's view of economics which also took into account how societies were provisioned (see also Georgescu-Roegan, 1966, 1970, Sen, 1984, and Boulding, 1986, who extended the notion of provisioning in various ways). A definition of economics that includes provisioning blurs the boundaries between the economic and the social, the public and the private (Nelson, 1995: 143). Other feminist writers like Merchant (1980), Keller (1985) and Bordo (1986, 1987) offer us a perspective that allows us to see the narrowness of the economic orthodoxy as reflecting gender-biases within science. Such biases have their roots in the development of western scientific thought that arose in the sixteenth and seventeenth centuries and are associated with Enlightenment philosophies and the growth of industrial capitalism. During this early transition period the previous connectedness of humans with a female, living nature changed to a detachment, whereby men became objective observers and controllers of nature, which itself became redefined. While still female, nature took on a passive image. The new worldview that emerged represented an understanding of science associated with masculinity, detachment and domination and femininity with nature, subjectivity and submission (Keller, 1985).

Underpinning this view of science is the acceptance of a way of thinking and knowing based on a Cartesian-type reason, often referred to as Cartesian, emanating from the philosopher Descartes. Feminists have strongly critiqued this view on the grounds of its gendered character. For example, Bordo (1986) has described this form of reason as the 'pure masculinization of thought'. Quoting from Hillman she demonstrates the way western, rational, scientific thought has been consciously depicted as masculine and superior:

> The specific consciousness we call scientific, Western and modern is the long sharpened tool of the masculine mind that has discarded parts of its own substance, calling it 'Eve', 'female' and 'inferior' (Hillman, cited in Bordo, 1986: 441).

In the Cartesian view, scientific thinking has come to be identified with all that is rational, detached, abstract and masculine, and clearly viewed as superior to the material reality inhabited by women, which is viewed as irrational, connected, concrete and emotional (see for example, McMillan, 1982; Lloyd, 1984; Hekman, 1994). While some feminists have focused on the development of such dualisms in the thought of the male Enlightenment philosophers, others, such as Irigaray (1985) trace it back to the ancient Greeks. Regardless, there is definite agreement that such dualisms are not constructed innocently, but are asymmetric, with the masculine side of the dualism perceived as superior and the feminine side subordinate. It is commonly argued by feminists that the rationality/irrationality (or rationality/emotionality) dualism is just one of many such dualisms like culture/nature, mind/body, public/private and aggression/passivity, that have come to be accepted as intrinsic descriptors associated with gender differences (see for example Sydie, 1988).

Feminist economists have been equally critical of the centrality of rationality in orthodox assumptions.[2] For example Nelson (1996: 22), in her discussion of the contemporary definition of economics, differentiates what she terms a core model of economics from a marginalized model. The subject of the core economic model is the self-interested, autonomous, rational, choice-making individual, the REM, while the subject of the marginalized model is social, other-oriented, dependent, emotional and directed by 'an intrinsic nature'. Hewitson (1995: 143) underscores the almost inhuman quality of the REM when she describes him as 'a logically asocial being; his relationships in no sense define him, being simply instrumental in the achievement of his self-defined ends'. Hyman (1994) offers a further critique of the rationality assumption of the economic orthodoxy, highlighting that what is important is not what the models include, but rather what factors are ignored. Included are such factors as selfishness and competition and ignored are non-economic motives, interdependence among individuals and concern for others, all characteristics most often associated with women's behaviour.

In the following section we outline our interdisciplinary alternative to the rationality foundation of neoclassical economics. However, it is important to emphasize that our intention is not to dismiss rationality *per se*. Nor should our substitution of the concept of constrained entrepreneurship imply irrationality. To do this, would be to indulge in a form of dichotomization of thought that does not mesh with the feminist perspective from which we are operating. Instead, our concept of constrained entrepreneurship is intended to complement (and extend) bounded rationality and to reinforce the usefulness of the TCE approach, if due recognition is given to the fact that running a successful business cannot rely simply on either transaction cost economizing or entrepreneurial activity, but must involve both these activities.

Transition to 'Constrained Entrepreneurship'

In this section we develop our construct, constrained entrepreneurship, providing not only a necessary complement to bounded rationality, but also an inclusive framework from which to analyse the running of a business. Our initial transition is from TCE to a focus on entrepreneurship. This focus is empirically advantageous and allows for a way of framing analyses that are more outward looking, context oriented and dynamic. Within this entrepreneurial focus, to complete the conceptual transition to constrained entrepreneurship, we extend the idea of 'boundedness' to the idea of constraints, which is capable of capturing both macro and micro level analyses of the new institutionalism, as well as incorporating a more feminist perspective.

The development of TCE followed from Coase's original emphasis that firms exist in order to save on transaction costs (Coase, 1937). A core aspect of transaction cost economizing revolves around contractual arrangements, which also determines the relative efficiency of particular organizational forms. This contractual focus of TCE, however, has led to a tendency to downplay other significant aspects of the activity of firms. Coase himself, much later in his career drew attention to this, with what appears to us to be an element of regret:

> The way in which I presented my ideas has, I believe, led to or encouraged an undue emphasis on the role of the firm as a purchaser of the services of factors of production and on the choice of the contractual arrangements which it makes with them. As a consequence of this concentration on the firm as a purchaser of the inputs it uses, economists have tended to neglect the main activity of a firm, running a business (1988a: 37-38).

Jones (1998) argues that 'running a business' translates into being an entrepreneur. This, however, does not imply dismissal of the significance of transaction cost economizing, which is especially important in relation to the purchase of inputs. In fact our earlier applications of TCE (de Bruin and Dupuis, 1999a, 1999b) which studied women street vendors in the informal sector, identified the economization of transaction costs as an important facet of their economic activity. Nevertheless, the narrow focus of TCE tends to underplay both entrepreneurial qualities at an individual level, as well as the conduct of entrepreneurial activity at a broader contextual level. Considering women's entrepreneurial activity within a broader contextual approach might involve an examination of such factors as: the impact of economic restructuring; the rise of feminism and the accompanying idea that 'girls/women can do anything'; enhanced skill development largely brought about by higher educational levels and attainment and thus an increase in human capital; and changes in both attitudes and practices in funding and lending institutions that better support women's entry into new business ventures. The current context, even if it is characterized by change and uncertainty, still affords greater 'choice' for economic activity than previously possible, albeit within constraints. It is the ability to perceive and take advantage of opportunities to create and add value, while simultaneously economizing on transaction costs, that we argue is the hallmark of successfully running a business. We acknowledge this as entrepreneurship.

The change of focus from transaction cost economizing to entrepreneurship is empirically advantageous in that it allows for a way of framing analyses that are more outward looking, context oriented and dynamic. A further advantage of shifting the TCE emphasis to entrepreneurship is that this better conveys that the market too involves institutional structures and entrepreneurial activity. Harking back to another Coasian remonstration that '[A]lthough economists claim to study the working of the market, in modern economic theory the market itself has an even more shadowy role than the firm' (1988b: 7). Taking up the challenge of giving more substance to the working of the market, Wang (1999: 783) leaves no doubt that 'the provision of the market itself requires entrepreneurial efforts' and institutional structures that economize on transaction cost. Our shifted focus is capable of capturing both these entrepreneurial and institutional requirements of market exchange.

As discussed in the 'Introduction' to this text, defining entrepreneurship is notoriously difficult task. However, the non-specific entrepreneurship framework we have developed can fit not only the heroic stereotype of the 'swashbuckling business adventurer' (Casson, 1982: 6) but also the Schumpetarian innovator who initiates new permutations, be it organizational form, product, process or supply source (Schumpeter, 1934), and can additionally provide a useful vehicle for taking into account the contemporary phenomenon of corporate entrepreneurship, the concept which is exemplified in yet another Coasian observation: '[w]hat I meant by the entrepreneur is the hierarchy in business which directs resources and includes not only management but also foremen (sic) and many workmen (sic) ...

no single individual is responsible for the final control of the firm' (Coase, 1991: 59). The framework we adopt for the analysis of entrepreneurship is thus an overarching one that can subsume a variety of classifications and taxonomies. It fits neatly with the notion of entrepreneurship as a continuum of activity we presented in the 'Introduction'. Thus, for example, following Sharma and Chrisman (1999) it can encompass both independent entrepreneurship, whereby an individual or group commence a stand alone new business, and corporate entrepreneurship which can be a varied process within an existing organization, whereby an individual or group act as a catalyst for innovation or renewal within the organization itself, or the creation of a new, usually subsidiary, organization. We have, however, added to the individual/corporate distinction with the concepts of community entrepreneurship, municipal-community entrepreneurship and state entrepreneurship (see Chapters 7, 8 and 9). Similarly, the framework can incorporate Thornton's classification of entrepreneurship into the supply side perspective, which focuses on individuals, their characteristics and suitability to occupy entrepreneurial roles and the demand side perspective, which emphasizes the number and nature of the entrepreneurial roles themselves that need to be filled (Thornton, 1999: 20).

Shifting the TCE focus to entrepreneurship can also embrace risk and uncertainty in a more positive fashion than through recourse to opportunism. In the Williamson TCE version, behavioural uncertainty arises from opportunism, i.e. 'self-interest seeking with guile' (1985:47), and has a significant impact on the magnitude of transaction costs. In Chapter 8 we argue that entrepreneurship can, but need not necessarily, be based on risk taking. In fact, with regard to entrepreneurship on the part of local and national states, we endorse the position that entrepreneurship should involve seizing opportunities or setting in place strategies that are responsive but measured, and do not rely on risk taking. While opportunism can occur, it is not a necessary assumption for incorporating uncertainty into the analytical framework. Furthermore, entrepreneurship in allowing for the incorporation of embeddedness subsumes the use of embedded ties as a means of attenuating uncertainty. Thus, for instance, relational embeddedness can mitigate against uncertainty by serving both as an information conduit and a trust mechanism (see, for example, Uzzi, 1996).

Having already made the link between TCE and entrepreneurship we take up again the bounded rationality assumption of TCE, to complete the transition to constrained entrepreneurship. Bounded rationality is the 'cognitive assumption' that lies at the core of TCE (Williamson, 1985: 45). The distinction between the neoclassical orthodox view of rationality and the revisionist approach of TCE is well captured by Simon's definition of bounded rationality as '*intendedly* rational, but only *limitedly* so' (1961: xxiv). It is almost self-evident that especially in the face of imperfect knowledge, behaviour is boundedly rational or satisficing, or 'rule-following', rather than maximizing (Langlois and Csontos, 1993). To some extent this rationality concept erodes the atomistic model of economic activity central to the economic orthodoxy, since inherent in the notion of 'boundedness' is an implicit recognition of the constraints of the wider social context. Nevertheless, it still represents an undersocialized view of the economic actor. It does, however, provide an intermediary link to the incorporation of a broader, as well as more explicit perspective of constraints which our concept embodies.

In our application of TCE to the study of women in street vending, mentioned earlier, we argued that these vendors exhibited bounded rationality, in that they used their 'limited' competence to best advantage (de Bruin and Dupuis, 1999a). However, we eschewed the use of limited as 'cognitive competence' in the sense used by Williamson (1985: 46). In our view, the women street vendors in our study were perfectly competent cognitively. The only limitations we discovered were to do with information bounds and formal educational training. This focus on 'limitations', however, left no room for the entrepreneurial spirit they demonstrated, which our concept of constrained entrepreneurship can readily incorporate.

We now turn to the question of our choice of the word constrained. We believe that the choice of words selected to express concepts is quite crucial, intrinsically carrying with it imagery and word pictures. Viewed from a feminist perspective for instance, the term 'bounded' conjures up images of entrapment and constriction, as for example in the past Chinese practice of binding women's feet. It is a masculinist-oriented terminology. By contrast, we view the term 'constrained' as less restrictive, allowing for flexibility, explicitly taking account of context and offering avenues for entrepreneurial opportunities.

Our choice of the term constrained is also consistent with the way sociologist Zygmunt Bauman uses the term. Bauman sees social action as operating within a context of both freedom and dependence, and importantly, that group membership is a condition through which social action occurs. There are certain similarities between Bauman's insights and Granovetter's views on embeddedness, in that they both provide the context in which social action takes place. Bauman argues that while group membership enables freedom, as it provides the possibilities and frameworks in which action can occur, it is also simultaneously constraining, in that it draws borders around freedom, by fixing 'the territory within which ... freedom may be properly exercised' (Bauman, 1990: 23-24). Thus Bauman provides a somewhat different view of constraints, the double-edged aspect of which we find appealing and appropriate when connected with entrepreneurship. Hence our notion of constraints as an area in which action can be 'properly exercised'.

An additional benefit of incorporating constraints as integral to our concept is its ability to subsume the TC critique of the micro perspective within the new institutionalism of organization studies and in particular take account of the 'constrained-efficiency framework' (Roberts and Greenwood, 1997). The crux of the TCE explanation for the existence of a specific organizational form lies with the efficiency of its governance structure relative to other alternatives (Winter, 1991). This is a comparative-efficiency framework for understanding organizational design adoption. It incorporates constraint chiefly through its behavioural assumption of bounded rationality, but does not explicitly consider institutional constraints, though as we acknowledged earlier, bounded rationality implicitly takes account of context and hence constraint. By contrast, the more dynamic constrained-efficiency account of organizational design adoption and evolution integrates the TC and institutional perspectives, to purposefully recognize cognitive limitations and the institutional environment. Analyses which explicitly embody a more encompassing view of constraint can also explain why less than optimally efficient organizational designs persist.

Finally, a significant feature of constrained entrepreneurship is that it provides a bridge between TCE and challenges to rationality constructs from outside the discipline of economics. It may be viewed as a possible synthesis of TCE ideas with embeddedness in economic sociology, and is more feminist oriented (de Bruin and Dupuis, 2000).

Contemporary Consumer Society

This penultimate section sets out the underlying features of the current consumer age, to contend that our notion of 'constrained entrepreneurship' better meshes with this consumer culture. Ritzer pointed out that the essence of contemporary capitalism, at least in the advanced, mature capitalist economies, 'may not be so much maximizing the exploitation of workers as the maximization of consumption' (1998: 68). Thus:

> The distinctive mark of the consumer society and its consumerist culture is not, however, consumption as such; not even the elevated and fast-rising volume of consumption. What sets the members of consumer society apart from their ancestors is the emancipation of consumption from its past instrumentality …In the consumer society, consumption is its own purpose and so is self-propelling (Bauman, 2001: 12).

An investigation of the history of consumerism reveals that the principal motive of consumption moved from 'need', which was finite, and set limits on the extent of consumption, to the less circumscribed and more flexible, 'desire', which has now been discarded in favour of 'wish' (Ferguson, 1992, 1996; Bauman, 2001). The recognition of wish as the principal motive force for consumption has, as Bauman so neatly phrases it, meant that:

> Consumer society has achieved a previously unimaginable feat: it reconciled the reality and pleasure principles by putting, so to speak, the thief in charge of the treasure box. Instead of fighting vexing and recalcitrant but presumably invincible irrational wishes, it made them into faithful and reliable (hired) guards of rational order (Bauman, 2001: 16).

In today's consumer society or as Beck (1992) would argue the 'risk society', there is also a continual search for finding ways and means of obtaining assurances of certainty. There is an ontological yearning for predictability. Holiday companies that sell pre-packaged 'action holidays', and McDonalds restaurants, in that they offer a sense of security within a controlled environment, have comprehended this consumer wish (Ritzer, 1998). At the same time, however, as Bauman points out so forcefully with his example of the Y2K bug, or the 'millennium (hum) bug' as he cynically calls it, 'uncertainty generated anxiety is the very substance that makes individualized society so fertile for consumerist purposes. ...More often than not, production of consumers means the production of 'new and improved fears' (Bauman, 2001: 27).

The nature, complexity, paradoxes and demands of this contemporary consumer society, is the general environment that running a business must take account of, either explicitly or implicitly. All entrepreneurship is thus constrained at an overarching level in that it must work within the bounds of the consumer society and cater to the 'wish' of the consumer. Yet, just as the consumer has choice in the fulfilment of wish, so too the entrepreneur can exercise choice within constraints, in so much as it is possible to create and manipulate consumer wish, for example, through calming anxieties or providing secure havens in a sea of uncertainty.[3] The concept of constrained entrepreneurship has the capacity to recognize both the impediments and opportunities afforded by the present day form of consumerism. Similarly, by moving into the shadows, yet acknowledging the bounded rationality underpinnings of entrepreneurial activity, it provides a better fit with the acceptance that in contemporary consumer society irrational wishes could be part of rational order.

Conclusion

Constrained entrepreneurship supplies a broad underpinning notion that simultaneously moves away from the optimizing free rein of the neoclassical economic actor, to encompass a perspective that explicitly accounts for not only the cognitive limitations of the individual, but also the broader restraints to economic activity, such as social norms and values. It may be worthwhile to point out here, however, that this notion of constraints is distinct from the idea of obstacles or barriers to entrepreneurship (for instance the lack of venture capital, limited networks and social capital etc.) that are frequently discussed in the body of entrepreneurship/self-employment literature.

More specifically, we present constrained entrepreneurship as a two fold conceptual extension to TCE and its behavioural assumption of bounded rationality. First, we elaborate on Coase's recent insight that the narrow focus on TCE has neglected consideration of the main activity of the firm, that of running a business. Here we pick up on the idea that running a business translates into being an entrepreneur. Second, we expand the idea of boundedness with that of constraints. Our reason for this is not simply whim, or for the sake of novelty, but rather one that recognizes the subtle power of words and the imagery they conjure up, as well as the notion that possibilities exist within the context of constraints. Thus the concept of constrained entrepreneurship, while still retaining worthwhile aspects of TCE, offers a complement to the narrow path that TCE has traversed. The value of the concept lies not only in that it is less confining and more adaptable than bounded rationality, but also in the fact that it gives explicit consideration to context and entrepreneurialism.

Furthermore, at the micro level of business organization, the explicit incorporation of constraints in our notion of constrained entrepreneurship, can explain either the selection of particular organizational designs, or why adoption of efficient design may be hindered. By offering connections to social network analysis in economic sociology and to institutionalism in organization studies, as well as being a more feminist oriented construct, the concept moves an interdisciplinary synthesis a step forward and away from 'the boundaries of particular doctrines and the narrow confines of a single point of view' (Ferber and Nelson, 1999: 782). In the true spirit of interdisciplinary scholarship we draw on, for example, the sagacious insights of economist Ronald Coase and sociologist Zygmunt Bauman. Finally, we assert that the concept is able to work within the all-enveloping climate of consumerism, which driven as it is by consumer wishes, imposes constraints, yet in its very malleability also affords choice. Thus, as we highlighted, 'constrained' does allow for flexibility and the proper exercise of action, albeit within limited territory – in this latter instance, consumer society. Entrepreneurship, despite being constrained, retains an elemental dynamism that can both take advantage of and create opportunity.

Notes

1. The term transaction costs have attracted a number of different definitions. In fact it has been observed that 'few words in the economic language have been more abused or fought over' than the term transaction costs (Allen, 1998: 2 of 31). Swedberg (1990: 115) defines transaction costs as 'costs other than price incurred in trading goods and services'. Coase (1988b: 38) focuses more on the function of transaction costs, which he defines as 'the cost of using the price mechanism'. Williamson's contractual focus is demonstrated in his definition of transaction costs as 'the ex ante costs of drafting, negotiating, and safeguarding an agreement and, more especially, the ex post costs of maladaption and adjustment that arise when contract execution is misaligned as a result of gaps, errors, omissions, and unanticipated disturbances' (Williamson, 1994: 103).
2. Feminist economics is a broad area made up of numerous strands. These range from the reformist stance taken by neoclassical feminists to transformationist positions which are significantly more critical of the orthodoxy. Economics, like the other social sciences, has been influence by postmodernist and poststructuralist positions views. There are also feminist economists who have been strongly influenced by Marxist, institutionalist and post-Keynesianist approaches. In this chapter we have adopted an eclectic approach.
3. We highlighted in the previous section other instances of choice within constraints for entrepreneurs.

References

Allen, D. (1998), '0740, Transaction Costs', *Encyclopedia of Law and Economics: Literature Review*, http://encyclo.findlaw.com (accessed 22 February, 2000).

Baak, S. (1999), 'Tests for Bounded Rationality with a Linear Dynamic Model Distorted by Heterogeneous Expectations', *Journal of Economic Dynamics and Control*, Vol. 23, pp. 1517-1543.

Bauman, Z. (1990), *Thinking Sociologically: An Introduction to Everyone*, Blackwell, Oxford.

Bauman, Z. (2001), 'Consuming Life', *Journal of Consumer Culture*, Vol. 1(1), pp. 9-29.

Beck, U. (1992), *Risk Society*, Sage, London.

Bordo, S. (1986), 'The Cartesian Masculinization of Thought', *Signs*, Vol. 11, Spring, pp. 439-56.

Bordo, S. (1987), *The Flight to Objectivity: Essays on Cartesianism and Culture*, State University of New York Press, Albany.

Boulding, K. (1986), 'What Went Wrong with Economics', *American Economist*, Vol, 30, pp. 5-12.

Brennan, G. and Loamsky, L. (1985), 'The Impartial Spectator Goes to Washington: Toward a Smithian Theory of Economic Behaviour', *Economics and Philosophy*, Vol. 1, pp. 1189-211.

Burt, R. (1992), *Structural Holes: The Social Structure of Competition*, Harvard University Press, Cambridge, MA.

Casson, M. (1982), *The Entrepreneur: An Economic Theory*, Martin Robertson, Oxford.

Coase, R. (1937), 'The Nature of the Firm', *Economica*, Vol. 4, pp. 386-405.

Coase, R. (1988a), 'The Nature of the Firm: Influence', *Journal of Law, Economics and Organizations*, Vol. 4, pp. 33-47.

Coase, R. (1988b), *The Firm, the Market and the Law*, University of Chicago Press, Chicago.

Coase, R. (1991), 'The Nature of the Firm: Meaning', in O. Williamson, and S. Winter (eds), *The Nature of the Firm: Origins, Evolution, and Development*, Oxford University Press, New York, pp. 48-60.

Coase, R. (1994), *Essays on Economics and Economists*, University of Chicago Press, Chicago.

de Bruin, A. and Dupuis, A. (1999a), 'Towards a Synthesis of Transaction Cost Economics and a Feminist Oriented Network Analysis: An Application of Women's Street Commerce', *American Journal of Economics and Sociology*, Vol. 58, pp. 807-827.

de Bruin, A. and Dupuis, A. (1999b), 'An Extension of Transaction Cost Analysis to Women's Informal Sector Activity: A Merger of Feminism with the New Economic Sociology', Working Paper Series No 99.23, ISSN 1174-5320, Department of Commerce, College of Business, Massey University, Albany, August, 1999.

de Bruin, A. and Dupuis, A. (2000), 'Constrained Entrepreneurship: An Interdisciplinary Extension of Bounded Rationality', *The Journal of Interdisciplinary Economics*, Vol. 12, pp. 71-86.

Dequech, D. (1999), 'Rationality and Irrationality', in P. O'Hara (ed.), *Encyclopedia of Political Economy*, Routledge, London and New York, pp. 957-960.

Dupuis, A. and de Bruin, A. (2000), 'A Re-examination of the Behavioural Assumption of Bounded Rationality', in E. Hölzl (ed.), *Fairness and Cooperation, International Association for Research in Economic Psychology/Society for the Advancement of Behavioral Economics, Vienna, Austria, Conference Proceedings*, pp. 87-91.

Etzioni, A. (1988), *The Moral Dimension: Toward a New Economics*, The Free Press, New York.

Ferber, M. and Nelson, J. (1999), 'Where Do We Go from Here?', in M. Ferber and J. Nelson (eds), *Quarterly Review of Economics and Finance*, Vol. 39, pp. 781-783.

Ferguson, H. (1992), 'Watching the World Go Round: Atrium Culture and the Psychology of Shopping', in R. Shields (ed.), *Lifestyle Shopping: The Subject of Consumption*, Routledge, London.

Ferguson, H. (1996), *The Lure of Dreams: Sigmund Freud and the Construction of Modernity*, Routledge, London.

Friedman, D. (1998), 'Modeling Bounded Rationality', *Southern Economic Journal*, Vol. 65, pp. 366-368.

Georgescu-Roegen, N. (1966), *Analytical Economics*, Harvard University Press, Cambridge, MA.

Georgescu-Roegen, N. (1970), 'The Economics of Production', *American Economic Review*, Vol. 60, pp. 1-9.

Granovetter, M. (1985), 'Economic Action and Social Structure: The Problem of Embeddedness', *American Journal of Sociology*, Vol. 91, pp. 481-510.

Granovetter, M. (1990), 'The Old and the New Economic Sociology: A History and an Agenda', in R. Friedland, and A. Robertson (eds), *Beyond the Marketplace: Rethinking Economy and Society*, Aldine de Gruyter, New York, pp. 89-112.

Granovetter, M. (1992a), 'Economic Institutions as Social Constructions: A Framework for Analysis', *Acta Sociologica*, Vol. 35, pp. 3-11.

Granovetter, M. (1992b), 'Problems of Explanation in Economic Sociology', in N. Nohria and R. Eccles (eds), *Networks and Organizations: Structure, Form and Action*, Harvard Business School Press, Boston, pp. 25-56.

Gulati, R. (1998), 'Alliances and Networks', *Strategic Management Journal*, Vol. 19, pp. 293-317.

Hekman, S. (1994), 'The Feminist Critique of Rationality', in *The Polity Reader in Gender Studies*, Polity Press, Cambridge, pp. 50-61.

Hewitson, G. (1995), Neo-classical Economics: A Feminist Perspective, in N. Grieve and A. Burns (eds), *Australian Women*, Oxford University Press, Australia, pp. 142-150.

Hindess, B. (1988), *Choice, Rationality and Social Theory*, Unwin, London.

Hyman, P. (1994), *Women and Economics: A New Zealand Feminist Perspective*, Bridget Williams Books, Wellington.

Irigiray, L. (1985), *Speculum of the Other Woman*, Cornell University Press, Ithaca, NY.

Jones, G. (1998), 'Don't Throw the Baby Out with the Bath Water: A Positive Interpretation of Transaction Cost Theory', Working Paper, Department of Management, Texas A&M University, June.

Kaufman, B. (1999), 'Emotional Arousal as a Source of Bounded Rationality', *Journal of Economic Behavior and Organization*, Vol. 38, pp. 135-144.

Keller, E. Fox, (1985), *Reflections on Gender and Science*, Yale University Press, New Haven, CT.

Knudsen, C. (1993), 'Modelling Rationality, Institutions and Processes in Economic Theory, in U. Mäki, B. Gustafsson, B. and C. Knudsen (eds), *Rationality, Institutions, and Economic Methodology*, Routledge, London, New York.

Langlois, R. (1986a), 'The New Institutional Economics: An Introductory Essay', in R. Langlois (ed.), *Economics as a Process: Essays in the New Institutional Economics*, Cambridge University Press, Cambridge, MA, pp. 1-25.

Langlois, R. (1986b), 'Rationality, Institutions and Explanation, in R. Langlois (ed.), *Economics as a Process: Essays in the New Institutional Economics*, Cambridge University Press, Cambridge, MA, pp. 225-255.

Langlois, R. and Csontos, L. (1993), 'Optimization, Rule-following, and the Methodology of Situational Analysis', in U. Mäki, B. Gustafsson and C. Knudsen (eds), *Rationality, Institutions, and Economic Methodology*, Routledge, London, New York, pp. 113-132.

Lloyd, G. (1984), *The Man of Reason*, University of Minnesota Press, Minneapolis, Minn.

Loasby, B. (1989), *The Mind and Method of the Economist*, Edward Elgar, Hants.

MacLeod, W. (1996), 'Decision, Contract, and Emotion: Some Economics for a Complex and Confusing World', *Canadian Journal of Economics*, Vol. 29(4), pp. 788-810.

McMillan, C. (1982), *Women, Reason and Nature*, Basil Blackwell, Oxford.

Merchant, C. (1980), *The Death of Nature*, Harper and Row, San Francisco.

Nelson, J. (1993), 'The Study of Choice or the Study of Provisioning? Gender and the Definition of Economics', in M. Ferber and J. Nelson (eds), *Beyond Economic Man: Feminist Theory and Economics*, University of Chicago Press: Chicago, pp. 23-36.

Nelson, J. (1995), 'Feminism and Economics', *Journal of Economic Perspectives*, Vol. 9(2), spring, pp. 131-148.

Nelson, J. (1996), *Feminism, Objectivity and Economics*, Routledge, London.

North, D. (1990), *Institutions, Institutional Change and Economic Performance*, Cambridge University Press, Cambridge, MA.

Oatley, K. (1992), *Best Laid Schemes: The Psychology of Emotions*, Cambridge University Press, New York.

Polanyi, K. (1944), *The Great Transformation*, Holt Rinehart, New York.

Polanyi, K., Arensberg, C. and Pearson, H. (1957), *Trade and Market in the Early Empires*, Free Press, New York.

Posner, R. (1972), *Economic Analysis of Law*, Little, Brown and Co, Boston.

Radner, R. (1996), 'Bounded Rationality, Indeterminacy, and the Theory of the Firm', *Economic Journal*, Vol. 106, pp. 1360-1373.

Ritzer, G. (1998), *The McDonaldization Thesis*, Sage, London.

Roberts, P. and Greenwood, R. (1997), 'Integrating Transaction Cost and Institutional Theories: Toward a Constrained-efficiency Framework for Understanding Organizational Design Adoption, *Academy of Management Review*, Vol. 22, pp. 346-374.

Rubinstein, A. (1998), *Modeling Bounded Rationality*, MIT Press, Cambridge, MA.

Schumpeter, J. (1934), *The Theory of Economic Development*, Harvard University Press, Cambridge, MA.

Selten, R. (1998), 'Features of Experimentally Observed Bounded Rationality', *European Economic Review*, Vol. 42, pp. 413-436.

Sen, A. (1977), 'Rational Fools: A Critique of the Behavioral Foundations of Economic Theory', *Philosophy and Public Affairs*, Vol. 6, pp. 317-44.

Sen, A. (1984), *Resources, Value and Development*, Harvard University Press, Cambridge, MA.

Sen, A. (1987a), 'Rational Behavior', in J. Eatwell, M. Milgate and P. Newman (eds), *The New Palgrave: A Dictionary of Economics*, Macmillan, London.

Sen, A. (1987b), *On Ethics and Economics*, Blackwell, Oxford; MIT Press, Cambridge, MA.

Sharma, P. and Chrisman, J. (1999), 'Toward a Reconciliation of the Definitional Issues in the Field of Corporate Entrepreneurship', *Entrepreneurship Theory and Practice*, Vol. 23, pp. 11-27.

Simon, H. (1957), *Models of Man*, Wiley, New York.

Simon, H. (1961), *Administrative Behavior* (2nd Edition), Macmillan, New York.

Simon, H. (1987), 'Satisficing', in J. Eatwell, M. Milgate and P. Newman (eds), *The New Palgrave: A Dictionary of Economics*, Vol. 4, MacMillan, New York, pp. 266-268.

Simon, H. (1992), 'Introduction', in M. Egidi and R. Marris (eds), *Economics, Bounded Rationality and the Cognitive Revolution*, Edward Elgar, Brookfield, pp. 3-8.

Swedberg, R. (1990), *Economics and Sociology: Redefining their Boundaries: Conversations with Economists and Sociologists*, Princeton University Press, Princeton, NJ.

Sydie, R. (1988), *Natural Women, Cultured Men: A Feminist Perspective on Sociological Theory*, Nelson Canada, Toronto.

Thornton, P. (1999), 'The Sociology of Entrepreneurship', *American Review of Sociology*, Vol. 25, pp. 19-46.

Uzzi, B. (1996), 'The Sources and Consequences for the Economic Performance of Organizations: The Network Effect', *American Sociological Review*, Vol. 61, August, pp. 674-698.

Wang, N. (1999), 'Transaction Costs and the Structure of the Market: A Case Study', *American Journal of Economics and Sociology*, Vol. 58, pp. 783-806.

Williamson, O. (1985), *The Economic Institutions of Capitalism: Firms, Markets, Relational Contracting*, Free Press, New York.

Williamson, O. (1994), 'Transaction Cost Economics and Organization Theory', in N. Smelser and R. Swedberg (eds), *The Handbook of Economic Sociology*, Princeton University Press, Princeton, NJ, pp. 77-107.

Winch, D. (1978), *Adam Smith's Politics*, Cambridge University Press, Cambridge.

Winter, S. (1991), 'On Coase, Competence and Corporation', in O. Williamson and S. Winter (eds), *The Nature of the Firm*, OUP, New York, pp. 179-195.

Wolozin, H. (2002), 'The Individual in Economic Analysis: Toward Psychology of Economic Behavior', *Journal of Socio-Economics*, Vol. 31(1), pp. 45-57.

Chapter 3

Ethical Entrepreneurship

Chris Moore and Anne de Bruin

Introduction

While there is a large and burgeoning literature on business ethics and corporate social responsibility, this chapter aims to contribute to understanding in the area mainly by highlighting three aspects of the ethical entrepreneurship picture. Firstly, the dual level impact of the ethical dimension on entrepreneurship is drawn out: at the more micro level, the ethical principles and perceptions of the individual entrepreneur that influence the conduct of business; at the overarching macro level, the ethical values and agendas of the consumer society that influence entrepreneurial activity. Secondly, our discussion links in with the theoretical conceptualization of 'constrained entrepreneurship' presented in Chapter 2, to argue ethical entrepreneurship as constrained entrepreneurship in action. Thirdly, ethical conduct is viewed not only from the dual ethical and constrained perspectives but also from a transaction cost perspective.

At the outset we indicate the adoption of a simple interpretation of entrepreneurship − to mean running a business. While simple this is not an unreasonable interpretation. As Coase draws attention to, 'the main activity of a firm', is 'running a business' (1988: 38). Ethical entrepreneurship is similarly a straightforward specification: running a business in an ethical manner. The entrepreneur is not conceived only in the capacity of the individual entrepreneur but can include more collective forms such as corporate entrepreneurship where running a business is a team effort and tribal entrepreneurship as discussed in Chapter 10.

The Dual Level Ethical Dimension

While necessarily an artificial dichotomy, since there is usually an interactive flow of influence between the levels of micro/individual and broader societal ethical considerations, the dual level differentiation is analytically convenient. Thus at the micro level, the contention here is that there is an ethical core, which underpins the entrepreneurial activities of individuals. This can derive from both the context of socialization of the entrepreneurs themselves and the site and locale of operation of their business. By contrast, the societal ethical perspective comprises the overarching expectation and increasingly an insistence, that businesses operate within ethical norms that conform to what is perceived to be the 'social good', often implicitly incorporating the needs of future generations as well. The ethical requirements of direct customers of the business could thus be only a small subset, or may not even feature within these ethical expectations.

A complex intertwining of religious, cultural, social and economic considerations shape the ethical foundation at the micro level. Hence, there are different understandings and interpretations of what is, in fact, ethical for various individuals. Thus for example, in running an indigenous business, ethical principle could be woven with kinship customs, a collective vision for tribal prosperity, tribal tradition and customary lore, the collective understanding of living in harmony with the nature, the spiritual and the inner-self, which in turn are influences which are dynamically being reshaped by other influences such as global capitalism and neo-tribalism (Mataira, 2000). Similarly, cultural and religious influences, such as Confucian traditions or Christian principles, may intertwine to influence the ethical perspective of individual entrepreneurial activity.

As the world's economies become more integrated through globalization, entrepreneurs find themselves, by necessity, doing business in a variety of countries with differing ethical, moral and cultural norms. For the entrepreneur, day to day business dealings often mean having to make ethical and moral choices outside their own known and familiar ethical framework. Whose ethics do you use? One's own or that of the host country where business operations are conducted? At one extreme the entrepreneur could adopt the position of cultural relativism, that is, no one culture's ethical values are better or worse than another's and so adopt local ethics. For an unethical entrepreneur this could be a convenient choice, for it may well create opportunities for pecuniary gain through, for example, exploitation of labour or the environment. However, relativism is ultimately unacceptable as it can give rise to nontrivial unethical outcomes, such as the use of child labour or the dumping of toxic waste, that breach more universally accepted ethical norms. On the other hand, neither is it appropriate to adopt a stance of cultural absolutism, or one's own ethical and moral code. Donaldson (1993) suggests a middle course between relativism and absolutism by the adoption of a moral threshold expressed as universal principles for corporate behaviour and framed in terms of rights, like the United Nations's Universal Declaration of Human Rights. Such principles establish minimum standards of behaviour but are flexible enough to allow for economic and cultural differences, including differing economic responses to developmental and environmental issues.

Donaldson (1993: 74) points out that moral rationality is bounded in a sense similar to Herbert Simon's bounded rationality concept, where behaviour is '*intendedly* rational, but only *limitedly* so' (Simon 1961: xxiv). If this is indeed the case, then entrepreneurs called upon to make an ethical call, will inevitability make a less than perfect decision because they have only a finite ability to understand

and process the infinite complexity and consequences involved. Further, as economic systems and practices are artifacts of cultures, and so naturally reflect varying ethical values and beliefs, the 'rules of the game' will inevitably vary from one culture to another. From this Donaldson asserts that the boundedness of moral rationality implies no one culture can claim the moral high ground when it comes to economic affairs, and therefore, cultures are allowed, within limits, to define their own economic morality. However, the 'within limits' argument stops this assertion from defaulting to relativism. But what are the limits? It is suggested they could take the form of 'hypernorms' – norms so fundamental to the human condition that they transcend culture. Their list includes:

> Core human rights, including those to personal freedom, physical security and well-being, political participation, informed consent, and the ownership of property; and the obligation to accord equal dignity to each human person (Donaldson, 1993: 75).

Fundamental norms like these hypernorms are an appropriate starting point for creating a basis for cross-cultural business ethics. Such principles could be taken up and incorporated into business practice and behaviour that takes cognizance of cultural differences in applying the principles. The challenge for the ethical entrepreneur, at the micro level, therefore, is to find that middle ground between home and host ethical values that allows for differing customs. In recent writings, Donaldson and Dunfee (1999) have expressed their thinking in terms of an Integrative Social Contracts Theory – a framework for resolving ethical dilemmas in business. This theory acknowledges the legitimacy of social contracts that hold corporations, communities and economies together but deems them illegitimate, or unethical, if they exist outside the boundaries of transcultural truths, or the hypernorms that define core human values.

At the overarching macro level, societal ethical demands impinge on the conduct of business. Thus for example, concerns for the natural environment and ecological systems, the advent of green consumerism and the actions of human rights groups and the anti-globalists are linked to an emerging global consciousness that the exploitation of the environment and humans is both unsustainable and unethical. There is ample evidence, both scientific and social, to support the argument that unfettered economic growth, including globalization, is unsustainable unless social and environmental constraints are incorporated into the growth equation. In the twenty-first century this is taken as self-evident and not up for debate. What is up for debate, however, is *how* sustainability and a just world should be achieved. For some, utilitarianism and free-market solutions are appropriate, for others, corporations and governments have a more direct and leading role to play by making ethical and moral behaviour part of their corporate culture and thinking. The actions of activist groups, combined with stakeholders' calls for ethical and moral leadership from institutions and entrepreneurs, has seen ethical considerations become embedded in trade and investment agreements, and multinational corporations' codes of ethics. Continued pressure from stakeholders for yet higher levels of corporate social responsibility (CSR) is pushing ethical behaviour ever higher up the corporate agenda and making managers aware that ethical behaviour is good business. As Frederick (1999: 79) observes, the lobbying efforts of environmental and CSR groups worldwide are far more likely to bring about marginal gains (and convergence) in ethical business behaviour globally than any ethical theory is likely to achieve.

Despite the compelling moral and ethical arguments underpinning CSR it has its critics. There is a philosophical view, espoused notably by Milton Friedman (see for example 1970), that maximizing shareholder value is the prime responsibility of business in a free enterprise system. The implication here is that unless it can be demonstrated that the inclusion of environmental and social objectives enhance profits or shareholder value then they should not play a role in business decision making. Nonetheless, today most corporate managers and entrepreneurs have accepted that they have moral and ethical obligations to society and the stakeholders in their business dealings with respect to the environment, owners, customers, suppliers and employees. Obligations, it can be argued, arise from the fact that entrepreneurs have a 'contract' with society and hence duties and responsibilities are created. Nevertheless, not all writers agree. Henderson (2001), for example, interprets the drive for ever-greater corporate citizenship as misguided virtue. It is claimed that the increasing list of stakeholders (in addition to owners) to satisfy; the adoption of broader objectives; more complex procedures; and more demanding standards impact negatively on costs and revenues and hence reduce shareholder value. Even the legitimacy of increasing societal expectations of businesses' dealings with society and the environment are questioned. In particular, there is a resentment of the need to adopt CSR as a defence against costs associated with say loss of reputation in society when society's expectations are deemed misguided or even anti-business. It is curious, however, that business is deemed the right to economic freedom in the pursuit of profit, yet society's right to hold or express its preference for greater social responsibility from business is questioned. It is perhaps ironic that the need for CSR is criticized when the function of business is to maximize shareholder wealth by satisfying customer demands, one of which is the desire for greater CSR.

The critics of CSR form a minority group. Most entrepreneurs and corporations, acknowledge that they have ethical and moral obligations to society and the environment. The adoption of ethical codes of conduct, CSR statements, and corporate strategies with an ethical ethos is evidence of this. A number of researchers have attempted to find an empirical relationship between ethical behaviour and financial performance. The results have been mixed. McWilliams and Siegel (2000) cite findings ranging from negative, through neutral to positive for studies using event study methodology, that is, the short-run financial impact of socially responsible or irresponsible acts. Other studies employing measures of a corporation's CSR performance, for example, an index of social performance and longer-term financial performance using accounting data, have also produced inconsistent results. McWilliams and Siegel are not surprised, as they claim many of the econometric models used are misspecified because they fail to take account of research and development (R&D) investment which is often highly correlated with measures of corporate social performance. R&D investment and CSR are likely to be correlated because corporations engaging in CSR are those pursuing differentiation strategies that involve R&D spending. Once R&D investment is controlled for, then they found that CSR has a neutral impact on performance. For entrepreneurs looking for guidance to the level of CSR they should adopt, McWilliams and Siegel (2001) suggest a pragmatic cost-benefit approach to deciding on an optimum level of CSR engagement. That is, entrepreneurs can maximize profit and satisfy all stakeholder demands by investing in CSR to a level where additional revenue, from increased demand for its products and services equals the additional costs of the resources used in providing CSR. At the more general level of ethics, Chami *et al.* (2002) assert that ethical considerations underpin the efficient functioning of not only corporations but economies too, and point out that behaving in an ethical way may be costly at times, but that the costs of behaving unethically may be far higher in terms of lost opportunities and inefficiencies.

No matter whether the relationship is negative, neutral or positive, entrepreneurs are increasingly constrained by societal expectations of what does and does not constitute ethical behaviour. Like any change in societal taste, mores, customs and needs, society's demands for more ethical business behaviour in its dealings with the environment and stakeholders opens up commercial opportunities for entrepreneurs to serve markets for ethically-based products and services, as well as win new customers and investors who are prepared to support ethically-minded entrepreneurs. Of course, the converse is true for those who behave in an unethical way. Costs in terms of loss of reputation, consumer boycotts, litigation etc, can be very damaging, even fatal, in the age of active environmental and consumer rights groups and instant global communication. In the next section we examine this opportunity/choice-within-constraint aspect of ethical entrepreneurship.

The Constrained Entrepreneurship Construct

Ethical entrepreneurship may be viewed in terms of the 'constrained entrepreneurship' construct presented in Chapter 2, where it was pointed out that entrepreneurship occurs within constraints at both the micro and macro levels. Constraints include, at the micro level, cognitive limitations of individuals and at the macro level, constraint emanates from the overarching operational context of entrepreneurship and encompasses social processes, institutional restraints and takes account of the functioning of contemporary consumer society. It was also highlighted that, '"constrained" does allow for flexibility and the proper exercise of action, albeit within limited territory' (de Bruin and Dupuis, Chapter 2; de Bruin and Dupuis, 2000).

We believe the constrained entrepreneurship framework suits analysis of ethical entrepreneurship for three reasons. Firstly, in adopting the constrained entrepreneurship framework we acknowledge that ethical entrepreneurship cannot work within the neoclassical paradigm and its rationality assumption of maximization of a single utility. Rather, we align ourselves strongly with the 'new economics' advanced by Amitai Etzioni that considers the 'irreducibility of moral behaviour' (1988: 67-87). There is pursuit of at least two irreducible 'utilities' or goals in choice and decision-making. There are 'two sources of valuation: pleasure and morality' (Etzioni, 1988: 4). People seek an appropriate balance or judicious mix of their moral commitments and pleasures rather than attempting to maximize either. Secondly, in presenting ethical imperatives as constraints we wish to convey ethical standards as 'not-negotiable', especially in the new global era. Thirdly constraint by no means rules out opportunity and thus attention to ethics and fulfilling moral commitments allows plenty of scope for the exercise of action, not only of benefit to society, but also to the business itself.

The growing imperative for meaningful CSR for example, which is not 'misguided virtue' (Henderson, 2001), but a condition for long-term firm survival in the global age, may be conceived of as a constraint. In particular, entrepreneurs are accountable to both society through implicit and explicit contracts that give them legitimacy, and increasingly, to the varying, and often conflicting goals and objectives of stakeholders – including those of individual and institutional owners, customers, suppliers, employees, local communities, government and NGOs. The 'constraint' of the societal ethical dimension nevertheless presents opportunities. The demand for socially responsible behaviour, environmentally friendly products and services, and the sustainable use of inputs creates new markets for entrepreneurs to serve. It also gives scope for entrepreneurs to develop creative differentiation strategies as a means to gaining competitive advantage in attracting new consumers and investors for whom ethics is an important consideration in their buying or investing decision.

There are many ways entrepreneurs may differentiate themselves to make them attractive to consumers on the basis of what might be classified as socially and environmentally responsible. For example, they can market products and services that have an ethical augmentation like GM-free food or recycled paper, as discussed in Crane (2001). Alternatively, the use of inputs that are derived from sustainable sources and/or combined with eco-efficient production processes could be another path to differentiation. Similarly, investing in CSR, and gaining a reputation as a good corporate citizen is another way to differentiate oneself and add value to a company's operations through increasing revenue and reducing such risks and costs as lower staff turnover and less litigation.

It is often assumed that investors in capital markets are not concerned with ethical issues but only the financial returns the markets offer. This is a misconception, as the growth in socially responsible investment (SRI) funds and SRI funds under management indicate. There are a rapidly growing number of investors and institutions around the globe that are prepared to invest their savings or funds with entrepreneurs or corporations that run their business in an ethical manner, or provide goods and services that align with investors' ethical views. To assist investors there are a number of indices that rate corporate performance (or sustainability) on environmental and social criteria. The Dow Jones Sustainability Index (DJSI) World, for example, is made up of three hundred companies (drawn from the 2,500 companies in the Dow Jones Global Index) and represents the top ten per cent of companies in sixty four groups across thirty three countries. There are similar indices such as the FTSE4Good. The rewards for a company being in such an index are, first, it gains financial benefit from investments based on the index, second, it gets recognition and kudos as a leader in sustainability practice in its industry, and third it lifts the company's profile with its stakeholders such as customers, suppliers, employees and legislators. In addition to indices like the ones mentioned, there are many SRI vehicles available globally to suit all ethical investment needs. In most cases the funds comprise a portfolio of companies selected, or screened, on the basis of the funds' advertised SRI criteria which exclude companies involved in activities like tobacco, armaments, or nuclear power. The growing importance of SRI to capital markets can be judged from the jump in the level of SRI funds under management. In the USA alone funds in portfolios screened for SRI has climbed to $2.03 trillion in 2001 from $1.49 trillion in 1999, or almost one in very eight dollars invested in professionally managed funds is SRI (Social Investor Forum, 2001). The growth has been greatly assisted by the trend for pension fund mandates to stipulate some, or all funds, be invested in securities companies known to behave in a socially responsible way. In order to determine whether a corporation is socially responsible or not, fund managers can either research companies themselves, or use independent research houses that specialize in rating corporations on their social, environmental and stakeholder performance. The increasing flow of funds into SRI acts as an incentive for entrepreneurs and corporations to be seen as ethical and socially responsible.

While the capital market statistics quoted above demonstrate that large corporates benefit from social responsibility, working within the ethical 'constraint' is similarly both necessary and advantageous for small and medium enterprises (SMEs) and micro enterprises. For instance, there is growing potential for community enterprises based on Zero Waste and recycling and creating wealth from waste (Murray, 1999).

Entrepreneurs can capitalize on the opportunities arising from serving a heightened ethical conscience in an economically integrated world. Running a business in an ethical manner can involve costs as well as benefits. In the next section we elaborate on this in terms of transaction cost economization opportunities and frame the constraint-exercise of action/opportunity of the ethical dimension, from a transaction cost approach.

The Transaction Cost Framework

The Coasian rationale for the existence of firms is economization on transaction costs: 'The main reason why it is profitable to establish a firm would seem to be that there is a cost of using the price mechanism' (Coase, 1937: 336). Williamson, (1975, 1981a) a prominent exponent of transaction cost (TC) analysis, has explained the formation of 'hierarchies' and the nature of the modern corporation chiefly in terms of internalizing transaction costs within the organization and thus saving on these costs, which for him are linked mainly to contracting costs. In fact, Williamson goes so far as to claim that 'the economic institutions of capitalism have the main purpose and effect of economizing on transaction costs' (1985: 17).

Despite a growing use of the TC approach, there is no consensus on the definition of transaction costs (TCs). As Allen maintains 'few words in the economic language have been more abused or fought over' than TCs (Allen, 1998: 2 of 31). For the purposes of our analysis, both micro-firm operation and contractual focused definitions of TCs and more macro views of TCs are suited. The latter perspective is captured in the definition of Arrow (1969, cited in Williamson 1985: 18), who sees TCs as the 'costs of running the economic system'. This definition serves to emphasize the point we make that the overall context of entrepreneurial operation within the ethical imperatives of societal demands in a global village, has significant TC implications.

It is not new to bring in the TC perspective to bear on ethical behaviour. Etzioni (1988: 68-69) discusses the relationship between ethics, or moral commitment and TCs, pointing out that higher levels (or stickiness) of individual and societal moral commitment leads to lower TCs. The rationale is that high levels of moral commitment by economic actors means there is less need to purchase hedge protection against a broken promise (contract) or spend money on lawyers to draft or enforce contracts. In this sense, higher levels of moral commitment lead to increased productivity and economic growth as fewer resources are dedicated to 'policing' economic activity.

Rather similar to our dual ethical dimension approach discussed earlier, we might distinguish between the impact on TCs and TC reduction opportunities that arise from micro level ethical operation and hence an enhanced climate of trust, at the level of the firm; and the TC implications of the overarching macro context of operation of businesses. In order to differentiate the latter impact of more societal level ethical considerations and their TC influences we term these social transaction costs (STCs). Our notion of STCs is intended to convey the idea that there are 'costs' imposed by wider societal ethical expectations and relate to the operation of an organization within these constraints.

In standard TC economics analysis, it is possible for some firm specific TCs – chiefly those costs related to exchanges that a business would otherwise conduct in markets, to be economized through internalization within the organization (Coase, 1937; Williamson, 1975). As Williamson (1981b: 568) suggests, 'there are so many kinds of organizations because transactions differ so greatly and efficiency is realized only if governance structures are tailored to the specific need of each type of transaction'. By contrast STCs cannot be internalized through choice of a particular governance structure.

Censure of a business by segments of society for a lack of CSR can raise STCs. Similarly when it is perceived that an entrepreneur's activity is one which contributes positively to social and environmental goals, such as sustainable development, this can lower STCs. Brown *et al.* (2002) identify eight areas where ethical behaviour, in the form of good corporate citizenship, can reap financial benefits. They show that sound ethical practice can benefit an entrepreneur in the areas of reputation management, risk management, recruitment and retention of quality staff, investor relations and the ability to attract capital, organizational learning and innovation, competitiveness, operational efficiency and the licence to operate. The benefits largely manifest themselves in superior performance by reducing costs, either direct or transactional, and/or by enhancing revenue.

The Brown *et al.* (2002: 8 of 11) discussion on 'licence to operate' provides neat illustration of our notion of STCs. For example, they cite the case of the pulp and paper industry in the 1990s, when the sector suffered from poor reputation, was linked to rainforest destruction and the creation of carcinogenic compounds and was placed under the spotlight of international campaigns against the lack of CSR. This led to the industry facing reduced access to land and timber and to added costs associated with responding to critics. The industry, however, reacted by commissioning an independent study on the economic, social and environmental sustainability of the sector and engaged in purposeful dialogue with its critics. This, in turn, resulted in improved understanding among the various groups of stakeholders and a willingness to work with the industry to find viable solutions, thus enhancing licence to operate, improving industry reputation and reducing STCs. Warhurst highlights the increasing trend toward civil society groups conceding a 'social licence to operate alongside normal regulatory licences and permits' (2001: 72). Formalizing such social licence and actively demonstrating positive contribution to sustainable development goals, through for instance tri- sector partnerships for social investment and sustainability performance indicators, could be the proactive way toward a 'sustainability licence' to operate (Warhurst 2001: 72). We would argue that obtaining a sustainability licence could significantly reduce STCs. In similar vein, Jupp (2002) believes corporations should move from a 'bolt-on' view of CSR to one of Corporate Social Innovation (CSI), where their experience and expertise in innovation can be used, in partnership with government, to create social value.

The maxim that 'reputation is all in business' is borne out by research. Dowling (2001: 1) reports the findings using *Fortune's* 'America's Most Admired Companies' data to answer the question 'does having an above-average reputation translate into superior financial performance?'. The answer is yes according to Roberts and Dowling (1997) who found that above-average *Fortune* reputation scores lead to a greater ability to sustain above-average returns as measured by return on assets (ROA), and a greater ability to attain above-average ROA. Of course, gaining a sound reputation involves more than just behaving ethically, although it is clearly a necessary prerequisite. As Dowling (2001) points out, a reputation, good or bad, is a result of a company's net activities, which in turn reflects its culture and performance. Brickley *et al*. (2002) emphasize that markets impose substantial costs on individuals, entrepreneurs and corporations that behave unethically, so creating private incentives to behave in an ethical way. Although such incentives do not guarantee ethical behaviour, they do, according to the authors, explain why most participants in markets behave ethically. Their analysis shows that it is a mistake to lower ethical standards to match those of competitors, for an ethical-based reputation is a source of differentiation that can lead to higher prices, higher sales and profits.

In a technical sense a corporation's reputation is an intangible asset whose value may vary over time, and therefore either add or detract from a corporation's market value. In recent years, intangible asset growth has been the major driver of corporate market value, with some estimates suggesting that intangible assets account for more than 80 per cent of market value. This being the case, reputation and by implication ethical behaviour and corporate responsibility, is a definite source of competitive advantage for many companies. Dowling (2001) mentions a number of operational and financial advantages a corporation or entrepreneur may enjoy from having a high reputation with stakeholders. An excellent reputation can, for example, give a company's products and services a competitive edge in the market by adding psychological value in terms of trust, reduced purchase risk, and making a positive difference when choosing between products and services which are functionally similar, or where it is difficult to rate service levels between companies.

A good reputation also creates other benefits for a company, ranging from attracting better quality employees to lower staff turnover as a result of higher job satisfaction. In the case of crisis, a company with a solid reputation is more likely to bounce back or be given the benefit of the doubt by government agencies, investors and consumers. What is certain is that a poor reputation is not good for business. Companies with poor reputations tend to attract negative responses from market analysts and the news media, leading to poor market valuations and more often than not, poor employee morale. In the age of the Internet bad news travels fast with activist websites like http://www.corporations.org that document and analyze corporate ethics and wrongdoings and reference databases dedicated to researching corporations' activities around the globe that make available 'how to' manuals to aid activism. There are websites that help organize consumer boycotts of products and services of companies deemed to have breached accepted ethical standards. In recent years a number of companies like Nike (labour practices), Shell (Brent Spar and Nigeria), Texaco (Exxon Valdez spill), Monsanto (genetically modified crops, PCB contamination), and of late accounting irregularities at Enron, Xerox, and WorldCom, to name just a few, had their reputations tarnished with, in some cases, substantial loss of shareholder wealth.

Inextricably linked to the functioning of the market and TC approach is the importance of ethics and trust. As Arrow highlights:

> ... Ethical elements enter in some measure into every contract; without them, no market could function. There is an element of trust in every transaction; ... It is not adequate to argue that there are enforcement mechanisms, such as police and the courts; these are themselves bought and sold, and it has to be asked why they will in fact do what they have to contracted to do (Arrow, 1973, cited in Williamson, 1985: 405).

At the micro level of the business, the generation of trust through an ethical stance acceptable to all stakeholders of a business including consumers and partners can reduce TCs as well as lead to other beneficial outcomes. If trust-based relationships can be successfully established with stakeholders then entrepreneurs can reduce substantially the TCs of monitoring and enforcing contracts that often arise where trust in absent.

Alan Greenspan forcefully makes the point in a commencement speech to graduands at Harvard University, that trust is crucial not only at the more micro levels of conducting business operations but also at broader societal levels:

> Trust is at the root of any economic system based on mutually beneficial exchange. In virtually all transactions, we rely on the word of those with whom we do business. Were this not the case, exchange of goods and services could not take place on any reasonable scale. Our commercial codes and contract law presume that only a tiny fraction of contracts, at most, need be adjudicated. If a significant number of businesspeople violated the trust upon which our interactions are based, our court system and our economy would be swamped into immobility (Greenspan, 1999).

A significant positive outcome of trust is the fostering of an environment of innovation in products, services and processes so important to a company's continued survival in a competitive world. It has been observed (Cooke and Wills, 1999) that creating an innovative workplace is dependent on the development of positive relationships within and between employees and management, and between the company and its suppliers and business partners. Establishing trust is at the heart of positive relationship building. Chami and Fullenkamp (2002) demonstrate, through the use of mathematical models, that trust (modeled as mutual altruism) between employees in a firm leads to greater job satisfaction, higher productivity and lower costs. The authors point out that for trust to work in this way trust must be valued by the organization and form part of its culture, to the extent that employees are matched and rewarded on the basis of their trustworthiness.

Corporate partnerships, where care is taken to fit and safeguard the ethical aspirations of partners, are moving in the right direction to grow trust and build mutually beneficial outcomes. In this connection it is worth mentioning that ethics and pragmatism can effectively co-exist. As outlined in Chapter 10, an 'assertively pragmatic approach' that assures preservation of the core cultural values and principles of partners can be adopted, such as with partnership arrangements entered by First Nations across Canada (Anderson, 1997). Here ethical and cultural imperatives of the indigenous stakeholder are incorporated within a project participation agreement.

Lower levels of generalized trust and morality in a society increase the TCs of conducting business for all entrepreneurs in such a society. Platteau (1994) argues that the norms of generalized morality rather than moral norms in small groups must prevail in order to sustain honest behavior through building trust and generating the right kind of preferences. Mutual trust among people is necessary in order to uphold the market order in the longer-term 'and at reasonable (transaction) costs' (Plattéau, 1994: 757). Platteau, however, also contends that '[U]nfortunately, generalized morality is not a commodity which can be easily called for as the need arises. It is actually embedded in the historically-determined cultural endowment of a society (1994: 802). Perhaps given such difficulties in building generalized morality, the solution of John Ralston Saul (2001) who urges the normalization of ethical behaviour and 'responsible individualism' may well be the way forward.

Concluding Comments

Operating within a meaningful ethical framework is an integral part of any strategy for long-term firm survival in the global age. Indeed the increasing awareness of wider societal ethical responsibilities against the backdrop of the accelerating pace in the use and accessibility of the Internet as a source of information and mass communication, makes it foolhardy to disregard such obligations.

This chapter has signaled the importance of explicitly considering the ethical dimension in entrepreneurship study and research. In fact, the position that we hinge this chapter on is that the centrality of ethics must be intrinsic to, rather than an exogenous imposition on the exercise of entrepreneurship and the conduct of business. The constrained entrepreneurship concept that we operationalize to incorporate the ethical dimension sets limits, yet also provides direction for seeking opportunities that arise from intentionally observing ethical mores. It is perhaps unfortunate that the transactions cost approach we use has more negative *cost* connotations, since adopting an ethical stance brings substantial benefit, such as the building of trust and good repute and fostering innovation, albeit simultaneously contributing to economization of transaction costs. We hope, however, that the transactions cost and constrained entrepreneurship approaches we highlight, offer useful new paths for incorporation of ethical considerations in the study of entrepreneurship.

Nobel Prize winner in economics, Amartya Sen laments that the nature of economics 'has been substantially impoverished by the distance that has grown between economics and ethics' (Sen, 1987: 7). As the study of entrepreneurship moves from adolescence to greater maturity, it must not suffer a similar fate.

References

Allen, D. (1998), '0740, Transaction Costs', *Encyclopedia of Law and Economics: Literature Review*, available at http://encyclo.findlaw.com (accessed 22 February, 2000).

Anderson, R. (1997), 'Corporate/Indigenous Partnerships in Economic Development: The First Nations in Canada', *World Development*, Vol. 25(9), pp. 1483-1503.

Brickley, J., Smith Jr, C. and Zimmerman, J. (2002 in press), 'Business Ethics and Organizational Architecture', *Journal of Banking and Finance*, Vol. 26(9), pp. 1821-1835.

Brown, D., Keeble, J. and Roberts, S. (2002), *The Business Case for Corporate Citizenship*, Arthur D Little Limited, http://www.environment-risk.com/articles (accessed 17 July, 2002).

Chami, R., Cosimano, T. and Fullenkamp, C. (2002), 'Managing Ethical Risk: How Investing in Ethics Adds Value', *Journal of Banking and Finance*, Vol. 26(9), pp. 1697-1718.

Chami, R. and Fullenkamp, C. (2002), 'Trust and Efficiency', *Journal of Banking and Finance*, Vol. 26(9), pp. 1785-1809.

Coase, R. (1937), 'The Nature of the Firm', *Economica*, Vol. 4, pp. 386-405.

Coase, R. (1988), 'The Nature of the Firm: Influence', *Journal of Law, Economics and Organizations*, Vol. 4, pp. 33-47.

Cooke, P. and Wills, D. (1999), 'Small Firms, Social Capital and the Enhancement of Business Performance Through Innovation Programmes', *Small Business Economics*, Vol. 13(3), pp. 219-234.

Crane, A. (2001), 'Unpacking the Ethical Product', *Journal of Business Ethics*, Vol. 30, pp. 361-373.

de Bruin, A. and Dupuis, A. (2000), 'Constrained Entrepreneurship: An Interdisciplinary Extension of Bounded Rationality', *The Journal of Interdisciplinary Economics*, Vol. 12, pp. 71-86.

Donaldson, T. (1993), 'When in Rome, Do...What? International Business and Cultural Relativism', in P. Minus (ed.), *The Ethics of Business in a Global Economy*, Kluwer Academic Publishers, MA.

Donaldson, T., Dunfee, T.W. (1999), *Ties that Bind: A Social Contracts Approach to Business Ethics*, Harvard University Business School Press, Cambridge, MA.

Dowling, G. (2001), *'Creating Corporate Reputations: Identity, Images, and Performance'*, Oxford University Press, New York.

Etzioni, A. (1988), *The Moral Dimension: Toward A New Economics*, The Free Press, New York.

Frederick, R. (1999), 'An Outline of Ethical Relativism and Ethical Absolutism', in R. Frederick (ed.), *A Companion to Business Ethics*, Blackwell Publishers, Oxford.

Friedman, M. (1970), 'The Social Responsibility of Business is to Increase its Profits', *New York Times Magazine*, 13 September, pp. 122-126.

Greenspan, A. (1999), *Commencement Address*, Harvard University, Cambridge, MA, http:// www.allstocks.com/agreenspan.html (accessed 20 July, 2002).

Henderson, D. (2001), *Misguided Virtue: False Notions of Corporate Social Responsibility*, New Zealand Business Roundtable, Wellington.

Jupp, R. (2002), 'Getting Down to Business: A New Agenda for Corporate Social Innovation', Demos, London, http://www.demos.co.uk/ (accessed 3 August, 2002).

Mataira, P. (2000), *Nga Kai Arahi Tuitui Maori: Maori Entrepreneurship: The Articulation of Leadership and the Dual Constituency Arrangements Associated with Maori*

Enterprise in a Capitalist Economy, Unpublished PhD thesis, Massey University, Albany, New Zealand.

McWilliams, A. and Siegel, D. (2000), 'Corporate Social Responsibility and Financial Performance: Correlation or Misspecification?', *Strategic Management Journal*, Vol. 21, pp. 603-609.

McWilliams, A. and Siegel, D. (2001), 'Corporate Social Responsibility: A Theory of the Firm Perspective', *Academy of Management Review*, Vol. 26(1), pp. 117-127.

Murray, R. (1999), *Creating Wealth from Waste*, Demos, London.

Platteau, J-P. (1994), 'Behind the Market Stage where Real Societies Exist – Part II: The Role of Moral Norms', *The Journal of Development Studies*, Vol. 30 (July), pp.753-817.

Roberts, P. and Dowling, G. (1997), 'The Value of a Firm's Corporate Reputation: How Reputation Helps Attain and Sustain Superior Profitability', *Corporate Reputation Review* (Summer), pp. 72-6.

Saul, J.R. (2001), *On Equilibrium*, Penguin Books, Canada.

Sen, A. (1987), *On Ethics and Economics*, Basil Blackwell, Oxford.

Simon, H. (1961), *Administrative Behavior* (2nd Edition), Macmillan, New York.

Social Investor Forum (2001), '2001 Report on Socially Responsible Investing Trends in the United States', http://www.socialinvest.org.

Warhurst, A. (2001), 'Corporate Citizenship and Corporate Social Investment: Drivers of Tri-Sector Partnerships', *The Journal of Corporate Citizenship*, Vol. 1, Spring, pp. 57-73.

Williamson, O. (1975), *Markets and Hierarchies, Analysis and Antitrust Implications: A Study in the Economics of Internal Organization*, Free Press, New York.

Williamson, O. (1981a), 'The Modern Corporation: Origins, Evolution, Attributes', *Journal of Economic Literature*, Vol. 19(4), pp. 1537-1568.

Williamson, O. (1981b), 'The Economics of Organization: The Transaction Cost Approach', *American Journal of Sociology*, Vol. 87, pp. 548-577.

Williamson, O. (1985), *The Economic Institutions of Capitalism: Firms, Markets, Relational Contracting*, Free Press, New York.

Chapter 4

Entrepreneurial Capital

Patrick Firkin

Introduction

A myriad of approaches have been adopted to study and better understand entrepreneurship. From an early focus on the personality of the entrepreneur there has been a shift to a broader examination of the nature and characteristics of the entrepreneurial process (Bygrave and Hofer, 1991). This chapter follows such a shift by examining the process from a resource-based perspective. In doing so it adopts a very broad view in conceiving of entrepreneurship as the pursuit of 'new endeavors, which may range from self-employment to the creation of substantial organizations' (Reynolds, 1991: 48).

Based on the view that organizations are made up of heterogeneous bundles of resources, themselves defined as a firm's relatively permanent tangible and intangible assets (Brush *et al.*, 1997: 316), Resource-Based Theory (RBT) is a perspective that is being used increasingly in the study of entrepreneurship (Dollinger, 1995; Lichtenstein and Brush, 1997; Alvarez and Busenitz, 2001). In this vein, Oinas (2001) describes entrepreneurship as the mobilization of resources, a function deemed fundamental to the very idea of entrepreneurial activity. Brush *et al.* (1997) sum up the RBT position that an enterprise is created through the actions of an entrepreneur in relation to resources. Morris (1998) summarizes these actions as determining, accessing and employing the necessary and appropriate resources. The roles of the entrepreneur in relation to resources can, therefore, be very challenging (Brush *et al.*, 2001). Morris (1998: 32) goes on to argue that although the 'natural tendency is to assume that the principal resource required for any entrepreneurial event is money, the critical resources are typically non-financial'. Brush *et al.* (2001: 65) affirm this view by noting the importance of not only money, but also people and information, to the launching of an entrepreneurial venture.

To conceptualize the various financial and non-financial forms that these resources can take, this chapter adopts the concept of capital. In its common usage, capital is taken to represent material wealth that is owned, and that can be used to generate further wealth, and to normally describe the monetary value of that wealth (Bullock *et al.*, 1988). However, just as Morris argues for a wider view of resources, so I want to employ a broader view of capital to also encompass a range of non-financial assets and resources that can be used in the entrepreneurial process. As well as economic capital, four other forms of capital feature in this discussion: human, social, physical and cultural capital. Collectively, these five forms make up a person's total capital, parts of which will have entrepreneurial value. This worth, in relation to the entrepreneurial process and enterprise, constitutes what I conceptualize as the entrepreneurial capital of an individual.

While, as will be seen, employing notions of capital in the study of entrepreneurship is not unique, entrepreneurial capital represents a novel concept. Certainly, aspects of human capital have been considered as entrepreneurial human capital (see for example Nafziger and Terrell, 1996; Gimeno *et al.*, 1997; Iyigun and Owen, 1999), but this is a much narrower and less cohesive concept than that developed here. Similarly, although Mosakowski (1998) employs the idea of entrepreneurial resources, these are restricted to an individual's propensity to act creatively and with foresight, to use intuition and to be alert to new opportunities.

In order to develop the entrepreneurial capital approach in more detail and highlight its distinctive character, the body of this chapter is divided into three major sections. The first of these undertakes a brief overview of the ways in which capital has been employed in the study of entrepreneurship. General and RBT approaches are considered. In the second section the discussion focuses on the components that make up the concept of entrepreneurial capital. First, aspects of the five forms of capital which taken together comprise the core component of entrepreneurial capital are discussed. While the decision to employ the idea of capital as a central motif for this model is based on the work of Bourdieu (1986), the contributions of a number of other theorists and researchers will be considered and incorporated. A further key facet of entrepreneurial capital, the convertibility of capital, is considered next. The final component that makes up the concept of entrepreneurial capital, the idea of entrepreneurial value, is then delineated.

The third section introduces interview data from a study conducted as part of the Labour Market Dynamics (LMD) Research Programme.[1] Three case studies are drawn from this material and presented in order to provide some empirical grounding of what has been, to this point, a theoretically orientated discussion. The chapter concludes with a section that suggests further developments of, and uses for, the model of entrepreneurial capital.

Notions of Capital and the Study of Entrepreneurship

Employing concepts of capital is not new to the study of entrepreneurship. Two broad approaches are summarized in this section.[2] The first focuses on more general instances of the use of forms of capital in the literature and research, while the second considers how these forms have been employed in relation to RBT.

Where one or other forms of capital are employed in entrepreneurial research or literature, it is quite common for them to be considered in isolation. Thus, the role of one form of capital in the entrepreneurial process is examined. Although they also look at other non-capital factors, this is the approach of Brüderl *et al.* (1992) who consider the influence of human capital on the mortality rates of newly formed businesses. Sometimes the inter-relationship with another form of capital, particularly economic capital, is contemplated. For instance, under what Brüderl and Preisendörfer (1998) would term the metaphor of social capital, Steier (2000) examines the roles of networks in business start-ups and, although he adopts a broad focus, his particular interest is in their function in relation to finance.

While a single orientation is common, efforts to examine the role of more than one form of capital can also be found. There is, for example, the work of Sanders and Nee (1986) who explore the impact of social and human capital on self-employment among Asian and Hispanic immigrants to the United States. Alternatively, Honig (1998) researches the effects of human, social and financial capital on the success of Jamaican microentrepreneurs.

Two further issues regarding how notions of capital are employed in the general entrepreneurship literature are also worth considering. Firstly, the forms of capital are usually defined quite narrowly. Honig (1998), for example, considers social capital in terms of marriage and close church affiliation, and human capital solely in terms of educational levels. Although these are undoubtedly aspects of the forms of capital under consideration, at best what is being considered are aspects of each form. While it can readily be seen that adopting such narrow or limited conceptualizations might have methodological advantages, it can also be argued that including a broader array of features under the categories of social or human capital makes for a more complete picture of the entrepreneur's social and human capital. The second and related issue is concerned with the differences in how the forms of capital are conceptualized across studies. For example, I would struggle to find other instances where social capital is operationalized as church associations, as Honig (1998) does in his research. Sanders and Nee (1986) use the same concept, but restrict their interpretation to family make up. Once again, while there may be sound methodological reasons for these approaches, such disparate interpretations of the same terms generate a fragmented sense of what constitutes the forms of capital and makes comparisons across research difficult.

While resources are not always conceptualized as forms of capital within the RBT literature, it has given rise to an integrated model of resources based on multiple forms of capital that are broadly defined (Dollinger, 1995; Brush *et al.*, 1997; Greene and Brown, 1997; Lichtenstein and Brush, 1997; Brush *et al.*, 2001). Over time the original typology, which comprised five forms of capital, has been expanded to include a sixth by the separating of technology from physical assets (Brush *et al.*, 2001):

- Financial Capital: Start-up and ongoing funding.
- Human Capital: Attributes, skills, education and experience, as well as the reputation of the entrepreneur(s).

- Social Capital: Relationships and networks – within the family, as well as social, ethnic, professional and political associations and the like.
- Physical Capital: Tangible assets such as facilities and equipment.
- Organizational Capital: Organizational relationships, structures, routines, culture, and knowledge.
- Technological Capital: Can be knowledge and process based.

The key points of this approach, in contrast with the more general use of the forms of capital in entrepreneurship research, are threefold. Firstly, though only a brief definition has been given here, each form of capital incorporates a wide range of resources. Secondly, these have been drawn together into a comprehensive resource-based model. Finally, they are employed collectively to analyze the nature of entrepreneurial activity in a range of ways.

Despite each of these three points mirroring aspects of the model of entrepreneurial capital that I develop in the next section, certain features differentiate it from the RBT approach. An important point of differentiation relates to the notions of capital that are utilized. As will be seen, cultural capital is added to the mix, while not all the forms of capital outlined above are incorporated. Following Lichtenstein and Brush (1997), technological capital is seen, depending on its make-up, to be either part of the entrepreneur's human capital or their physical assets. Organizational capital is also not included as a distinct category given the interview data that form the empirical underpinning of the model. These data focus heavily on businesses founded by individuals or couples and which mostly remained very small – sole operators, or employing only family or one or two employees, and seems to suggest that in these circumstances organizational capital might remain very much a part of the entrepreneurs themselves. The notion of organization capital, however, is not discarded entirely. Rather, a concluding section explores wider applications of the model of entrepreneurial capital, some of which might necessitate the incorporation of organizational capital. A key distinguishing feature of the entrepreneurial capital is the introduction of convertibility as a conceptual mechanism. This is explored in the next section. Briefly, it recognizes that entrepreneurs use different forms of capital as an alternative to financial expenditure, where financial expenditure might not be able to realize the same benefits, and to enhance profitability. It also means that aspects of a person's total capital can be converted to an entrepreneurial purpose. A final difference is the development of the novel concepts of entrepreneurial value and capital.

Entrepreneurial Capital: Developing the Model

The various features that make up the concept of entrepreneurial capital are now explored in some detail, beginning with the five forms of capital utilized in this model. Though a number of other theorists are drawn on in order to outline the forms of capital used here, the French theorist Bourdieu is central to these discussions as it was his writings that served as the initial stimulus. Bourdieu (1986) proposes three forms of capital – economic, social and cultural – and all three are employed in the model. That said, although cultural capital is often used in relation to educational attainment, it does not have a prominent place in the entrepreneurship literature. Rather, the institutional aspects of cultural capital – educational attainment and qualifications – are more usually captured in terms of human capital. Thus, human capital represents the fourth form utilized here. It is the embodied and material states of cultural capital, not encompassed by the concept of human capital, but which still have some value in relation to entrepreneurship, that are retained and which form a novel aspect of this model of entrepreneurship. The fifth form of capital that is employed, physical capital, is taken from the RBT typology. It seems an important addition to the model as it encompasses capital not covered in any of the other forms. As well, Bourdieu outlined the important notion of convertibility, which is also incorporated into this discussion. Finally, the concept of entrepreneurial value and its mediating role in determining entrepreneurial capital is developed.

Economic Capital

Economic capital refers to financial assets of any form that are directly convertible into money (Bourdieu, 1986; Jary and Jary, 1995). As such, it requires little further elaboration. While Morris' (1998) caution against seeing entrepreneurial activity solely in terms of financial resources has already been noted, as Light and Karageorgis (1994) show, in respect of ethnic entrepreneurship, financial capital has a prominent role as both a focus of study and as an explanatory variable. As well as being of considerable importance at start-up, economic capital is an ongoing issue and is also sometimes implicated in the closure of businesses. This form of capital can be seen in terms of the equity people have in their business and their business related borrowings (Reynolds and White, 1997). Likely sources of the latter include the entrepreneur(s) and other members of the initial enterprise at start-up; friends, family and business associates; and institutional arrangements through banks and other financial companies, private investors, venture capitalists, stockholders, and government agencies.

Human Capital

Human capital is often limited in meaning to ideas about formal qualifications, skills and work experience. Indeed Becker (1993) in his key work in this area, opens with a broad notion of what human capital might encompass, but then goes on to reinforce this narrower conception. However, human capital can be seen to entail a great deal more than education and training: 'It is a compendium of all traits and abilities that make human beings economically productive in a society'

(Shanahan and Tuma, 1994: 746). This includes both innate characteristics and those that are acquired.

Like social capital, the concept of human capital is well established within the field of entrepreneurship. However, there are wide variations in how this concept is operationalized and employed. The concept of entrepreneurial human capital is sometimes used, though here, too, there is considerable variation in its usage (for example compare Nafziger and Terrell, 1996; Gimeno *et al.*, 1997; Iyigun and Owen, 1999). While not necessarily intended as such, Brüderl *et al.* (1992) provide a basis for summarizing the various ways that human capital is used in relation to entrepreneurship. Following Becker (1993), their model incorporates general and specific human capital. General human capital encompasses a person's formal education and prior work experience. A range of personal attributes could also be included in this category. Specific human capital is made up of industry-specific and entrepreneur-specific components. As the term suggests, industry-specific human capital is knowledge, training, skills and experience related to a particular industry or sector. Entrepreneur-specific human capital includes a person's previous experience and family background in entrepreneurship. As well, the approach of Brüderl *et al.* (1992) could be extended to include personal characteristics necessary for self-employment. Two examples of such characteristics include a willingness to work hard and commit long hours (Gilbertson *et al.*, 1994).

Social Capital

Some confusion exists over the meaning of the term social capital (Portes, 1998, 2000a, 2000b; Schuller, 2000; Lin 2001; Adler and Kwon, 2002). At one level, this is the result of social capital being used in two senses – one with a communal emphasis, and the other more individually orientated. In response, Lin (2001: 26) argues that the widely held view is that social capital can be both a collective and individual good. It becomes important in any discussion of social capital, therefore, to make clear how the concept is being employed in that particular context. Thus, in this chapter the concept is more individually orientated. Additional confusion is likely to arise from what Lin describes as the tendency for social capital to be employed as another trendy term in the broad context of improving or building social integration and solidarity. In this sense, Lin sees it as often used to represent notions such as culture, trust or norms with problems arising because such interchangeability cannot always be assumed.

Social capital has been defined in a number of ways (see Adler and Kwon, 2002) from which Portes (1995, 1998, 2000a, 2000b) offers what he calls a consensus position. He conceptualizes social capital as the ability to secure resources, or benefits as he prefers to call them, consequent upon people's membership in social networks or other social structures. How much social capital a person has depends, according to Bourdieu (1986), on the size of their networks and the volume of capital (in the three forms he identifies) that members of that network have. It is produced through people's ongoing efforts at establishing and sustaining relationships with others in their family, neighbourhoods, workplaces, sporting and social clubs, and so on, though these may not be conscious efforts at generating social capital per se. According to Lin (2001), a number of factors determine the value of social capital for an individual. These include the circumstances of its usage, the make-up of the social structures and networks that the person is part of, their location relative to other members, and the nature of the relationships they share with them.

In relation to entrepreneurship, social capital is used most commonly to describe 'network-mediated benefits beyond the immediate family' (Portes, 1998: 12). That is, the benefits and resources that accrue from the entrepreneur's efforts at being part of and utilizing a wide range of relationships (Birley, 1985; Aldrich and Zimmer, 1986). Brüderl and Preisendörfer (1998) usefully coin the idea of a social capital metaphor to capture the range of approaches that consider networks in business. Some of these use various related concepts (such as ties or embeddedness, for instance) while others work within the more specific framework of social capital described above.

Though less prominent, a second way that social capital is used in relation to entrepreneurial activity is associated with relationships within the family. Bourdieu clearly includes this as one of the 'socially instituted' relationships that is a source of particular resources and benefits enjoyed by relatives, by virtue of their being part of that family (1986: 249). Sanders and Nee (1996) explicitly employ this idea in their study of family and extended family relationships in respect of small business activity in immigrant populations. An exclusive focus on the social capital between spouses or partners has been developed elsewhere (Firkin, 2001a; see also Chapter 6).

Cultural Capital

Bourdieu (1986) identifies cultural capital as having three states. Since one of these, the institutional state, has been incorporated into human capital, it is the remaining two states which are of greater interest in this context. The objectified state of cultural capital concerns 'cultural goods (pictures, books, dictionaries, instruments machines etc)' (Bourdieu, 1986: 243). While these have a material character, and can thus be owned simply by utilizing economic capital, for them to be appropriated or consumed as they were intended, that is, for their symbolic value to be realized, presupposes the embodied state of cultural capital. This comprises 'long lasting dispositions of the mind and body' (Bourdieu, 1986: 243-244). Harker (1990: 34) identifies some of these as 'the body of knowledge, the tacit understandings, the style of self-presentation, language usage, values etc', that are shared among groups. DiMaggio helpfully summarizes them as 'prestigious forms of knowledge or style' (1994: 39). The process of embodiment occurs across time and forms part of our ongoing socialization; it involves considerable investment by others and is heavily dependent on the family (Bourdieu, 1986: 244).

In developing an expanded notion of human capital theory that incorporates embodied cultural capital de Bruin and Dupuis (1995) and de Bruin (1999)[3] also open up the idea of cultural capital. Whereas Bourdieu emphasizes its class nature, these authors pay attention to the notion of ethnicity and argue that though people from outsidé the dominant culture are often at a disadvantage, they still possess embodied cultural capital that is shared with others because of common ethnicity. Rather than focusing solely on how a lack of dominant cultural capital disadvantages groups, the emphasis shifts to the way that cultural capital shared by non-dominant groups can, under certain conditions, provide positive resources and the basis for opportunity. Cultural capital is then seen to have the potential to be utilized in an entrepreneurial sense to provide goods and services in particular ways and forms that are preferred and valued by groups.

If the term ethnic is opened up to include those collectives whose 'members have some awareness of group membership and a common origin and culture, or that others think of them as having these attributes' (Aldrich and Waldinger, 1990: 112), then it becomes possible to consider a range of groups that could possess cultural capital. For example, local communities exhibit characteristics that fit this definition. Thus, though they might share many of these with a wider population, there might be features that are more specific to, or characteristic of, a particular locality and its citizens. The cultural capital they share could then be utilized in an entrepreneurial sense. While de Bruin and Dupuis (1995), and de Bruin (1998) make just this point in relation to community entrepreneurship (see Chapter 7), here I concentrate on its applicability at the individual level, a similar orientation I have been keen to highlight in respect of social capital. Unlike the other forms of capital, cultural capital does not have a strong presence in the literature on entrepreneurship.

Physical Capital

This form of capital is drawn from the RBT typology outlined in the previous section. It includes the 'tangible assets necessary for the operation of the business' (Greene and Brown, 1997) or, in other words, facilities and equipment. In addition, Dollinger (1995: 32) includes the location of those facilities and equipment and the amenities available at that location. Lichtenstein and Brush (1997) point out that since some of these assets can be difficult to obtain, the availability of, or accessibility to, physical resources can shape certain decisions within the process of starting and running a business. Often the physical capital necessary for a venture is not explicitly considered.

Convertibility

A key characteristic of Bourdieu's discussion of capital, and one that has important implications here, is the notion of convertibility – how each form of capital can be transformed from, and into, other forms of capital. They can also be held and used in concert. While most interest centres on the economic convertibility of other forms of capital, Portes (1998: 4) points out that 'though Bourdieu insists that the outcomes of the possession of social and cultural capital are reducible to economic capital, the processes that bring about these alternative forms are not'. That is, the benefits of social and cultural capital may be translated into monetary forms, but money alone, if at all, cannot immediately lay claim to social and cultural capital. Any conversion that does eventuate is likely to occur across considerable periods of time and be the outcome of a complex, multifarious and contingent process. Convertibility is also an inherent feature of entrepreneurial value, as discussed next.

Entrepreneurial Value

The concept of entrepreneurial capital is based on the total capital that an individual possesses, which is, in turn, made up of the sum of their economic, human, social, cultural, and physical capital. As is apparent, the broad definitions of each form allow for this total capital to encompass a wide range and number of resources. Not every aspect of a person's total capital, however, will be useful in an entrepreneurial sense. For example, for one of the LMD interviewees, being a qualified meat inspector had no benefits when he ran his own house painting business. Nor does every person have access to the same sorts and levels of capital. For instance, those entrepreneurs not married or in like-relationships cannot draw on the social capital that is available through a spouse or partner. Thus, the entrepreneurial capital a person possesses is made up of the components of their total capital that have an entrepreneurial value in that they have some worth in an entrepreneurial context and in relation to the entrepreneurial process.

While some aspects of this capital, such as the desire to be self-employed or prior entrepreneurial experience, are entrepreneurial in orientation, others are neither necessarily, nor automatically, entrepreneurial in nature. For instance, people can have a trade or profession without being self-employed. However, there are circumstances where such attributes or qualifications can be converted to an entrepreneurial use. Thus, depending on circumstances, various components of an individual's capital can be converted to an entrepreneurial purpose or advantage. Those parts which can be so converted possess varying degrees of entrepreneurial value – for instance, some are essential, others very useful, and some helpful, but not essential.

Entrepreneurs act to identify and develop their entrepreneurial capital by extracting the entrepreneurial value from their total capital or, in other words, converting the various forms of capital they can access to derive entrepreneurial value. Generating entrepreneurial capital is a key role for entrepreneurs since it is the 'identification, acquisition and combination of resources that results in the unique identity of the business' (Greene and Brown, 1997: 163). As this implies, the particular mix of capital required in a venture will be different depending on the nature of an enterprise and the entrepreneur. Moreover, it can change across time in relation to the lifecycle of the enterprise, as well as internal and external circumstances. Thus, the ideas of entrepreneurial value and capital must be seen as dynamic concepts since, as Brush *et al.* (1997) describe it, over time 'some resources are re-organized, new ones are acquired, some become specialized and others may become idle'. It is also the case that when people do not possess particular forms of capital necessary for starting or running a business, they may acquire or access these in various ways. For instance, many of the entrepreneurs in the LMD Research Project were engaged in the ongoing development of networks that would be of some advantage to the business. As well, some of them learned skills necessary for running their enterprise. Though a number of the entrepreneurs benefited from their wives or female partners doing the accounts for a business, they were not all skilled in this respect at the outset and often had to obtain the necessary knowledge and skills to help with their partner's business.

Finally, it is worth noting that this approach has a useful fit with the notion of constrained entrepreneurship as developed by de Bruin and Dupuis (2000; also see Chapter 2). The idea of 'constraint' acknowledges that entrepreneurs always have to operate within various limits. Such limits do not, however, necessarily curtail entrepreneurial drive or activity, but rather shape the form and processes that result. Thus, as the case studies will show and as de Bruin and Dupuis (2000: 11) point out, 'possibilities exist within the context of constraint', including the constraints imposed by the make-up and depth of a person's entrepreneurial capital.

Case Studies

Three short case studies are now presented to illustrate how the model of entrepreneurial capital, that has been theoretically developed thus far, can be practically used in the analysis of entrepreneurial activity. They are drawn from interviews in the Hawkes Bay regional component of the LMD study, in which 24 of the 96 households in the sample contained self-employed people (Shirley *et al.*, 2001a, 2001b, 2001c). The entrepreneurial activities that these interviewees were engaged in were predominantly small businesses, often owner-operated, involving in the main professional services, trades, or agricultural/horticultural activities.

Before reviewing the case studies it is worth noting that the original data set provided limited examples of the kind of ethnic cultural capital discussed earlier in the chapter. Neither of the businesses run by people who identified themselves as Maori[4] drew on ethnic cultural capital. Despite this reservation regarding evidence of cultural capital at work in an entrepreneurial sense, the first case does provide a hint of what benefits this form of capital might offer, when associated with belonging to a particular community. This business, a specialist meat processing, distribution and marketing enterprise, was primarily run by a husband and wife, Allan and Carol,[5] together with an outside partner. The cultural capital that Allan drew on in starting and running the business was based on a strong knowledge of what the region could provide and of its residents. In this way he could draw on resources within the region to exploit the particular tastes and preferences, and parochial nature, of the people who lived there.

The company was primarily engaged in processing goat and lamb meat and had grown out of Allan's long involvement in the livestock industry. He had previously run his own business trading livestock and had then established this business with his partner. As well as his background and expertise, the previous experience Allan had in running a business was a critical asset. So, too, were the many personal attributes he brought to the enterprise, including his innovative and risk taking disposition. To Allan's mind, though, the risks he took in business were very calculated and based, in particular, on his extensive industry-specific human capital.

Though Allan and his business partner had been deliberately growing this business quite slowly, financial capital was still an issue.

> We've put all our own money into it and [our partner's] put his money into it and we've just been doing it on our own resources and borrowing ourselves. ...When you've got continual outgoings and nothing coming in it does get quite frustrating ... [but] as long as we can maintain generating some sort of income for the business then we'll just live on what we need each week.

While much of the business was run from Allan and Carol's home, they had also leased a former butcher's shop and transformed this into their processing plant. Thus, physical capital was made up of the family home as well as rented premises and the purchase of specialized equipment.

The couple's precarious financial position was somewhat alleviated by a frugal lifestyle and, at one point, Carol's involvement in part-time paid employment, while she was also helping out in the business. However, the demands of the enterprise saw Carol give up her part-time job to become more involved in their own enterprise. Her performing of a range of administrative and other tasks freed Allan to promote and develop the company. To facilitate this change they used up economic capital in the form of valuable savings.

Social capital from within the family was, therefore, vitally important for this business. So, too, was social capital arising out of more general networks. Much of the husband's role involved establishing and maintaining a whole host of relationships to benefit the business. This often drew on his background and networks in the livestock industry. Networking was also vital for developing a customer base. At times this man's heavy involvement in the community through sporting, service and church organizations was of use. As well as existing networks, he was always keenly aware of opportunities that might arise in a range of settings.

The second case involves a horticultural enterprise that was also run by a husband and wife, Dave and Fran. In wanting a lifestyle where they could share work and domestic responsibilities, Dave and Fran's motivations and intentions were somewhat different from those of Alan and Carol. As such, this could in many respects be considered a copreneurial venture (Marshack, 1994; Baines and Wheelock, 1998; Smith, 2000) though the interviews revealed that the shift to self-employment and the subsequent running of the business was very much instigated, led, and heavily influenced by Dave. After having been a schoolteacher for many years, including several as a principal, he had decided to attempt self-employment through a mixed horticultural venture that grew flowers, vegetables and fruit commercially for export. In wanting such a radical change Dave did not look to base any venture on his industry-specific human capital in the area of education. A shift from school teaching to horticulture is quite significant, however, and though he brought general business management skills from his previous work, Dave had to go about deliberately acquiring the more specific skills and knowledge he needed. This was done, in part, by experimenting on a property the couple had previously owned. In addition, Dave drew on personal attributes such as being prepared to take a risk and, as will be shortly illustrated, willing to work extremely hard.

As this type of enterprise cannot be run from just anywhere, the initial step involved the purchase of a larger property. Though over time Dave and Fran had had good incomes and developed equity through the prior ownership of property, the new enterprise still required a substantial mortgage, a fact that had major implications for the venture. Initially it was intended that Dave would continue to supplement their income with part-time teaching while growing the business. Fran would help while caring for their child. However, the country's economy deteriorated and interest rates rose sharply forcing a radical change in plans.

> Our budgets were blown a bit and it meant we needed to earn a lot more money than we had thought. We developed the flower growing side, the horticultural side of the property, quickly. Money started coming in but not enough to pay all the bills. I stopped work first of all to actually devote more time to establishing the business and [my wife] started work. ...[She] was teaching at a primary school. ... I looked after the baby and worked during the day. ... I was also driving the school bus. It was quite a busy time.

In addition Dave worked at the business during the evenings, as did Fran, though she also assumed responsibility for childcare once she had finished her day's teaching.

This transition from full-time mother to full-time worker was a difficult one for Fran, something that Dave readily acknowledged. It was necessary, however, for their financial survival and the fact that she did this, despite its effects on her, illustrates the strength of social capital in a marriage or like relationship. It also highlights a negative outcome.

> [My wife] hated going off to work and leaving the baby at home and the baby hated [her] going off to work and I hated seeing it all.

Ultimately it would contribute to the couple's decision to quit the business. Though both put up with these arrangements for a time, in the hope that they could overcome this difficult period, eventually Dave and Fran decided the price was too high. It was a decision not based solely on financial considerations, however. Rather, it centred on the emotional and physical costs of using other forms of capital in order to cope with the financial stresses.

Other types of social capital did not seem to play as large a role in this enterprise, though extended family helped with some extra finance. The disjuncture between Dave's background and the business he started may help account for a lack of networks that he could utilize in the new field. As they exported their produce, developing customers in the local area was not an issue. When the decision was made to end the business, Dave's teaching qualifications and networks in the field of education proved invaluable for him in making a smooth transition back to full-time paid employment. Thus, though at best they had limited entrepreneurial value, these aspects of his personal and social capital were still very useful in other contexts.

Drawing on the experiences of one of the four female entrepreneurs, the final case involves a woman who had spent many years in office and secretarial work, but had wanted for some time to have her own small business. Frustration with employers and wanting to be at home more for her adolescent children, finally prompted Helen to start a small company offering secretarial services. Clearly she drew on her general and specific training, skills and experience to establish this venture. As time went on, Helen invested in some computer training to enhance these skills. Lacking any prior experience of self-employment and, unlike the other entrepreneurs, with very little personal confidence that she could succeed, Helen coped with the apprehension she felt over this move by treating her business as a 'hobby'.

To set up her business, Helen borrowed what seemed like a lot of money to her at the time, in order to buy a typewriter and photocopier. She also took a number of measures to minimize the financial outlay including identifying the physical capital available at home. The goodwill of her family allowed Helen to turn a recreation room into a rather spartan office with the barest of furnishings. Though cost effective and convenient, working from home had come to generate a sense of isolation at times, though any plans to move into a commercial area would have required an injection of economic capital.

Social capital within Helen's family provided other resources as well. Her son and daughter helped out at busy times in various ways. In addition, her husband was extremely supportive and she knew she could rely on his income. Since she had started the business specifically with the intention of being better able to combine some form of paid work with caring for the children, Helen's husband did not have to provide additional input in this area. Later, once the children had left home, some changes did occur. With the business now full-time he had gradually taken over cooking the evening meal and doing the grocery shopping in order to free her for more work.

Although experienced in secretarial work, Helen had no networks that would provide clients for her new business. Thus, she initially took some very pragmatic steps to get work, advertizing in the business pages of the local telephone directory and local newspapers. When interviewed many years later she had a firmly established clientele, many of whom would just 'drop by'. However, servicing this group of regular customers had created expectations that she would always be available. Like all the other entrepreneurs Helen often had to work long hours to complete work on time. She was also increasingly concerned that a work-related health condition would affect her ability to type and thus continue in the business.

Comparing and contrasting these three cases shows what can be uncovered by employing the model of entrepreneurial capital in an analysis. Collectively, they demonstrate the variety of forms of capital that can comprise a person's entrepreneurial capital and how this is uniquely related to the people involved, the businesses concerned, the timeframes being considered, and other contextual factors. Though the examples regarding cultural capital are limited, the cases otherwise well illustrate the nature and place that each of the five forms of capital outlined earlier can have in the entrepreneurial process. In addition, as Allan and Carol's circumstances reveal, these component forms can themselves be a mix of various elements. Social capital, for instance, was evident within and outside the home. Outside the family, it was drawn on in relation to developing and maintaining networks of suppliers, distributors and customers. Within the family, social capital provided important resources, with Carol informally, and then formally, helping out in the enterprise by carrying out a range of administrative and other roles. She also earned income through a part-time job. In terms of economic capital, the mix comprised Carol's income, the couple's savings, their very frugal budgeting, and some borrowings. Allan and Carol contributed to their physical capital by running the business in part, from their own home, though specialized premises and equipment were also needed.

The second and third cases illustrate the different qualities and dimensions that entrepreneurial capital can assume. Apart from a small loan, Helen's entrepreneurial capital is largely based on various components that she already had. Dave and Fran, in contrast, had to access and obtain extensive amounts of various forms of capital – for instance, substantial economic capital in the form of a mortgage to purchase sizeable physical capital, as well as developing significant human capital outside their usual areas of work and expertise. Thus, entrepreneurial capital may often have to be made up of acquired components rather than simply being that which a person already possesses. Helen's health concerns also have some relevance here. Her fears that a physical condition she was developing would negatively affect her ability to work illustrate that the loss of, or failure to secure, particular resources can be as influential as having or obtaining others. In comparison with Dave and Fran's situation, Helen's case additionally demonstrates that even low levels of capital can have entrepreneurial value.

All the cases clearly show the convertibility of various forms of capital to an economic value or, in some other way, to a benefit for the business. The use of homes to run businesses is an example of this in relation to physical capital. As well, convertibility is frequently and obviously seen in relation to social capital within the family and the roles that spouses perform, be they in the business, in the home, or in other employment. In this form, social capital often relies on the capital possessed or acquired by spouses. Dave and Fran's case presents a further dimension of social capital between spouses[6] by highlighting the negative effects of having to rely so heavily on it, in their case to overcome financial difficulties.

While all the cases show how forms of capital have an entrepreneurial value and can thus be converted to entrepreneurial capital, Dave's circumstances neatly illustrate that not all the capital a person possesses is of this kind. While providing some general skills and experience, little of Dave's industry-specific human capital had entrepreneurial value and thus lacked convertibility. Rather, he had to acquire the skills and knowledge necessary to run the business. As the only one of the three businesses to close, this case provides a chance to see how capital can operate in such a context. In this instance, Dave's specific human and social capital in relation to his background in teaching eased the transition back to employment.

As a final observation, it is worth noting that the approach to business evidenced by Helen, in the third case study, showed some similarities with the other female entrepreneurs in the LMD study, but was in contrast with the men's cases. Helen, like the other women, drew on her entrepreneurial capital to develop a business that would fit with her domestic responsibilities – her business was initially and deliberately organized on a part-time basis, so that she worked only during school hours, and was run from home. The male entrepreneurs, in contrast, made no such allowances or considerations and in concentrating on their businesses they left the bulk of domestic responsibilities to their wives or partners. Unlike others, over time Helen's husband did increase his domestic responsibilities as her business grew.

Conclusion

As has been shown, employing notions of capital in the study of entrepreneurship is hardly novel. However, the concept of entrepreneurial capital, as developed here, consolidates and extends existing work. Entrepreneurship becomes, as it were, the exercise of that capital. Key features of this concept are the addition of cultural capital as a further form worth considering in relation to entrepreneurial activity, and the introduction of the mechanism of convertibility and the concept of entrepreneurial value.

While developed and illustrated at the individual and family level, this model could easily be applied to group, firm or other entrepreneurial entities (see Chapter 5 for further individual and firm level application and extension). Elsewhere in the text the ideas of community, municipal-community and cultural entrepreneurship are discussed (see chapters 7, 8 and 10). Though obviously a larger task, the shift into identifying, via the notion of entrepreneurial value, the entrepreneurial capital possessed by such entities is made possible by the groundwork presented here. In such contexts, the idea of organizational capital could well be added to the mix. This refers to 'the skills, knowledge and learning embodied within the firm over time or brought by the employees' as well as organizational relationships (Lichtenstein and Brush, 1997: 332). Dollinger (1995: 34) also includes the firm's structure, routines and systems under this rubric. Replacing the term 'firm' with 'community' or 'group' would not alter the implied nature of this form of capital.

Given the importance that entrepreneurial activity has for any economy a range of approaches to its conceptualization and investigation is needed. In respect of the former, the model developed in this chapter serves to conceptualize entrepreneurship in general terms, as well as providing a means of describing particular instances of the entrepreneurial process. As an investigative tool the model could be employed in a number of ways. Research designed with it in mind would, in comparison with the data used in the chapter, produce far greater detail concerning the forms of capital, and the component aspects of each form, that were utilized in such instances. It is also possible to move beyond description and to compare and contrast cases, as was briefly demonstrated using the case studies. This could be in terms of entrepreneurs, the enterprises they are engaged in, and the processes that unite the two. Thus, an entrepreneur's identification, possession, acquisition and exercise of capital could be examined in relation to particular factors (e.g. locality, age, gender, and ethnicity), the type of enterprise (e.g. products and services, type, and size) and the process by which that enterprise is founded and managed. While not only enhancing our knowledge of the entrepreneurial process, the data gathered in these ways are also likely to be of value in the development of policy and programmes to monitor and assist entrepreneurs and business creation.

Notes

1. The Labour Market Dynamics and Economic Participation (*LMD*) Programme, funded by the New Zealand Foundation for Research, Science and Technology, is an interdisciplinary research project that was initially designed to explain the dynamics of economic participation by exploring the interface between households and the labour market in three regional labour markets in New Zealand. The first phase of the *LMD* programme sought to explain how individuals made decisions about access and participation in the labour market, with emphasis on the life cycle of the household. The

interview data used here is from this first phase. See Shirley *et al.*, 2001a; 2001b; 2001c; and Firkin 2001a and 2001b for further details.

2. Rather than being a review of the literature *per se*, it is intended that this discussion illustrates, in brief and general terms, the issues being considered.
3. See Farkas (1996) for an alternative approach to the reconciliation of these two concepts.
4. Maori are the indigenous people of New Zealand (see Chapter 10).
5. The names used here are fictitious.
6. Chapter 6 of this text examines the idea of familial social capital, including its negative aspects, in greater detail.

References

Adler, P. and Kwon, S-W. (2002), 'Social Capital: Prospects for a New Concept', *Academy of Business Review*, Vol. 27(1), pp.17-40.

Aldrich, H. and Waldinger, R. (1990), 'Ethnicity and Entrepreneurship', *Annual Review of Sociology*, Vol. 16, pp. 111-135.

Aldrich, H. and Zimmer, C. (1986), 'Entrepreneurship Through Social Networks', in D. Sexton and R. Smilor (eds), *The Art and Science of Entrepreneurship*, Ballinger Publishing Company, Cambridge, MA.

Alvarez, S. and Busenitz, L. (2001), 'The Entrepreneurship of Resource-Based Theory', *Journal of Management*, Vol. 27, pp. 755-775.

Baines, S. and Wheelock, J. (1998), 'Working For Each Other: Gender, the Household and Micro-business Survival and Growth', *International Small Business Journal*, Vol. 17(1), pp. 16-35.

Becker, G. (1993), *Human Capital* (3rd Edition), The University of Chicago Press, Chicago and London.

Birley, S. (1985), 'The Role of Networks in the Entrepreneurial Process', *Journal of Business Venturing*, Vol. 1(1), pp. 107-117.

Bourdieu, P. (1986), 'The Forms of Capital', in J. Richardson (ed.), *The Handbook of Theory and Research for the Sociology of Education*, Greenwood Press, New York.

Brüderl, J., Preisendörfer, P. and Ziegler, R. (1992), 'Survival Chances of Newly Founded Business Organisations', *American Sociological Review*, Vol. 57, pp. 227-242.

Brüderl, J. and Preisendörfer, P. (1998), 'Network Support and the Success of Newly Founded Businesses', *Small Business Economics*, Vol. 10, pp. 213-225.

Brush, C., Greene, P., Hart, M. and Edelman L. (1997), 'Resource Configurations Over the Life Cycle of Ventures', in P. Reynolds, W. Bygrave, N. Carter, P. Davidsson, W. Gartner, C. Mason, and P. McDougall (eds), *Frontiers of Entrepreneurship Research 1997*, Proceedings of the Seventeenth Annual Entrepreneurship Conference, Babson College, MA.

Brush, C., Greene, P. and Hart, M. (2001), 'From Initial Idea to Unique Advantage: The Entrepreneurial Challenge of Constructing a Resource Base', *Academy of Management Executive*, Vol. 15(1), pp. 64-78.

Bullock, A., Stallybrass, O. and Trombley, S. (1988), *The Fontana Dictionary of Modern Thought* (2nd Ed.), Fontana, London.

Bygrave, W. and Hofer, C. (1991), 'Theorising about Entrepreneurship', *Entrepreneurship: Theory and Practice*, Vol. 16(2), pp. 13-22.

de Bruin, A. (1998), 'Entrepreneurship in a New Phase of Capitalist Development', *The Journal of Interdisciplinary Economics*, Vol. 9, pp. 185-200.

de Bruin, A. (1999), 'Towards Extending the Concept of Human Capital: A Note on Cultural Capital', *The Journal of Interdisciplinary Economics*, Vol. 10, pp. 59-70.

de Bruin, A. and Dupuis, A. (1995), 'A Closer Look at New Zealand's Superior Economic Performance: Ethnic Employment Issues', *British Review of New Zealand Studies (BRONZS)*, No. 8, pp. 85-98.

de Bruin, A. and Dupuis, A. (2000), 'Constrained Entrepreneurship: An Interdisciplinary Extension of Bounded Rationality', *The Journal of Interdisciplinary Economics*, Vol. 12, pp. 71-86.

DiMaggio, P. (1994), 'Culture and Economy', in N. Smelser and R. Swedberg (eds), *The Handbook of Economic Sociology*, Princeton University Press, Princeton, NJ and Russell Sage Foundation, New York.

Dollinger, M. (1995), *Entrepreneurship – Strategies and Resources*, Austin Press and Richard D. Irwin Inc., IL.

Farkas, G. (1996), *Human Capital or Cultural Capital: Ethnicity and Poverty Groups in an Urban School District*, Aldine de Gruyter, New York.

Firkin, P. (2001a), *'Doing the Books' – Social Capital Between Spouses in Business-Owning Families*, Working Paper No. 6 – Labour Market Dynamics Research Programme, Massey University, Albany and Palmerston North.

Firkin, P. (2001b), *Entrepreneurial Capital: A Resources-Based Conceptualisation of the Entrepreneurial Process*, Working Paper No. 7 – Labour Market Dynamics Research Programme, Massey University, Albany and Palmerston North.

Gilbertson, D., Wright, H., Yska, G., Gilbertson, D., *et al.* (1994), *Kiwi Entrepreneurs: A Study*, Graduate School of Business and Government Management Working Paper Series 1/95, Victoria University of Wellington, Wellington.

Gimeno, J., Folta, T., Cooper, A. and Woo, C. (1997), 'Survival of the Fittest? Entrepreneurial Human Capital and the Persistence of Underperforming Firms', *Administrative Science Quarterly*, Vol. 42, pp. 750-783.

Greene, P. and Brown, T. (1997), 'Resource Needs and the Dynamic Capitalism Typology', *Journal of Business Venturing*, Vol. 12, pp.161-173.

Harker, R. (1990), 'Schooling and Cultural Reproduction', in J. Codd, R. Harker and R. Nash (eds), *Political Issues in New Zealand Education* (2nd Edition), Dunmore Press, Palmerston North.

Honig, B. (1998), 'What Determines Success? Examining the Human, Financial and Social Capital of Jamaican Microentrepreneurs', *Journal of Business Venturing*, Vol. 13, pp. 371-394.

Iyigun, M. and Owen, A. (1999), 'Entrepreneurs, Professionals, and Growth', *Journal of Economic Growth*, Vol. 4, pp. 213-232.

Jary, D. and Jary, J. (1995), *Collins Dictionary of Sociology* (2nd Edition), Harper Collins Publishers, Glasgow.

Lichtenstein, B. and Brush, C. (1997), 'Salient Resources in New Ventures: A Longitudinal Study of the Composition and Changes of Key Organizational Resources in Three Entrepreneurial Firms', in P. Reynolds, W. Bygrave, N. Carter, P. Davidsson, W. Gartner, C. Mason, and P. McDougall (eds), *Frontiers of Entrepreneurship Research*, Babson College, MA.

Light, I. and Karageorgis. S. (1994), 'The Ethnic Economy', in N. Smelser and R. Swedberg (eds), *The Handbook of Economic Sociology*, Princeton University Press, Princeton, NJ and Russell Sage Foundation, New York.

Lin, N. (2001), *Social Capital: A Theory of Structure and Action*, Cambridge University Press, New York and Cambridge.

Marshack, K. (1994), 'Copreneurs and Dual-Career Couples: Are They Different?', *Entrepreneurship: Theory and Practice*, Vol. 19(1), pp. 49-69.

Morris, M. (1998), *Entrepreneurial Intensity: Sustainable Advantages for Individuals, Organisations, and Societies*, Quorum Books, Westport, CT.

Mosakowski, E. (1998), 'Entrepreneurial Resources, Organizational Choices, and Competitive Outcomes', *Organization Science: A Journal of the Institute of Management*, Vol. 9(6), pp. 625-643.

Nafziger, E. and Terrell, D. (1996), 'Entrepreneurial Human Capital and the Long-Run Survival of Firms in India', *World Development*, Vol. 24(4), pp. 689-696.

Oinas, P. (2001), 'Entrepreneurship as Mobilization of Resources: The Case of e-Commerce', in *Conference Proceedings, RENT XV, Research in Entrepreneurship and Small Business, 15th Workshop, November 22-23*, Vol. 2, pp. 127-138, Small Business Institute, Turku School of Economics and Business Administration, Turku, Finland.

Portes, A. (1995), 'Economic Sociology and the Sociology of Immigration: A Conceptual Overview', in A. Portes (ed.), *The Economic Sociology of Immigration: Essays on Networks, Ethnicity and Entrepreneurship*, Russell Sage Foundation, New York.

Portes, A. (1998), 'Social Capital: Its Origins and Applications in Modern Sociology', *Annual Review of Sociology*, Vol. 24, pp. 1-24.

Portes, A. (2000a), 'The Two Meanings of Social Capital', *Sociological Forum*, Vol. 15(1), pp. 1-12.

Portes, A. (2000b), 'Social Capital: Promise and Pitfalls of its Role in Development', *Journal of Latin American Studies*, Vol. 32, pp. 529-547.

Reynolds, P. (1991), 'Sociology and Entrepreneurship: Concepts and Contributions', *Entrepreneurship: Theory and Practice*, Vol. 16(2), pp. 47-70.

Reynolds, P. and White, S. (1997), *The Entrepreneurial Process: Economic Growth, Men, Women and Minorities*, Quorum Books, Westport, CT.

Sanders, J. and Nee, V. (1996), 'Immigrant Self-Employment: The Family as Social Capital and the Value of Human Capital', *American Sociological Review*, Vol. 61(2), pp. 231-249.

Schuller, T. (2000), 'Social and Human Capital: The Search for Appropriate Technomethodology', *Policy Studies*, Vol. 21(1), pp. 25-35.

Shanahan, S. and Tuma, N. (1994), 'The Sociology of Distribution and Redistribution', in N. Smelser and R. Swedberg (eds), *The Handbook of Economic Sociology*, Princeton University Press, Princeton, NJ and Russell Sage Foundation, New York.

Shirley, I., Firkin, P., Cremer, R., Eichbaum, C., de Bruin, A., Dewe, P., Dupuis, A. and Spoonley, P. (2001a), *Transitions in the Hawkes Bay Labour Market: Education and Training – Research Report*, Labour Market Dynamics and Economic Participation Research Programme, Massey University, Albany and Palmerston North.

Shirley, I., Firkin, P., Cremer, R., Eichbaum, C., de Bruin, A., Dewe, P., Dupuis, A. and Spoonley, P. (2001b), *Transitions in the Hawkes Bay Labour Market: Welfare and Unemployment – Research Report*, Labour Market Dynamics and Economic Participation Research Programme, Massey University, Albany and Palmerston North.

Shirley, I., Firkin, P., Cremer, R., Eichbaum, C., de Bruin, A., Dewe, P., Dupuis, A. and Spoonley, P. (2001c), *Transitions in the Hawkes Bay Labour Market: Unpaid Work and Paid Work – Research Report*, Labour Market Dynamics and Economic Participation Research Programme, Massey University, Albany and Palmerston North.

Smith, C. (2000), 'Managing Work and Family in Small "Copreneurial" Businesses: An Australian Study', *Women in Management Review*, Vol. 15(5/6), pp. 283-289.

Steier, L. (2000), 'Entrepreneurship and the Evolution of Angel Financial Networks', *Organization Studies*, Vol. 21(1), pp. 163-192.

Chapter 5

Electronic Entrepreneurship

Anne de Bruin

Introduction

The global age is an age marked by rapid innovation and the spread of new computer-based electronic technology, communications and information systems (IS). This phenomenon in itself opens up a wealth of entrepreneurial opportunities. For instance, the pervasiveness of the internet, which Castells (2001: 2) neatly conveys by pointing out that it is 'a communication medium that allows, for the first time, the communication of many to many, in chosen time on a global scale', has presented both new ways of working and entrepreneurial possibilities. The rise and growth of electronic commerce or e-commerce characterizes business development in the global age.

The definition of e-commerce can be quite encompassing. For instance, according to Ostasiewski (n.d.: 1) '[I]t is a process where two or more parties conduct business transactions via computer and some type of communications network, often the Internet. The transactions can include business-to-business, online retail, financial, and transfer of information used in business activities'. Since it involves a rapidly evolving technology this definition is also a dynamic one. Moreover, as other forms of communication that utilize modern technology such as fax machines, telephones, television and video become computer-enabled, the idea of 'media convergence' (see for example Wilson, 2000; Fitzgerald, 2001; Jenkins, 2001) has also come to be debated, making the precise definition of e-commerce even more difficult and the impact of the new information and communications technology (ICT) even more wide-ranging.

This chapter is not intended, however, to discuss in detail issues of e-commerce or business start-ups, where the production or use of new innovations and electronic technologies, together with their related components, themselves form a direct base or product of the business e.g. companies growing from the design of new software, or production of office automation and network systems or the dot.com enterprise. Rather, the purpose of this chapter is to highlight 'electronic opportunity', especially from a resource-based perspective and mainly for small enterprises and the self-employed individual. The introduction of the personal computer and attendant software has made ICT more widely accessible and affordable. Information technology and electronic resources expand the capital base as a resource component in its own right, but also, importantly, through facilitating the conversion of other existing resources to derive 'entrepreneurial value' (Firkin, 2001; see also Chapter 4 – 'Entrepreneurial Capital'). A stages approach to resource reconfiguration through the idea of the 'entrepreneurial value chain' is also presented. This chapter therefore, further operationalizes and extends the theoretical conceptualization presented in Chapter 4.

The electronically based, entrepreneurial use of various forms of capital is demonstrated mainly by use of a case study approach. Examples from the electronic music industry are used to show how through access to reasonably priced equipment, there is conversion of embodied resources of the individual to a differentiated product. This industry is also used to exemplify the notion of the entrepreneurial value chain. Interview data from a study conducted as part of the Labour Market Dynamics (LMD) Research Programme[1] is utilized to illustrate how ICT impacts on entrepreneurial activity. The chapter additionally includes brief comment on the 'embeddedness' (see Chapter 1) implications of virtual or online networking and the importance of the effective use of IS resources.

A Resource-Based Approach

The types of resources necessary for growth of firms and innovation, the resource profile of the entrepreneur, resource ownership and control, and the resource mix are all considerations that feature prominently in the analysis of entrepreneurship (see for example Stevenson and Gumpert, 1985; Cooper *et al.*, 1994; Greene and Brown, 1997; Brush *et al.*, 1997, 2001). The resource classification adopted for this chapter is that of Brush *et al.* (2001). Resources comprise: financial capital, which is the financial resources for starting up and growing a business; human capital, which includes education, skills, experience; social capital, which consists of the networks of advisors and contacts in the industry, and other social and family contacts; physical capital, which incorporates the tangible assets such as equipment essential for the operation of the business; organizational capital, which involves the relationships, operational structures, routines and culture of the organization; and technological capital, which is differentiated from physical capital and is usually knowledge-based, entailing proprietary control of processes and/or technology, for instance via patent, license or trademark. Dollinger (1995) provides clarification of the nature of technological capital by specifying the difference between technological capital and intellectual capital, though intellectual capital is subsumed under human capital in the categorization adopted for this chapter: 'Intellectual capital is embodied in a person or persons and is mobile. If the person or persons leave the firm, so does the capital. Technological resources are physical or legal entities and are owned by the organization' (Dollinger, 1995: 33).

To the Brush *et al.* (2001) five forms of capital, cultural capital is added as a separate capital form. Although elsewhere it has been suggested that the state of embodied cultural capital may be included as part of human capital (de Bruin and Dupuis, 1995; de Bruin 1999a, 1999b), I now believe that it is important to consider culture and cultural capital more explicitly. As pointed out in the 'Introduction' and also in Chapter 10 – 'Indigenous Entrepreneurship', culture matters in the global age.

The notion of cultural capital used is that of Bourdieu (1986) who identifies three states of cultural capital: the institutional, objectified and embodied states. The institutional state is encompassed within human capital as it can be converted into educational qualifications. The objectified state comprises cultural goods such as pictures, books, instruments etc. and these can be sold to become financial capital. The embodied state of cultural capital (Bourdieu, 1986: 243-244; DiMaggio, 1994: 39) which is the body of understandings, knowledge and style of a group that becomes inherent in persons of that group over time and is integral to the socialization process, may also be harnessed for wealth creating purposes. Bourdieu, through his notion of convertibility, argues that both social and cultural capital can be transformed into other forms of capital, to have a monetary value. As Portes (1998: 4) highlights, the transformation route is not clearly evident and simple. It could be a long drawn out and complex process, and especially so for the conversion of embodied cultural capital. I contend, however, that electronic technology can facilitate transformation and shorten the route.

Firkin (2001; Chapter 4) introduces the idea of entrepreneurial value when he argues that not all of an individual's total capital will be useful in an entrepreneurial sense. Capital has 'entrepreneurial value' only when involved in the entrepreneurial process and converted to entrepreneurial purpose or advantage. Firkin terms the component of total capital that has entrepreneurial value, 'entrepreneurial capital'. To this analysis is now added the idea of an 'entrepreneurial value chain'. An entrepreneurial value chain emerges from the processes of deriving and adding entrepreneurial value to resources/capital at different stages. For instance, as Brush *et al.* (2001) emphasize, personal resources need to be transformed into organizational resources. A new resource bundle with organizational capital which comprises the 'skills, knowledge and learning embodied within the firm over time or brought by the employees' (Lichtenstein and Brush, 1997: 332) becomes necessary to derive further profit opportunities. There is thus mobilization of entrepreneurial value from different packages of total capital, so that profitable opportunities are sought at a variety of steps of entrepreneurial activity.

At this point, it is useful to elaborate further on organizational capital. Tomer (1987: 2) highlights the fact that organizational capital 'is embodied in either organizational relationships, [the skills of] particular organization members, the organizations repositories of information, or some combination of the above in order to improve the functioning of the organization'. In the 'e-conomy' (Castells, 2001: 90), which is a rapidly changing and evolving economy, the knowledge and information base embodied in the workers and other repositories requires constant reprogramming and modification to suit this environment. There is a widespread recognition of the value of on-the-job learning and the life-long learning of workers in this global age, but what is less recognized is the significance of the effective use of IS resources for the enhancement of organizational capital. Better use of IS resources is increasingly important for small and medium enterprises (SMEs) in an era of heightened competitive pressures.

Deriving Entrepreneurial Value

The electronic music industry provides useful examples of the use of the new technology of the global age, as affordable physical capital to enable the convertibility of cultural capital. It also can be used to illustrate the notion of the entrepreneurial value chain. It should be mentioned here, however, that the understanding of culture and hence cultural capital adhered to is one that is wider than the common identification of culture simply with ethnicity. In fact, as pointed out in the 'Introduction' to this book, cultural embeddedness and identity increasingly matters in the global age. I adopt here a broad definition of culture to include the possibility of multiple cultural identities. Thus for example, followers of 'Garage Music', discussed next, are culturally united across territorial boundaries and ethnicities. Broader interpretations of cultural capital correspondingly encompass wider possibilities and potential for harnessing this form of capital to derive entrepreneurial value.

The emergence and spread of a new music style and sound since the 1980s – garage music, which is a sub genre of electronic dance music – is used here as an example to highlight that opportunity creation and identification, directly linked in with the technological forms of the global age, is often a distinguishing feature of what I term 'electronic entrepreneurship'. Garage music is a distinctive dance music style created on electronic equipment. It is 'the continuation of Disco by other means. ... after the collapse of disco, disco music was proving too expensive to record live. Cheap synthesizers, sequencers and drum machines suited the now highly specialized dance market' (Brown, n.d.). With origins in Chicago and initially popularized in the New York dance club Paradise Garage, from where it is believed to derive its name, and through a small network of New York and New Jersey, U.S.A. record labels in the late 1980s, this DJ-based electronic music has now spread internationally.

Specialist, independent 'little record labels' have sprung up outside the US, such as in the UK, a phenomenon facilitated by technological developments. In common with many other industries, the garage music industry also uses the Internet and web sites extensively as a resource to promote and inform about the music and forthcoming garage events and also to sell products direct via the net. Reciprocal links to web sites serve as a form of networking as well. These include the vertical linkages in the industry from record labels, radio stations, dance clubs, DJs and DJ collectives, music downloads and other related goods and services.

One success story in the garage music scene is that of 21 year old Daniel Bedingfield who went to the top of the UK pop charts at the end of 2001 with his debut single 'Gotta Get Thru This'. In that this musician may be regarded as self-employed, components of his total capital may be perceived in terms of entrepreneurial value. Bedingfield is typical of many musicians who come from families and groups where music is a vital aspect of their lives and part of their embodied cultural capital. His family environment was steeped in music. As an interview with his grandmother highlighted, '...the whole family loved to sing, Daniel and sisters Natasha and Nicola had formed a synth pop band and released a single when he was 18. The Bedingfields also sang gospel songs at church' (Aronson, 2001: A3).

The hit dance track was recorded in Bedingfield's South London bedroom with only a computer and microphone costing £1000 (Aronson, 2001). In this way, the embodied cultural capital of the artist was combined with electronic physical capital and easily mobilized to yield entrepreneurial value and thus activating an entrepreneurial value chain. This resource mix yielded objectified cultural capital in the form of the dance track which could be more readily converted into financial capital for the artist. The next stage in extracting entrepreneurial value from a different package of total capital, and a re-bundling of resources, came when the independent London-based garage record label, Relentless Records, purchased the track for £400,000 (Anonymous, n.d.[a]). The organizational capital and other resources of the firm form a new mix of total capital and becomes yet another link in the entrepreneurial value chain. Technological capital also enters into the picture with copyright. In fact, at the levels of each firm in the supply chain, further resource mixes represent added links in the entrepreneurial value chain. For instance, Relentless Records contracted Aspect Marketing to help promote the Bedingfield, 'Gotta Get Thru This', release. Interestingly, however, this promotion used conventional means, distributing over 23,000 responsive postcard mailers (Anonymous, 2001). This supplemented Relentless Record's web site promotions. Thus non-electronic modes of business activity often complement the electronic medium.

A further example from the world of new popular music which provides an illustration of the mobilization of the entrepreneurial value of social capital is that of a top New Zealand, but now London-based, 'futurejazz' exponent, keyboardist, 27 year-old Mark de Clive-Lowe. This case demonstrates that typically, virtual networking and face-to-face social contact supplement and complement each other. de Clive-Lowe has made his own way into the 'Western London sound' – a diverse set of musical influences, such as break-beat, jazz, disco, Latin, house, rap and soul, that has fused into one unique style that is often referred to as the West London Sound. This sound is to be found in locales such as London's Notting Hill Gate, and is exemplified by music at the 'Off-Centre' Club (actually in East London) and has been popularized in the past few years by such producers as Restless Soul/Phil Asher, I.G. Culture, and 4Hero (Anonymous, n.d.[b]).

de Clive-Lowe quickly found his feet in the West London Sound scene through social networks cultivated through both virtual and real-time links. Arriving in London in 1998, he was soon welcomed as a regular player drawing initially on the networks of his friends and especially fellow musician, 30 year-old saxophonist, Nathan Haines, who was already there. Even before his shift to London, however, de Clive-Lowe had begun his virtual networks, through setting up and promoting himself and a website supporting and linking New Zealand jazz artists – jazz.co.nz. (de Bruin, 1998). Set up in the mid-1990s as a way of spreading information about the New Zealand jazz scene, de Clive-Lowe succeeded in creating the site as both a resource and springboard for virtual networking through an associated mailing list, *Jazztalk*, which often featured comment and information from both artists and fans. de Clive-Lowe is also a good exemplar of the 'do-it-yourself' Kiwi attitude. Early in his career, entrepreneurially drawing on his human, social and financial capital, he and engineer friend, Andrew Dubber, set-up and ran their own jazz label, Tap Records, which sold de Clive-Lowe's music and that of other artists such as veteran New Zealand jazz trumpeter, Kim Paterson. Tap Records, and its related infrastructures, also spawned compilation CDs to promote Auckland jazz such as *Manifesto Auckland Jazz Sampler (1997)* that was produced by the South Pacific Jazz Collective and Tap. Since 1998, de Clive-Lowe was slowly evolving to his current 'futurejazz' sound, as well as establishing important musical and promotional networks. Interestingly, he had also linked with garage music pioneer, Francois K, during a three-month trip to New York (de Bruin, 1999).

Both the Bedingfield and de Clive-Lowe examples serve to illustrate that the new electronic technology can open up entrepreneurial opportunity for younger people especially in sectors such as the creative sector, which have hitherto been difficult for the young to 'break into' on the basis of the their own capital base. It must be added here, however, that entrepreneurial activity of both elder and youth can be facilitated by ICT (see also Chapters 11 and 12 – 'Elder Entrepreneurship' and 'Youth Entrepreneurship' respectively).

Opportunities of the Electronic Medium

This section highlights how the e-conomy has been used for enhancing the flexibility of the work and business organization process. I draw here on interview data from a study conducted as part of the Labour Market Dynamics (LMD) Research Programme[2] to show how self-employment in the global age is often interwoven with ICT, which also provides the means for harnessing and growing the entrepreneurial value of an individual's capital base.

The current phase of the LMD research aims to explore, through in-depth interviews, the experiences of men and women involved in non-standard working arrangements in New Zealand. Generally, standard work has been defined as full-time employment with regular, permanent hours, largely carried out between Mondays and Fridays and with stability in the nature of employment. Non-standard work, therefore, includes aspects such as the lack of expectations of continued employment, workload fluctuations, flexibility, the location of employment and changing employment relationships. Recent research has demonstrated that increasingly, New Zealanders are employed under a range of conditions that depart significantly from standard employment conditions (Firkin *et al.*, 2002).

Participants for the study were chosen from people who lived in the greater Auckland area and who fulfilled three principal criteria. First, they were currently involved in non-standard ways of working. They may have experienced career transitions from standard to non-standard work or have never worked in the 'traditional way'. Second, the work they were involved in had to have either a knowledge or technology component (or both). Third, the sample represented a cross section of people who met the first two criteria. Participants were involved in semi-structured, in-depth interviews that lasted for about an hour. They were also asked to complete a short questionnaire that required them to rate their experiences in non-standard work. The research participants were fairly evenly split by gender (19 male and 21 female). They were aged between 21 and 52 years. The majority was clustered in the 35-45 year bracket (53 per cent) though this was more pronounced for females (62 per cent) as compared to males (42 per cent). Their educational backgrounds tended more towards tertiary (university or polytechnic based) qualifications with 60 per cent of people holding such credentials. Those whose highest qualifications were secondary school based made up 17.5 per cent of participants. Professional or trade certifications and the like accounted for the balance.

Although studies on entrepreneurship no longer focus exclusively on the characteristics of the entrepreneur, the personal resource endowment of the self-employed individual is important, as 'the entrepreneur is the primary resource' (Brush *et al.*, 2001: 65). The extent of personal resources could vary depending on the circumstances that lead to self-employment which may be entered into voluntarily (pull factors) or can be the result of retrenchment/redundancy and the like (push factors). Push factors are associated with poor employment alternatives, often the result of weak labour markets, and mean that people are forced into such a move. Other factors, such as personal circumstances, may also exercise a push towards this type of work.

In the LMD research into non-standard work, the majority of participants (60 per cent) were attracted (pulled), into alternative work arrangements. Males made up almost two-thirds of this group. Indeed, almost 80 per cent of all the male participants were prompted into alternative arrangements by pull factors. Most of the moves into self-employment – some form of contracting or small business operation – were driven by a desire to be employed this way. In some cases, this was implied in dissatisfaction with being an employee and motives were expressed in terms of hopes for an improvement of lifestyle and/or income. A small group saw alternative working arrangements as one way to balance other commitments, such as full-time study, sport and caring for a family. By contrast, only six transitions (15 per cent) can be identified as exclusively the outcome of people being pushed into non-standard work forms.

Opportunities presented by electronic technology played a significant role in creating and/or sustaining the work of the interviewees. Many of the interviewees in the LMD study highlighted the usefulness of so-called 'virtual' networking in providing a growing spectrum of opportunities not previously available. For example, one participant, commenting on networking noted:

> Really the Internet revolution has made that possible. It wasn't possible 15 years ago. There is all sorts available to you now, off shore, anywhere in the world, anybody you happened to have bumped into, which you can use for specific areas of expertise.

Furthermore, several of the participants in the study engaged people to provide a specific area of expertise without the client necessarily being aware of who was involved in the project. The contractor acquiring the work would be the contact and, as one participant suggested:

> Someone would contact me with a specific requirement and if I was interested in fronting for the job I could invisibly haul in behind me as many people as I choose.

Another commented that when considering a proposal for a contract:

> ...I would bring in someone to assist me if I thought I needed that. ...One needs to just maintain the thought of just acknowledging what you know and what you don't know and then you are able to provide the service that your client needs.

Thus virtual networks featured not only in relation to the expansion of an individual's social capital but also as a facilitator of the entrepreneurial process and a possible business organizational model. To quote Castells (2001: 67), this organizational model is the model of 'the network enterprise', which 'is neither a network of enterprises nor an intra-firm, networked organization. Rather, it is a lean agency of economic activity, built around specific business projects, which are enacted by networks of various composition and origin: *the network is the enterprise*'. The LMD interviews provided support for the operation of the network enterprise at the level of micro-enterprises.[3] Furthermore, the management of contract relationships, especially for some of the sole operator interviewees in the LMD programme, mainly through these virtual networks, also illustrates not only a new and added facet of social capital but also of organizational capital. Indeed, this dimension might be perceived as virtual organizational capital.

The ICT revolution that characterizes the global age has altered the way of work and opened up new horizons in lines of business with a long (and colourful) past. The following example from the LMD study is that of a self-employed woman running a horoscope business.[4] Thus, the age-old practice of astrology delivered and conducted in a way that fits the new electronic age. Interestingly, this person had been unemployed for several years, but now the electronic technologies and non-standard work has contributed to her transformation into a business entrepreneur. Also, similar to several other older women who enter business by drawing on their life experience (McKay, 2001), this woman drew on her life-long interest to go into self-employment. Although this worker had formal training as a beautician, she mobilized the knowledge built up through a lifetime hobby to obtain entrepreneurial value.

The interviewee perceives herself as a consultant and a sub-contractor. The business had two main aspects to it: phone consultations through an 0900 number and writing commissions involving astrologies for several different media websites. The latter segment of the business was personal computer and email and electronic document-based. Personal readings through email were a new area that the business had also branched into recently. The business receives credit card payment for services through a web site and reduces costs in this way. The web is used for further skill acquisition and information:

> I get a lot of information from the net. There are several really quite good sites that I use just to keep my hand in ... through the Internet there are courses but there is a lot of information through books as well as the Internet. But I suppose I would use the Internet more because it is free and I can do it at night when you are a little bit tired so it's sort of more an informal area ...

The second case presented is that of a self-employed teleworker in a small town in the South Island of New Zealand.[5] Qualified as a pharmacist, this woman worked as Dispensary Manager for a busy pharmacy for eleven years. With changing childcare responsibilities (the birth of two children), she began to look for home-based work. Her 'passion for writing' was 'long standing' (Hamilton, 2001) and she combined this passion with her pharmaceutical knowledge, to telework. She finds jobs through web sites, conducts research and obtains information through on-line libraries and FDA web sites. She taught herself web design, now maintains her own web site (http://globaltelecommute.com/) and has a weekly ezine – electronic newsletter, and her up-skilling is through e-learning. In a postscript to the interview, this worker, through a personal communication, informed me that she would re-locate to the United Kingdom after being 'head-hunted' via the internet. She also pointed out that since all her contacts were online 'I take them with me', thus illustrating how the new technology has enhanced the mobility of social capital.

The third interviewee profiled is a youth entrepreneur who runs the web-based company nzgirl Ltd.[6] At around 21 years of age, with no formal educational qualifications in the area and a couple of years work experience in a web development company, she began the venture, an online magazine, (targeted at a highly localized niche market – young sub-teen and teenage girls in New Zealand), which was a new concept for New Zealand (see http://nzgirl.co.nz/index.php). While at a superficial level, this case appears to be merely an IT commodity based enterprise, what is really relevant is that this example demonstrates that in bypassing the traditional medium (a hard copy magazine), the need for a larger resource base is also bypassed. Thus a smaller total capital base, especially in terms of human and financial capital, is harnessed for entrepreneurial purposes via the new technology. As the entrepreneur observes:

> The beauty about this industry is that nobody is qualified. It is such a new medium that nobody really has much experience. In fact I am classed as one of the older people in the industry because I had been in the business two years before doing *nzgirl*, so I have four years worth of experience which is pretty rare. ... Exactly, there are about ten people in New Zealand that have that much experience that are out there as consultants etc. It is kind of nice being in an industry that is so new. ... I am only 23 and when I go into publishers meetings and things I'm pretty sure they find it rather amusing.

Deriving entrepreneurial value from networking is also an important component of the growing entrepreneurial capital of this entrepreneur, who maintains that:

> Networks are extremely important. It's surprising in the last two years how many people have got to know me now, it's good. There are two folders now, one with the business side, Marketing Managers etc ... that's really good because we have never had any money to spend on advertising so it was really about aligning ourselves to certain things that go on out there and getting as much PR as we can.

New product spin-offs are also in the pipeline for nzgirl Ltd. There are nzgirl merchandising opportunities being explored. This is likely to lead to the creation of new links in this entrepreneurial value chain. Should the merchandise range include a license, this would bring a new form of capital, technological capital, into the entrepreneurial capital mix.

Virtual Networks and Embeddedness

As observed in the previous two sections, virtual networks enhance social capital and organizational capital, are an information source and provide valuable means for functioning of the network enterprise.[7] In this section, I comment on virtual networks from the embeddedness perspective.

An important advantage of embeddedness usually cited is the idea that embedded networks form an efficient information conduit, passing on more than just price and quantity information that would characterize simple arm's-length transactions (see Chapter 1 – 'Introduction', for an in-depth discussion of this concept). Valuable production information, market trends, organizational stratagem and detailed data on a partner's production function can also be relayed through the embedded link. With this fine-grained information transfer, and especially with the exchange of information regarding production functions, it is possible that firms might negotiate a fair price between them in the exchange (Uzzi, 1997: 45-46). Trust facilitates the removal of information asymmetry between network partners, with no firm having a major information advantage over another within an embedded network (Uzzi, 1997). This, in turn, can enable better co-ordination, curtailing inefficiencies (Clark and Fujimoto, 1991; Fruin, 1992; Nishiguchi, 1994). In some situations, however, firms within an embedded network tend to be isolated from information sources outside their network. Actors within the network may demonstrate a tendency to ignore, or be blocked from receiving, information from sources external to a firm's usual set of network contacts. It results in 'information isolation' (Uzzi, 1997: 59). 'Atrophied embeddedness' is an outcome where embedded ties become too entrenched, hinder growth, flexibility and adaptability to change and lead to information gaps (de Bruin and de Bruin, 2002). Virtual networking can, however, mitigate the dangers of atrophied embeddedness.

A unique advantage of many virtual networks is their dynamic and contestable nature, where contestability is freedom of entry into, and exit from, the network. Unlike formalized firm networks or face-to-face communication and personal contact, online communication can be more fluid and informal. Rather than information isolation, this medium allows for greater information sharing as 'some entrepreneurs may be more willing to share their thoughts with, or ask questions of 'cyber anonymous peers' who are not in the company' (Evans and Volery, 2001: 341). Online business forums, chat rooms and other online interactions offer industry and interest specific knowledge and guidance, often at no or trivial cost and with few barriers to entry.

It may be argued that the increasing use of virtual networks might pose a challenge in terms of how trust may be engendered. Although trust is difficult to quantify and assign a value to, it is an essential element in relations within and between firms (Nooteboom, 2002) and is inherent in embeddedness (Granovetter, 1985; Uzzi, 1997). There is no evidence to suggest, however, that virtual networking and the network enterprise is characterized solely by opportunism and does not involve trust. Neither need it be a faceless medium, what with teleconferencing and the like. Moreover project tasks well performed within a virtual team and repeat contracts build a sense of reliability and therefrom, trust. Furthermore, online networking can complement other forms of social capital and can also grow from, and into, personal contact.[8]

Brief Corollary Comment

If, as Alvarez and Busenitz (2001: 762) assert, 'the entrepreneurial problem is how to secure the best use of resources to obtain a profit', then the management of information technologies and the effective use of information systems (IS) by small enterprises is of vital importance. As Deshaies (1998: 315) highlights, '[T]he inadequate performance and unsatisfactory use of information systems applications and resources constitutes a major problem for many small businesses'.

In order to reduce this inefficiency, a strategic, participatory approach to the implementation of IS, realistic policy and management concepts, and tools to plan and organize the firm's information resources, including training, are necessary (Deshaies, 1998). In terms of the resource-based emphasis of this chapter it is also important to note that improvements in the effectiveness of IS augments organizational capital.

Business survival is increasingly dependent on the use and deployment of ICT. Slow response to the changes brought about by new electronic mediums and inability to effectively use IT and IS could mean that small and medium enterprises (SMEs) would lose their competitive advantage in serving small community or local niche markets as larger technologically enabled business encroach on this localized arena of operation (Kleindl, 2000). By the same token, Fariselli *et al.* (1999) argue that SMEs can reduce their competitive disadvantage, *vis-à-vis* larger firms in the global market-place, through the use of electronic commerce networks. For instance, smaller firms can group together to gain access to e-payment systems. They emphasize the 'important synergies between e-commerce (virtual) networks and (real) production networks' (Fariselli *et al.*, 1999: 261).

Concluding Comments

The key intention of this chapter was to convey an overall idea that ICT vitally impacts on and interacts with the entrepreneurial process in the global age. It is worth reiterating here that this chapter was not concerned with IT service and product enterprise possibilities. Rather, the main purpose was to highlight that electronic entrepreneurship opens up a range of new opportunities in terms of the resource-based perspective of entrepreneurial activity. The new ICT facilitates the mobilization of existing capital and fast-tracks the conversion of some forms of capital for entrepreneurial purposes. It also grows the capital base.

Through further operationalization and extension of the entrepreneurial capital concept presented in Chapter 4, this chapter confirms the usefulness of this resource-based theoretical construct. The notion of the entrepreneurial value chain offered here conveys the dynamism and evolution that characterizes entrepreneurship and shows that the concept of entrepreneurial capital is not a static one confined to the start-up phase of entrepreneurial activity. Given the electronic emphasis of this chapter, the entrepreneurial value chain can be set in motion with ICT featuring as an integral part of total entrepreneurial capital, or as a catalyst in harnessing entrepreneurial value from an existing total capital bundle. Organizational and social capital can also be augmented through the effective use of the IS resources and virtual networking. New links in the entrepreneurial value chain are created when different resource configurations result at different steps of entrepreneurial activity, often accompanied by an expansion of total entrepreneurial capital. New links can also be associated with new products or complementary services that spring from the original entrepreneurial activity.

The speed of change of the ICT revolution makes it difficult for academic research to keep pace. Therefore, the need exists for empirical studies on the unprecedented potential ICT presents for entrepreneurship. Furthermore, as Low (2001: 23) emphasizes, '...it is entrepreneurship scholars that should be developing frameworks for explaining the opportunity space of the Internet'. It is hoped that the resource based position of this chapter will go some way toward assisting in this future framework development.

As a final comment, I draw attention to the need to understand the dimensions and consequences of the 'digital divide' in a globally connected world (see, for example, Castells, 2001: 247-274). Mitigation of the digital divide, even in the most basic way, can have a far reaching impact especially for enterprise – 'like rain falling on parched earth' (Sansoni, 2002: 42), as starkly brought home by the spread of the information exchange for agricultural commodities in rural Mali, one of the poorest regions in sub-Saharan Africa. Indeed, I cannot phrase the need for bridging the digital divide better than Castells does: 'In a global economy, and in a network society where most things are dependent on these Internet-based networks, to be switched off is to be sentenced to marginality – or compelled to find an alternative principle of centrality' (Castells, 2001: 277), however, '[F]or as long as you want to live in society, at this time and in this place, you will have to deal with the network society. Because we live in the Internet Galaxy' (Castells, 2001: 282). As the global age progresses, there can be no doubt that ICT will be a fundamental aspect of the exercise of entrepreneurship.

Notes

1. The Labour Market Dynamics and Economic Participation (LMD) Programme, funded by the New Zealand Foundation for Research, Science and Technology, is an interdisciplinary research project at Massey University. The author has been on the research team since 1999. The interview data used here is from the current phase of the programme which delves into non-standard work (see Firkin *et al.*, 2002; Spoonley *et al.*, 2002). Chapter 4 presented data from the first phase of the programme which sought to explain how individuals made decisions about access and participation in the labour market, with emphasis on the life cycle of the household.
2. Ibid.
3. Online consulting services provided by multinational professional service firms, demonstrate a form of operation of the network enterprise in the setting of large firms and as distinct organizational sectors – arms, of the multinational. Ernst & Young's *Ernie*, set up in 1995, a subscription-based, password-protected web site which interactively supplies customized services and consulting is one such illustration (see www.eyonline.com).
4. Separate and additional consent for the inclusion of interview material originally gathered in the LMD study was gained from the interviewee profiled here, who has seen and approved what has been written on her personal experiences and business.
5. Ibid.
6. Ibid.

7. For an interesting exploration of the online services for entrepreneurs, including information gathering, networking, consulting, counseling, and education and training, see Evans and Volery (2001).

8. Large scale virtual networking can grow from personal networking. A good illustration is the First Tuesday initiative that started with an informal get together of around 50 like minded people in Britain, agreeing to meet as the name suggests every first Tuesday of the month in 1998, and this has grown to become 'First Tuesday: The World's Leading Business Forum Company in the Technologies Sector' (http://www.firsttuesday.com/), with thousands of members in the UK and Europe.

Acknowledgement

This chapter contains part of the research on non-standard work that has been funded by the New Zealand Foundation for Research, Science and Technology and I acknowledge, with gratitude, that support. I would also like to sincerely thank Patrick Firkin for his insightful comments.

References

Alvarez, S. and Busenitz, L. (2001), 'The Entrepreneurship of Resource-Based Theory', *Journal of Management*, Vol. 27, pp. 755-775.

Anonymous (2001), www.aspectmarketing.co.uk (accessed 1 June, 2002).

Anonymous (n. d. [a]) http://www.bbc.co.uk/radio1/artist_area/bedingfielddaniel/ (accessed 20 May, 2002).

Anonymous (n.d. [b]), 'Mark de Clive-Lowe: Biography', http://www.jazz.co.nz/tap/mark/bio.html (accessed 25 May, 2002).

Aronson, C. (2001), 'Kiwi at Heart Dances up Charts with DIY Single', *New Zealand Herald*, 4 December, p. A3.

Bourdieu, P. (1986), 'The Forms of Capital', in J. Richardson (ed.), *The Handbook of Theory and Research for the Sociology of Education*, Greenwood Press, New York.

Brown, C. (n.d.) 'What is Garage', http://www.garage-music.com/garage1.htm (accessed 20 May, 2002).

Brush, C., Greene, P., Hart, M. and Edelman L. (1997), 'Resource Configurations Over the Life Cycle of Ventures', in P. Reynolds, W. Bygrave, N. Carter, P. Davidsson, W. Gartner, C. Mason and P. McDougall (eds), *Frontiers of Entrepreneurship Research 1997*, Proceedings of the Seventeenth Annual Entrepreneurship Conference, Babson College, MA.

Brush, C., Greene, P. and Hart, M. (2001), 'From Initial Idea to Unique Advantage: The Entrepreneurial Challenge of Constructing a Resource Base', *Academy of Management Executive*, Vol. 15(1), pp. 64-78.

Castells, M. (2001), *The Internet Galaxy*, Oxford University Press, New York.

Clark, K., and Fujimoto, T. (1991), *Product Development Performance*, Harvard Business School Press, Boston.

Cooper, A., Gimeno-Gascon, F. and Woo, C. (1994), 'Initial Human and Financial Capital as Predictors of New Venture Performance', *Journal of Business Venturing*, Vol. 9, pp. 371-395.

de Bruin, A.R. (1998) 'Mark de Clive-Lowe', http://www.suite101.com/article.cfm/new_zealand_music_scene/5337) (accessed 25 May, 2002).

de Bruin, A.R. (1999), 'Six Degrees Away From Mark', http://www.suite101. com/article.cfm/new_zealand_music_scene/22410 (accessed 25 May, 2002).

de Bruin, A. (1999a), 'Cultural Capital', in P. O'Hara (ed.), *Encyclopedia of Political Economy*, Routledge, London and New York, pp. 169-171.

de Bruin, A. (1999b), 'Towards Extending the Concept of Human Capital: A Note on Cultural Capital', *The Journal of Interdisciplinary Economics*, Vol. 10, pp. 59-70.

de Bruin, A. and de Bruin, J. (2002), 'Atrophied Embeddedness: Towards Extending Explanation of Japan's Growth Slowdown', *The Journal of Interdisciplinary Economics*, Vol. 13, pp. 401-427.

de Bruin, A. and Dupuis, A. (1995), 'A Closer Look at New Zealand's Superior Economic Performance: Ethnic Employment Issues', *British Review of New Zealand Studies (BRONZS)*, No. 8, pp. 85-98.

Deshaies, L. (1998), 'Information Systems', in P. Julien (ed.), *The State of the Art in Small Business and Entrepreneurship*, Ashgate, Aldershot and Brookfield.

DiMaggio, P. (1994), 'Culture and Economy', in N. Smelser and R. Swedberg (eds), *The Handbook of Economic Sociology*, Princeton University Press, Princeton, NJ, and Russell Sage Foundation, New York, pp. 27-57.

Dollinger, M. (1995), *Entrepreneurship: Strategies and Resources*, Irwin, Boston.

Evans, D. and Volery, T. (2001), 'Online Business Development Services for Entrepreneurs: An Exploratory Study', *Entrepreneurship and Regional Development*, Vol. 13(4), pp. 333-350.

Fariselli, P., Oughton, C. Picory, C. and Sugden, R. (1999), 'Electronic Commerce and the Future for SMEs in a Global Market-Place: Networking and Public Policies', *Small Business Economics*, Vol. 12, pp. 261-275.

Firkin, P. (2001), *Entrepreneurial Capital: A Resources-Based Conceptualisation of the Entrepreneurial Process*, Working Paper No. 7 – Labour Market Dynamics Research Programme, Massey University, Albany and Palmerston North.

Firkin, P., McLaren. E., Spoonley, P., de Bruin, A., Dupuis, A., Perera, H., Cremer, R. and Overton, J. (2002), *Non-Standard Work: Alternative Working Arrangements Amongst Knowledge Workers*, Research Report Series 2002/1, Labour Market Dynamics Research Programme, Massey University, Albany and Palmerston North.

Fitzgerald, M. (2001), 'Media Convergence Faces Tech Barrier', *Editor and Publisher*, January 15, pp. 30, 31.

Fruin, W. (1992), *The Japanese Enterprise System*, Oxford University Press, New York.

Granovetter, M. (1985), 'Economic Action and Social Structure: The Problem of Embeddedness', *American Journal of Sociology*, Vol. 91(3), pp. 481-510.

Greene, P. and Brown, T. (1997), 'Resource Needs and the Dynamic Capitalism Typology', *Journal of Business Venturing*, Vol. 12, pp.161-173.

Hamilton, P. (2001), 'How I achieved telecommuting success', http://globaltelecommute. com/page_8.htm (accessed 2 May, 2002).

Jenkins, H. (2001), 'Convergence? I Diverge', *Technology Review*, June, p. 93.

Kleindl, B. (2000), 'Competitive Dynamics and New Business Models for SMEs in the Virtual Marketplace', *Journal of Developmental Entrepreneurship*, Vol 5(1), pp. 73-85.

Lichtenstein, B. and Brush, C. (1997), 'Salient Resources in New Ventures: A Longitudinal Study of the Composition and Changes of Key Organizational Resources in Three Entrepreneurial Firms', in P. Reynolds, W. Bygrave, N. Carter, P. Davidsson, W. Gartner, C. Mason, and P. McDougall (eds), *Frontiers of Entrepreneurship Research 1997*, Proceedings of the Seventeenth Annual Entrepreneurship Conference, Babson College, MA.

Low, M. (2001), 'The Adolescence of Entrepreneurship Research: Specification of Purpose', *Entrepreneurship: Theory and Practice*, Vol. 19(1), pp.17-25.

McKay, R. (2001), 'Women Entrepreneurs: Moving Beyond Family and Flexibility', *International Journal of Entrepreneurial Behaviour and Research*, Vol. 7 (4), pp.148-168.

Nishiguchi, T. (1994), *Strategic Industrial Sourcing*, Oxford University Press, London.

Nooteboom, B. (2002), *Trust: Forms, Foundations, Functions, Failures and Figures*, Edward Elgar, UK.

Ostasiewski, P. (n.d.), 'Electronic Commerce and the Entrepreneur', http://dl.wju.edu/aca/ecommerce.htm, pp. 1-7 (accessed 30 April, 2002).

Portes, A. (1998), 'Social Capital: Its Origins and Applications in Modern Sociology', *Annual Review of Sociology*, Vol. 24, pp. 1-24.

Sansoni, S. (2002), 'Silicon Mali', *Forbes Global*, 6 February, pp. 42-43.

Spoonley, P., de Bruin, A. and Firkin, P. (2002 – forthcoming), 'Managing Non-Standard Work Arrangements: Choices and Constraints', *The Journal of Sociology*.

Stevenson, H. and Gumpert, D. (1985), 'The Heart of Entrepreneurship', *Harvard Business Review*, March-April, pp. 85-94.

Tomer, J. (1987), *Organizational Capital*, Praeger, New York.

Uzzi, B. (1997), 'Social Structure and Competition in Interfirm Networks: The Paradox of Embeddedness', *Administrative Science Quarterly*, Vol. 42, pp. 35-67.

Wilson, T. (2000), 'Media Convergence: Watching Television, Anticipating Going On-Line', *Media Asia*, Vol. 27(1), pp. 3-9.

Chapter 6

Familial Entrepreneurship

Patrick Firkin, Ann Dupuis and Anne de Bruin

Introduction

A theme running throughout this text is that of the embedded nature of economic activity. While this perspective has been outlined in some detail in the introductory chapter, in short it serves as a counter to a view of individuals as homo economicus or the rational, independent, self-serving actor. Founded in the work of Polanyi (1944, 1992), who compared economic activity in pre-market societies with that in modern market societies, this idea was further developed by Granovetter (1985). Put quite simply, an embedded perspective demands that ongoing social relations are central to any analysis of economic activity since that activity is actually embedded in these relations. Given its prominence throughout the text, it is obvious that we consider entrepreneurship, as one type of economic activity, to be embedded in a range of social settings and relationships depending on the form that it takes. This chapter seeks to explore a particular instance of this wider phenomenon: how entrepreneurial activity is embedded within families.

As the name of this chapter makes obvious, our mechanism for conducting such an exploration is the idea of familial entrepreneurship. We use this concept to draw together two distinct but overlapping areas of business activity – entrepreneurship and family businesses (Hoy and Verser, 1994). Doing so raises certain issues, however, that need to be dealt with before proceeding. The first issue concerns how family businesses are defined since this has implications for what is considered under such a rubric (Heck *et al.*, 1999; Rowe and Hong, 2000). It is not our intention to review the literature in this area except to note that, as with entrepreneurship, considerable variation and disagreement exists over what constitutes a family business (Brockhaus, 1994; Upton and Heck, 1997; Sten, 2001).[1] In keeping with the broad approach to the meaning of entrepreneurship adopted throughout the text, we employ a similarly inclusive strategy by defining family businesses as those businesses owned and/or managed by one or more family members (Heck *et al.*, 1999). While family businesses can range in size from 'street-corner laundromats and ethnic restaurants to major corporations' (Rowe and Hong, 2000: 1), they represent a large proportion of the small and medium enterprise (SME) sector (Cameron and Massey, 1999). Increased attention to this sector has consequently focused greater attention on these types of enterprises (ibid).

Secondly, there is the debate over whether a family business can be considered entrepreneurial. In response to this issue, Dyer and Handler (1994) and Brockhaus (1994) find various connections between entrepreneurship and family business. Similarly, Upton and Heck (1997) demonstrate that different types of family firms satisfy various types of entrepreneurial activity, depending on how that activity is defined. In relation to this issue we adopt the position of Heck *et al.* (1999: 1) who observe that 'much of what is designated as entrepreneurship is often synonymous with or very closely related to family business'. This is clearly resonant with the broad definition of entrepreneurship outlined in the editors' introduction, which identifies this phenomenon as incorporating a range of activities from self-employment to the creation of substantial organizations (Reynolds, 1991).

The idea of familial entrepreneurship, then, clearly locates or embeds entrepreneurial activity within the context of the family. This is the position adopted by Sanders and Nee (1996), though their research was limited to immigrant families. They viewed 'the relationship between family composition and immigrant self-employment [as] a special case of the more general embeddedness tendency described by Granovetter (1985)'. Our contention is that this is a more widespread phenomenon than generally recognized. Though not using the language of embeddedness, as Heck *et al.* (1999: 1) put it, 'entrepreneurs are usually family members maneuvering in concert or disharmony with an array of other family members, sometimes even within the nonresidential, extended family arena'. While we acknowledge that an entrepreneur may have no contact with family of any kind, our broad definition of family businesses allows for this embeddedness to take a number of forms. By way of demonstrating the effects of entrepreneurial activity being embedded in families, in the next section we briefly examine two issues, those of succession and the influence of the entrepreneur's family of origin. To illustrate the various forms that embeddedness can take, we also outline the sorts of family relationships that can be implicated, and the roles and types of involvement undertaken by family members.

Our main focus in this chapter, however, is to explore one particular family relationship within the context of familial entrepreneurship. Our further goal in focusing exclusively on the spousal relationship is to explore in detail the various contributions that spouses[2] make to the entrepreneurial activities of their partners. As was done by Portes and Sensenbrenner (1993), we employ the concept of social capital as a means of operationalizing the notion of embeddedness. Thus, necessarily, the second section provides an overview of the concept of social capital. Included is a review of how social capital is employed in relation to family and to entrepreneurship, as well as some discussion of the notion of convertibility and the negative side of social capital. Bringing together the various threads of the discussion thus far enables us to offer the proposition that the embedded nature of entrepreneurial activity within the family can be conceived of in terms of familial social capital.

The third section develops this concept in some detail and illustrates it by drawing on interview material from the Hawkes Bay regional component of Labour Market Dynamics (LMD) study,[3] in which 24 of the 96 households in the sample were self-employed people. The entrepreneurial activities that these interviewees were engaged in can be broadly described as self-employed small businesses, often owner-operated, involving professional services, trades, or farming activities. Every enterprise clearly had a principal – someone who appeared to have the major role in, and primary responsibility for, the company. Aside from the three female owners/operators, in all the other cases the principal was the male partner in the relationship. Using this data, the section begins with an outline of the motivations for, and flows of, social capital in these circumstances. Next, a typology of the resources that consequently emerge is developed. Such a typology is a useful adjunct to research within this field. The idea that social capital can be converted into other resources, particularly economic capital, is then discussed. Finally, we explore the 'other side of embeddedness' (Waldinger, 1995). Though embeddedness is often uncritically seen as a positive feature of business activity, it can also have negative effects. This has been has been conceptualized as 'atrophied embeddedness' (de Bruin and de Bruin, 2002). Accordingly, we consider some possible negative outcomes of embeddedness in relation to the idea of familial social capital.

Embedding Entrepreneurial Activity in Families

There are various ways that entrepreneurial activity can be embedded in families. In this section we seek to illustrate the importance of this phenomenon by considering two issues – succession and the influence of the family of origin. By then exploring the relationships, roles and resources that may be involved, we also want to establish some parameters for this form of embeddedness.

Succession

Succession refers to the transferring of management or ownership from the business founder or current owner/manager to other family members, usually in the 'next' generation. Though we do not adopt this strategy here, succession is often considered a defining feature of family businesses (Heck *et al.*, 1999). It is also frequently identified as the main problem experienced by family businesses and, consequently, is an area of considerable interest to researchers (Dyer and Handler, 1994; Upton and Heck, 1997; Cameron and Massey, 1999; Sten, 2001). In particular, research has focused on the dynamics behind the frequent resistance of entrepreneurs and founders to any such transfer; the role and attitudes of family members and others in this process; and the process of succession itself (Dyer and Handler, 1994; Upton and Heck, 1997). As these issues suggest, the embedding of entrepreneurial activity within families is very apparent in relation to succession. Given that it can involve many aspects – from business, financial and economic through to emotional, psychological and inter-personal dimensions, for instance – the matter of succession also illustrates the depth, complexity and multi-faceted nature of this embeddedness.

The Family of Origin of the Entrepreneur

Dyer and Handler (1994) and Upton and Heck (1997) canvas the various approaches to considering what role a person's family of origin has in their move into some form of entrepreneurial activity. They outline three broad viewpoints. The psychodynamic view considers the influence of childhood family dynamics on the development of an entrepreneurial disposition. Such a disposition can emerge from negative and positive dynamics. Alternative perspectives explore the impact of having one or both parents who were self-employed, and of parents promoting entrepreneurial activity among children and adolescents. What this issue illustrates are the various ways that the embedded nature of entrepreneurial activity within families can be considered beyond just entrepreneurial events. Rather, it can occur at much earlier points in a person's life, and in less obvious, yet fundamental ways.

Relationships

Though people outside a family may be directly or indirectly involved in a family business, by their very nature these businesses also involve familial relationships of some kind and which are a key element in such enterprises (Cameron and Massey, 1994). These various relationships and connections can provide the basis for the nature and degree of involvement by family members in a family business. This involvement can have a range of benefits for these businesses. However, since it can also generate particular dynamics that are not apparent in non-family firms (Cameron and Massey, 1999), the often strong emotional component to family relationships may mean that there can be negative implications and effects as well.

Various ways can be used to distinguish such relationships. For instance, Heck *et al.* (1999) use the distinction between family members living inside or outside the household to calculate participation rates in their study of family businesses in the United States. They found participation by the latter group to be much lower that those living in the household. While this division may have some utility in a cross-sectional approach, longitudinally the composition of households can change over time (children move out of home and form their own families). Care too needs to be taken with different groups, since their attitude to particular living arrangements can markedly affect the composition of the household. Sanders and Nee (1996) for instance, identify spouses, children, and other related adults as living within some of the households they researched. An alternative approach might be to conceptualize relationships in terms of the strength of ties (Granovetter, 1973). Stronger ties are associated with those in one's close or immediate family – between parents and children, siblings, or spouses for instance. Weaker ties refer to more distant relatives. Here too, the strength of ties is also open to change over time and with events such as marriage. Our point here is not to align ourselves with one or other approach, but to acknowledge that family businesses may involve a range of relationships and that each piece of research needs to adopt appropriate ways of considering and conceptualizing these. In this discussion we are confronted with few issues in this regard, since the substantive part of the chapter deals only with the spousal relationship.

Roles and Resources

As Baines and Wheelock (1998) observe, there is a wide variety of roles through which family members can be involved in businesses. Out of these roles emerge resources that can be used directly, or indirectly, in relation to the family business. It may be useful to conceive of this involvement in terms of a continuum. At one extreme there is the family member who is the full business partner or joint entrepreneur. In this respect, the notion of copreneurs has been developed to describe couples who share the ownership of, contributions and commitment to, and responsibility for any business (Smith, 2000: 283). Then there are family members who invest in an enterprise but take no other role. Family members may also work in the business, both on a paid or unpaid basis. Finally there are the various forms of support that family members can offer. These might include giving advice and providing emotional support and encouragement. Also included in this broad category are activities that allow the entrepreneur to devote time and energy to the enterprise. As will be seen in the following sections, these activities are key contributions that spouses, in particular women, make to family businesses. Such activities include caring for children and the home, as well as engaging in other paid employment.

In noting that the entrepreneur 'depends on the supportive environment that other family members create', that 'other family members subsidize the business through sacrifice, physical efforts or money' and that 'all the family assets may be invested in the business', Rowe and Hong (2000: 1) neatly capture the diverse nature of these roles and the resources that are available as a result. Their observations also emphasize that family members can be involved in multiple roles and in providing a mix of resources. In a subsequent section we expand on the whole idea of roles and resources, including their categorization as direct or indirect. At this point it is important to note, however, that the idea of indirect roles and resources means that family members can contribute to a business, without any direct input to the enterprise.

Social Capital

Having outlined how entrepreneurial activity can be embedded within families, we now introduce the concept of social capital. Following Portes and Sensenbrenner (1993), we employ this concept as a means of operationalizing the idea of embeddedness. The work of Bourdieu (1986) is fundamental in relation to understanding the various forms of capital. A better account of the structure and functioning of the social world requires, according to Bourdieu, a broader view of the resources and assets that people possess than is possible with capital only conceived of in its monetary form. Instead, Bourdieu conceptualizes these various resources and assets, which in his terms amount to power, as not only economic, but also as cultural and social forms of capital. Since we will not be employing the idea of cultural capital, only the other two forms need explanation. The economic form represents what would usually be understood as capital.

Convertibility

Before defining social capital, another key characteristic of Bourdieu's (1986) approach to capital that is employed in this analysis is the convertibility of the different forms – how each can be transformed from and into other types of capital and how they can also be held and used in concert. Importantly, however, as Portes summarizes it, 'though Bourdieu insists that the outcomes of possession of social and cultural capital are reducible to economic capital, the processes that bring about these alternative forms are not' (1998: 4). That is, the benefits of social and cultural capital may be translated into monetary forms, but money alone, if at all, cannot immediately lay claim to social and cultural capital. As well, the conversion process may not always be explicit and can be concealed to varying degrees. Thus, any conversion that takes place is likely to be the outcome of a complex, multifarious and contingent process.

Defining Social Capital

Social capital has become a widely used and interpreted concept (see Adler and Kwon, 2002 for a detailed discussion). Indeed, some confusion exists over the meaning of the term social capital (Portes, 1998, 2000a, 2000b; Schuller, 2000; Lin 2001; Adler and Kwon, 2002). At one level, this is the result of social capital being used in two senses – one with a communal emphasis, and the other more individually orientated. In response, Lin (2001: 26) argues that the widely held view is that social capital can be both a collective and an individual good. Therefore, in any discussion of social capital it becomes important to make clear how the concept is being employed in that particular context. Additional confusion is likely to arise from what Lin (2001) describes as the tendency for social capital to be employed as another trendy term in the broad context of improving or building social integration and solidarity. In this sense Lin sees it as often used to represent notions such as culture, trust or norms, with problems arising because such interchangeability cannot always be assumed.

Given these issues, we acknowledge at this point that our use of the concept of social capital is more individually orientated. Following Portes (1998: 6), we define social capital as 'the ability of actors to secure benefits by virtue of membership in social networks or other social structures'. Portes argues that such a definition, based on the work of Bourdieu (1986) and Coleman (1988), represents a consensus that is emerging in the literature. The benefits of social capital can readily be seen to include roles and resources, two key features of the discussion that follows. However, some debate exists over whether the actual resources themselves should be included in the meaning of social capital, as opposed to it simply taking in the ability or opportunity to access those resources (Adler and Kwon, 2002). We adopt a middle position by identifying the types of resources in general terms, while noting that the specific make-up and amount of resources varies between cases, and for each case, across time. Factors that influence this variation include: the contexts in which the businesses are operating; the nature of each business and its changing circumstances; and the characteristics of the individuals involved.

Social Capital and Entrepreneurship

The embedded nature of entrepreneurial activity is often presented in terms of the identification, formation, maintenance and utilization of social networks for the benefits and resources that accrue from them (Birley, 1985; Aldrich and Zimmer, 1986; Brüderl and Preisendörfer, 1998; Thornton, 1999; Allen, 2000). Thus, for example, in terms of starting and running a business networks can be useful in relation to suppliers, customers, information and finance. Benefits can include settled and dependable relationships, favourable terms, and preferential treatment and access. Brüderl and Preisendörfer (1998) usefully put forward the idea of a social capital metaphor to capture the range of approaches to considering networks in business. Portes and Sensenbrenner (1993) explicitly use the idea of social capital to operationalize the concept of embeddedness to study the experiences of immigrants settling, living and working in new communities. Some of these experiences are concerned with entrepreneurial activity.

Developing the Idea of Familial Social Capital

While the consideration of social capital within business, and entrepreneurship in particular, is most commonly restricted to 'network-mediated benefits beyond the immediate family' (Portes, 1998: 12) other possibilities exist. One such possibility is the family. As Bubolz puts it, the family is 'source, user and builder of social capital' (2001: 129). Bourdieu (1986) was explicit in his view that families could be a source of social capital, though his main focus was in relation to educational attainment. Similarly, Coleman (1988) also acknowledged the importance of the family, though he was principally interested in how social capital contributed to the creation of human capital in the next generations. Portes (1998: 11-12) surveys a number of other explorations of social capital in a familial context that are concerned with issues such as, educational achievement, labour force participation, and coping with change. In order to set apart this particular type of social capital from the more general form, we refer to it as familial social capital.

The Negative Outcomes of Social Capital

As Portes points out in numerous places, it is all too easy to be seduced by the benefits of a particular concept (Portes, 1995; 1998; 2000a, 2000b; and with Sensenbrenner, 1993). Though he is specifically referring to social capital, the sentiment can easily be applied to embeddedness more generally, since less attention is paid to its costs or negative implications. Portes and Sensenbrenner

(1993: 1338) put it thus, 'the same social mechanisms that give rise to appropriable resources for individual use can also constrain action or even derail it from its original goals'. Greater balance is emerging, however, with literature and research focusing on both the positive and negative outcomes of embeddedness.

Waldinger (1995), for instance, illustrates the 'other side of embeddedness' in his examination of how the intersection of ethnicity and entrepreneurship can impede access to outsiders. As well as exclusion, Portes (1998) identifies three other negative outcomes from recent studies: excessive claims might be made on group members; individual freedom can be restricted as a result of group membership; and there is the possibility of downward levelling pressure on group members. In his examination of inter-firm relations, Uzzi (1997) identifies what he calls the paradoxes of embeddedness. Some examples of these include embeddedness changing from an asset to a liability with the unexpected loss of a network's core member. Alternatively, over-embeddedness can stifle economic action if the social aspects come to outweigh other aspects of the relationship. Similarly, if relationships that are over-embedded sour, then the firm can be derailed into all sorts of unproductive negative activity, such as spite and revenge.

The idea of atrophied embeddedness has been offered as a means of conceptualizing some of the negative aspects of embeddedness (de Bruin and de Bruin, 2002). As part of a complementary and supplementary explanation for the slowdown in economic growth in Japan in the 1990s, this concept captures the process whereby embedded ties become too entrenched, hindering competitiveness and compromising economic growth (de Bruin and de Bruin, 2002). Consequently, embedded ties can become an impediment to growth, flexibility and adaptability to change, and the potential that embeddedness offers is lost; it withers or is stifled. We see this concept as a useful means to capture the negative aspects of embeddedness.

Familial Social Capital Between Spouses in a Family Business

Whenever considered within the context of the family, social capital is virtually always looked at in terms of the parent-child relationship, and is usually in some way connected with education. Seldom is any such discussion focused on self-employment or entrepreneurial activity, and it is rare to see an emphasis on spousal relations. In the remainder of the chapter we seek to remedy these omissions by utilizing the concept of social capital to examine entrepreneurial activity within the family and by specifically focusing on the spousal relationship.

Increasing attention is being paid to the roles of spouses in family businesses in the literature (e.g. Marshack, 1994; Baines and Wheelock, 1998; Rowe and Hong, 2000; Smith, 2000; Römer-Paakkanen, 2001). The idea of copreneurship, as already mentioned, is one outcome of such a focus (Smith, 2000). In addition to considering spouses, Sander and Nee (1996) also research the role of teenage children and other related adults in relation to self-employment among immigrant families. Their work is significant in that they employ social capital as a conceptual mechanism. Though the analysis that follows builds on the work of Sanders and Nee, it differs in several key aspects. Firstly, whereas Sanders and Nee also included some consideration of human capital, we are focused solely on social capital, although our discussion of convertibility acknowledges other forms of capital can also be present. Secondly, we move outside of a concentration on immigration. Finally, since the interview data that are drawn on in the remainder of this section did not canvas the role of other family members, we limit our discussion to the social capital between spouses, where one or both of them is involved in some form of entrepreneurial activity. The following discussion outlines the flow of resources, the motives for providing them, and a typology of roles and resources that emerge from familial social capital. The convertibility of this form of capital is then focused on along with some consideration of its negative outcomes.

The Flow of Social Capital Between Spouses

Social capital between spouses can likely produce a range of benefits for both parties, regardless of the type of employment either person undertakes. However, the particular demands of self-employment mean that one party can come to rely quite heavily on the contributions of the other. Consequently, it is reasonable to conclude that in these circumstances the social capital between spouses is extremely important. Although both parties can be possessors (those who derive benefits) and providers (those who provide benefits) of social capital (Portes, 1995), in the cases drawn from the LMD study, the balance tended to be skewed towards the principals being the main beneficiaries. That is, the flow of benefits and resources that social capital produced, appeared to move predominantly in one direction: from the partner as provider, to the principal as possessor. Of course, when benefits of some sort from a successful business accrued to the partner – say through the income derived from the enterprise – then the flow of effects can be more balanced.

The Motivation for Social Capital Between Spouses

Marriage and like-relationships see spouses or partners providing significant and diverse forms of support for one another, from the emotional, through to the very practical. These can be offered and drawn on in different ways and for a range of reasons by both parties. This was directly mentioned or implied in the LMD interviews. The expectations of having access to, and the commitment to providing, such various forms of support can be seen as underpinned by certain values and norms associated with marriages. Portes (1995) identifies values as one form of altruistic motivation for the presence of social capital. In relation to families, Coleman (1988) suggests that prescriptive norms mean people forgo self-interest and act selflessly in the family's interest. A related proposition regarding the source and motives of this form of social capital is the sense that the strength and fulfilment of these commitments and expectations is due, in part, to the intimate nature of marriage. In his discussion of how people form a relationship,

Giddens talks of the inevitability of 'clos[ing] off of others, who become part of a generalised "outside"' (1992: 138). Such closeness and exclusivity could be a further source of social capital, since it has some fit with the idea of bounded solidarity, the second form of altruistic motivation identified by Portes (1995).

An alternative or complementary source, though more instrumental in orientation, may lie with the idea of reciprocity (Portes, 1995). Marriage is, of course, much more than the instrumental idea of accumulating and redeeming social chits. However, reciprocity is likely in the sense that one partner provides support, based partially on the expectation that some benefits will accrue to them and the family as a whole. While the LMD interviews did not directly assess the expectation of partners regarding future income, this sense of reciprocity seemed implicit in some interviews, although it appeared of lesser importance and was certainly not the only motivation.

Although developed independently, support can be found for all three of these propositions in the work of Sanders and Nee (1996). They characterize the family in terms of obligations, expectations and dependence, and acknowledge the small-group-like or bounded nature of the family and the solidarity that results. As well, they consider the place of reciprocity in terms of self-interest. In short, Sanders and Nee (1996) see 'collective interests and strong personal ties' as the keys to social capital within the family and their findings bear some similarity with the analysis of the LMD interview data.

Roles and Resources – A Typology

The roles and resources that emerged from the social capital between spouses were direct and indirect in nature. Direct resources can be further broken down into formal and informal types. Regardless of the type, these resources could be drawn on in a predictable fashion, or required unexpectedly. While support and encouragement appeared to underpin all that was made available by one partner to another, they are resources in themselves. Whether of a practical or emotional nature, they were the most common resources made available and utilized as a result of familial social capital.

The most obvious way that roles and resources were utilized was when they were applied directly to the enterprise. That is, the spouse took some active role. Interestingly, however, when both spouses were involved in the business each person carried out very different functions. Although there may have been some occasional or minor overlap of tasks, and while there was variation in the types and number of activities they performed, the spouse of a self-employed male usually performed ancillary roles; doing accounts, administration, answering phones, and so on. Despite the tasks appearing mundane, these were vital functions in relation to the business.

Any functions that a partner performed could be undertaken formally by them being employees of the business or, occasionally, business partners. Alternatively, they could be done in an informal fashion where the role had no legal or formal standing. While formal roles were remunerated, informal ones could be paid or unpaid, though even if spouses did not receive individual remuneration they could still share in the income generated by the company. Sometimes spouses were engaged with the business both informally and formally, and their status could change across time and with circumstances. For instance, partners might give up a formal role when it was no longer needed or could not be sustained. In the latter circumstance, they might continue this function informally. Often the spouses from the LMD study formally undertook a core function, such as the books, and then helped out in other ways on an informal basis.

In some cases there was no direct participation in the business by partners. For instance, none of the male partners of women principals were involved in their ventures. Similarly, just over a third of the male principals required no direct input from their female partners. However, even in such cases, social capital is still important as spouses can make other contributions through providing indirect resources, such as financial and emotional support and, more often, caring for the home and family.

These latter activities seem to have been the most significant indirect resources required of spouses in the more than 60 per cent of cases where children under 16 years were part of the household. This was particularly true for male principals. Unlike the three women principals, who each treated their businesses as 'sidelines', all the men conceived of their enterprises as providing the main income in the household. Given this perspective, they usually sought to devote considerable amounts of time and energy to the business in order to ensure its viability and success. With them so preoccupied, it seems that little, if any, time or energy was left for their families. Thus, their spouses were heavily involved in the care of children, in order to both free up their partner and to compensate for the inability of the self-employed person to be so involved. Although there is only a small group for comparison, in all but one instance the male partners of female principals did not increase their involvement in the care of children or the home.

Another form of indirect resource provided by spouses was the income they generated by working outside the business. While sometimes this could be channelled into the venture, more often it went to support the family. Hence, our decision to view it as an indirect resource. In order to bring in additional income such as this, women often worked part-time on top of their other responsibilities. This income could be very important during start up, when businesses require finance but are not yet generating any themselves, and during times of difficulty when cashflow can be poor. Two of the women principals acknowledged their husband's income as financial security while they were self-employed.

By breaking down roles and resources into direct or indirect types, we are not meaning to create an either or situation. More often, a mix of resources was in evidence, and this mix could vary over time and circumstance. Whether direct or indirect, the resources produced through social capital between partners could be drawn on in a predictable way, or unexpectedly. In the first sense, couples often undertook a great deal of planning and preparation before starting a small business, part of which involved some consideration of the resources that a spouse could contribute. Familial social capital thus became the basis of anticipated resources for a venture. It also appears to suggest that the expectation and utilization of social capital inherent in a relationship was in some way negotiated, rather than just appropriated. Even with planning and preparation, however, resources sometimes had to be drawn on unexpectedly, in terms of the type of resource required, or, in regard to the amount that was needed. Not only does this signal the often difficult and unpredictable nature of embarking on self-employment, it also highlights the very special nature of the bond between partners, and the benefits that can accrue from their relationship.

Although conceptualized within a social capital framework, the various findings of the LMD study bear striking similarities with other research in this area. As to the involvement and respective roles of spouses, in their British study, Baines and Wheelock (1988) found that 40 per cent of the businesses they examined had a high involvement by both partners. A little under half of this group (48 per cent), had a single owner and the balance was co-owned. In just over two-thirds of the former category, the partner's involvement amounted to them being employed by the company, and in the remaining cases it meant they provided substantial unpaid input. Of those businesses that were co-owned, less than a third fulfilled the complete equity requirements of true copreneurship where couples *shared* the ownership and running of, as well as responsibility for, any business (Smith, 2000: 283). Rather, the majority comprised cases where the female partner took an ancillary role, usually working in a clerical or support capacity. Similar findings were made by Marshack (1994) in her study of 83 copreneurial and 71 dual career couples. Instead of copreneurs forging a new form of egalitarian relationship, she found that they tended to have very traditional demarcations. Thus, the men were the leader and decision-maker at home and work, with the wife consistently filling the role of support person. Given that the men she studied worked long hours in the business, management of the household was left predominantly to the women. Smith's (2000) study of 20 Australian copreneur couples replicates the general thrust of these findings. In respect of indirect resources, Marshack (1994), Baines and Wheelock (1998), Smith (2000), and Römer-Paakkanen (2001) for instance, all found that women routinely assume the predominant role in managing the household and caring for children when they, and/or their partners, are in business. They can also be involved in other paid employment (Rowe and Hong, 2000). Both these roles can be critical to the operation and success of the venture, and their partner or husband's participation in it, since these indirect resources in some way allowed the self-employed person to commit time, energy and presence to the enterprise.

The Convertibility of Familial Social Capital

Although it might be argued that some of the roles or activities that partners engage in might actually represent economic rather than social capital, we feel instead that conversion can occur in these circumstances so easily as to mask the transformation. This is especially apparent in one case, where the family business collapsed and the wife quickly got a job. In focusing solely on the financial aspects of her working, what can be missed is that *one* of her motives for getting a job and not insisting that her husband get employment, seemed to be her ongoing support of his efforts at establishing another venture, despite the difficult times.

Convertibility can also be seen in relation to employing staff in a family business. This can easily be viewed as an economic decision, but if the employee is a spouse or partner then it is in the nature of their relationship to the self-employed person and, therefore, the business, that additional benefits can accrue. For instance, the interviews revealed that partners usually had a special commitment to the enterprise's success and were willing to perform a range of tasks outside of, or in addition to, what a paid employee might do. 'Recruiting' was easier, as was 'termination' if the extra expense could not be sustained. Even then, it was more than likely that the work would continue to be done but on an informal basis. As well, the employment of a partner did not need to be for set times, hours and so on, since they often worked as, and when needed.

An important feature of conversion is that it can be heavily concealed. As has been argued, indirect resources were often crucial to self-employed people being able to devote themselves totally to the enterprise. However, because the resources were indirect it is easy not to connect them with the economic gains made as a result. It is all too simple, for example, to see aspects of this as 'what women do in families'. Much later, in realizing the negative effects of their obsession with making their businesses a success, many men recognized the value and size of the contribution that women had indirectly made.

Finally, before leaving the matter of convertibility, it is important to note that this depended, to a degree, on the human capital of a spouse – that is, the education, training, skills, experience, qualities and attributes they possessed or that they acquired. Thus, for example, employing a spouse only became useful if they could do the job that was needed. Conversion in these circumstances was also dependent on the nature of the business, which could play a part in determining what, and how, a partner might contribute to it. As well, partners did not always have the skills and experience required of them – whether that related to special expertise needed in a particular business, or to more general skills such as bookkeeping. In those circumstances they had to be motivated and able to acquire the necessary skills. Similarly, the availability of indirect financial support relied on the partner being free to work (considering their other responsibilities) *and* their ability to get a job.

Atrophied Embeddedness

The LMD study also revealed various negative effects of familial social capital. Many of the men who were interviewed recognized, some years later, that their excessive commitment and involvement with their business – which the extra efforts and contribution of their partner had allowed – had had negative implications for them and their family. Later, on reflection, they voiced considerable regret over the situation. Their partners also sometimes experienced detrimental impacts. They may have found the other person's lack of involvement in family life saddening or disappointing, and the various demands they consequently experienced were often quite taxing. These could involve caring for the family and home as well as engaging in paid employment and they frequently came in addition to any direct involvement they had in the business and the activities that they had undertaken as a result. While no partner catalogued so explicitly these negative experiences, it was not unusual for them to acknowledge the pressure, stresses and demands created by looking after a home and children, perhaps working in paid employment, and possibly helping out with the business.

Though not explicitly mentioned in the interviews, we also identified a further, potentially negative outcome. This could occur when the resources that emerge from social capital between partners are used to sustain a financially untenable business that otherwise would not have survived. Such resources can be vital in helping a business overcome a difficult time. However, they alone cannot solve all the problems a business has. It is possible, therefore, that they may help plaster over the cracks but be unable to ultimately hold the enterprise together indefinitely. Such an action may blind those involved to alternative or necessary strategies.

Conclusion

At the beginning of this chapter we establish that entrepreneurial activity is embedded within the family and that familial entrepreneurship is widespread, especially in the realm of small, family-owned and operated businesses. Developing the notion of familial social capital between spouses and its convertibility lays the foundation for our understanding of familial entrepreneurship. The basis of familial social capital viewed in the context of the family business is that a proportion of the social capital that contributes to the running of the business is sourced from within the family structure. In this chapter we focused on the spousal relationship as the primary source of familial social capital.

The LMD study and other similar pieces of research strongly demonstrate that the spouse (i.e. the spouse who does not take principal responsibility for the business, most often the woman in the spousal relationship) is often an important contributor to the family business, a facilitator of the business' entrepreneurial activity. This is the case regardless of whether the spouse's contribution has a direct or indirect impact on the business, or whether the contribution is of a formal or informal nature. With such an understanding, the spouse's contributions could be performing any role or supplying any resource that impacts on the family business ranging from paid or unpaid input such as doing the accounts and answering telephones to caring for home and family, thus allowing the principal spouse more time to dedicate to the business. It is important to realize that the roles and resources produced through social capital between spouses are variable and can be adapted to the needs of the business at any particular time. However, negative effects of familial social capital are also apparent, such as allowing either spouse to take excessive time away from family in favor of the business or even extending the life of a financially untenable business.

Notes

1. The interested reader can see Heck *et al.* (1999) for just such a review.
2. By this term we also mean the partners of people in marriage-like relationships. For simplicity, however, we use the one term.
3. The Labour Market Dynamics and Economic Participation (*LMD*) Programme, funded by the New Zealand Foundation for Research, Science and Technology, is an interdisciplinary research project that was initially designed to explain the dynamics of economic participation by exploring the interface between households and the labour market in three regional labour markets in New Zealand. The first phase of the *LMD* programme sought to explain how individuals made decisions about access and participation in the labour market, with emphasis on the life cycle of the household. The interview data we use here is from this first phase. See Firkin (2001); Shirley *et al.* (2001a; 2001b; 2001c) for further details.

References

Adler, P. and Kwon, S-W. (2002), 'Social Capital: Prospects for a New Concept', *Academy of Management Review*, Vol. 27(1), pp. 17-40.

Aldrich, H. and Zimmer, C. (1986), 'Entrepreneurship Through Social Networks', in D. Sexton and R. Smilor (eds), *The Art and Science of Entrepreneurship*, Ballinger Publishing Company, Cambridge, MA.

Allen, W. (2000), 'Social Networks and Self-employment', *Journal of Socio-Economics*, Vol. 29, pp. 487-501.

Baines, S. and Wheelock, J. (1998), 'Working For Each Other: Gender, the Household and Micro-business Survival and Growth', *International Small Business Journal*, Vol. 17(1), pp. 16-35.

Birley, S. (1985), 'The Role of Networks in the Entrepreneurial Process', *Journal of Business Venturing*, Vol. 1(1), pp. 107-117.

Bourdieu, P. (1986), 'The Forms of Capital', in J. Richardson (ed.), *The Handbook of Theory and Research for the Sociology of Education*, Greenwood Press, New York.

Brockhaus, R. (1994), 'Entrepreneurship and Family Business Research: Comparisons, Critique, and Lessons', *Entrepreneurship: Theory and Practice*, Vol. 19(1), pp. 25-38.

Brüderl, J. and Preisendörfer, P. (1998), 'Network Support and the Success of Newly Founded Businesses', *Small Business Economics*, Vol. 10(3), pp. 213-225.

Bubolz, B. (2001), 'Family as Source, User, and Builder of Social Capital', *Journal of Socio-Economics*, Vol. 30, pp. 129-131.

Cameron, A. and Massey, C. (1999), 'Family Business in New Zealand: A Neglected Area', in P. Mellalieu (ed.), *Think Global! Act Global! The Role and Impact of Strategic Management in the Development of Small Enterprise and New Ventures: Proceedings of the Annual Educators Conference of the New Zealand Management Society, 7th Annual Conference*, 2-5 February, Graduate School of Business, Massey University, Palmerston North.

Coleman, J. (1988), 'Social Capital in the Creation of Human Capital', *American Journal Of Sociology*, Vol. 94, pp. S95-121.

de Bruin, A. and de Bruin J. (2002) 'Atrophied Embeddedness: Towards Extending Explanation of Japan's Growth Slowdown', *The Journal of Interdisciplinary Economics*, Vol. 13(4), pp. 401-427.

Dyer, W. and Handler, W. (1994), 'Entrepreneurship and Family Business: Exploring the Connections', *Entrepreneurship: Theory and Practice*, Vol. 19(1), pp. 71-83.

Firkin, P. (2001), *'Doing the Books' – Social Capital Between Spouses in Business-Owning Families*, Working Paper No. 6, Labour Market Dynamics Research Programme, Massey University, Albany and Palmerston North.

Giddens, A. (1992), *The Transformation of Intimacy: Sexuality, Love and Eroticism in Modern Societies*, Polity Press and Blackwell Publishers, Cambridge and Oxford.

Granovetter, M. (1973), 'The Strength of Weak Ties', *American Journal of Sociology*, Vol. 78, pp. 1360-1380.

Granovetter, M. (1985), 'Economic Action and Social Structure: The Problem of Embeddedness', *American Journal of Sociology*, Vol. 91, pp. 481-510.

Heck, R., Trent, E. and Kaye, K. (1999), 'The Prevalence of Family Business from a Household Sample', *Family Business Review*, Vol. 12(3), pp. 209-228.

Hoy, F. and Verser, T. (1994), 'Emerging Business, Emerging Field: Entrepreneurship and the Family Firm', *Entrepreneurship Theory and Practice*, Vol. 19(1), pp. 9-23.

Lin, N. (2001), *Social Capital: A Theory of Social Structure and Action*, Cambridge University Press, Cambridge and New York.

Marshack, K. (1994), 'Copreneurs and Dual-career Couples: Are they Different?', *Entrepreneurship Theory and Practice*, Vol. 19(1), pp. 49-69.

Polanyi, K. (1944), *The Great Transformation*, Holt Rinehart, New York.

Polanyi, K. (1992), 'The Economy as Instituted Process', in M. Granovetter and R. Swedberg (eds), *The Sociology of Economic Life*, Waterview Press, Boulder, CO.

Portes, A. (1995), 'Economic Sociology and the Sociology of Immigration: A Conceptual Overview', in A. Portes (ed.), *The Economic Sociology of Immigration: Essays on Networks, Ethnicity and Entrepreneurship*, Russell Sage Foundation, New York.

Portes, A. (1998), 'Social Capital: Its Origins and Applications in Modern Sociology', *Annual Review of Sociology*, Vol. 24, pp. 1-24.

Portes, A. (2000a), 'The Two Meanings of Social Capital', *Sociological Forum*, Vol. 15(1), pp. 1-12.

Portes, A. (2000b), 'Social Capital: Promise and Pitfalls of its Role in Development', *Journal of Latin American Studies*, Vol. 32, pp. 529-547.

Portes, A. and Sensenbrenner, J. (1993), 'Embeddedness and Immigration: Notes on the Social Determinants of Economic Action', *American Journal of Sociology*, Vol. 98, pp. 1320-50.

Reynolds, P. (1991), 'Sociology and Entrepreneurship: Concepts and Contributions', *Entrepreneurship: Theory and Practice*, Vol. 16(2), pp. 47-70.

Römer-Paakkanen, T (2001), 'Family Entrepreneur in Cross-Fire of Multiple Goals and Needs', in *Conference Proceedings, RENT XV, Research in Entrepreneurship and Small Business, 15th Workshop, November 22-23*, Vol. 2, pp. 127-138, Small Business Institute, Turku School of Economics and Business Administration, Turku, Finland.

Rowe, B. and Hong, G-S. (2000), 'The Role of Wives in Family Businesses: The Paid and Unpaid Work of Women', *Family Business Review*, Vol. 13(1), pp. 1-13.

Sanders, J. and Nee, V. (1996), 'Immigrant Self-employment: The Family as Social Capital and the Value of Human Capital', *American Sociological Review*, Vol. 61(2), pp. 231-249.

Schuller, T. (2000), 'Social and Human Capital: The Search for Appropriate Technomethodology', *Policy Studies*, Vol. 21(1), pp. 25-35.

Shirley, I., Firkin, P., Cremer, R., Eichbaum, C., de Bruin, A., Dewe, P., Dupuis, A. and Spoonley, P. (2001a), *Transitions in the Hawkes Bay Labour Market: Education and Training: Research Report*, Labour Market Dynamics and Economic Participation Research Programme, Massey University, Albany and Palmerston North.

Shirley, I., Firkin, P., Cremer, R., Eichbaum, C., de Bruin, A., Dewe, P., Dupuis, A. and Spoonley, P. (2001b), *Transitions in the Hawkes Bay Labour Market: Welfare and Unemployment*, Research Report, Labour Market Dynamics and Economic Participation Research Programme, Massey University, Albany and Palmerston North.

Shirley, I., Firkin, P., Cremer, R., Eichbaum, C., de Bruin, A., Dewe, P., Dupuis, A. and Spoonley, P. (2001c), *Transitions in the Hawkes Bay Labour Market: Unpaid Work and Paid Work*, Research Report, Labour Market Dynamics and Economic Participation Research Programme, Massey University, Albany and Palmerston North.

Smith, C. (2000), 'Managing Work and Family in Small 'Copreneurial' Business: an Australian Study', *Women in Management Review*, Vol. 15, pp. 283-289.

Sten, J. (2001), 'Examining Loss and Replacement in Business Families: Towards a Conceptual Framework on Transfers of Family Businesses', in *Conference Proceedings, RENT XV, Research in Entrepreneurship and Small Business, 15th Workshop, November 22-23*, Vol. 2, pp. 127-138, Small Business Institute, Turku School of Economics and Business Administration, Turku, Finland.

Thornton, P. (1999), 'The Sociology of Entrepreneurship', *Annual Review of Sociology*, Vol. 25, pp. 19-46.

Upton, N. and Heck, R. (1997), 'The Family Business Dimension of Entrepreneurship', in D. Sexton and R. Smilor (eds), *Entrepreneurship 2000*, Upstart Publishing Company, Chicago.

Uzzi, B. (1997), 'Social Structure and Competition in Interfirm Networks: The Paradox of Embeddedness', *Administrative Science Quarterly*, Vol. 42, pp. 35-67.

Waldinger, R. (1995), 'The "Other Side" of Embeddedness: A Case Study of the Interplay of Economy and Ethnicity', *Ethnic and Racial Studies*, Vol. 18, pp. 555-580.

Chapter 7

Community Entrepreneurship

Ann Dupuis and Anne de Bruin

Introduction

There is a large body of literature which contends that the world has entered a new global age, based on very different economic, societal and ideological principles from those that characterized industrial capitalism (Dicken, 1998; Held *et al.*, 1999). Variously described as postmodernist (Seidman, 1994; Best and Kellner, 1997), post-Fordist (Amin, 1995), post-industrial (Bell, 1974), the information age (Wilson, 1999; Castells, 2000a), the network society (Castells, 2000b) and the global age (Albrow, 1996), the new phase, in its various guises, is characterized by flexibility (Felstead and Jewson, 1999), pluralism (McLennan, 1995) and a harnessing of new technology (Castells, 2000a, 2000b). Accompanying this shift have been major changes to the traditional production base in developed western nations which have had uneven impacts on certain population groups, as industries and organizations were restructured and rationalized in their efforts to remain viable. Of relevance to this chapter, are those groups which had previously provided the labour force for large-scale, Fordist-type manufacturing businesses, or major state sector enterprises, and were hardest hit by the ensuing unemployment, as industrial and manufacturing plants closed, downsized, or moved off-shore, and restructuring of the state sector was undertaken. In New Zealand, as in a number of other western nations, the resultant unemployment exhibited strong ethnic dimensions and has been concentrated spatially within specific ethnic localities (de Bruin and Dupuis, 1995a, 1995b; de Bruin, 1998). A further widespread concern has been the lack of portable work related skills and entrepreneurial intent among these groups.

In this chapter we seek to advance a framework that proposes an alternative conceptualization of employment creation to those based on employment training schemes that train workers to fill employers' demands. Instead the employment creation we discuss has a grassroots base, whereby community or local level input is linked with entrepreneurial initiatives, and is often based on the possession of cultural capital resources, rather than those derived solely from human capital.

While the need for employment creation at the local level has been recognized in official quarters, such as the OECD in its Local Initiatives for Employment (ILE) programme (OECD, 1990), efforts to stimulate entrepreneurship have remained focused on building and strengthening the entrepreneurial capacity of the individual. In some labour market disadvantaged communities, however, where individuals initially lack the skills and other prerequisites for successfully pursuing new ventures, even with enabling mechanisms, such as business assistance centres and financing programmes for new small ventures, the expectation that entrepreneurship would be stimulated in the short term to create jobs may be unrealistic. This expectation also often ignores the importance of effective demand in sustaining businesses in such communities. In order to overcome such obvious difficulties to the creation of entrepreneurial responses by individuals in these communities, we offer the approach of 'community entrepreneurship'. As depicted in this chapter the concept of community entrepreneurship is a fruitful framework through which current community employment creation initiatives can be analyzed. At the same time it provides a conceptual rationale to drive new entrepreneurial ventures in employment creation at the local level.

The following section of this chapter critiques orthodox approaches to employment creation based on human capital theory, which stress greater education and training for individuals as being too narrow and inflexible and with insufficient emphasis on the character of the local community and the broader context in which the community is located. Community entrepreneurship is proposed as a viable alternative to such approaches. Before outlining the key features of the concept of community entrepreneurship in a later section, we provide a brief discussion of its genesis. Here we focus on both the local economic conditions in New Zealand that led to our concern with local ethnic unemployment issues, and the theoretical catalyst, namely Schumpeterian-type ideas on entrepreneurship. The latter are delineated and extended to examine their contemporary relevance. Finally, the chapter provides examples of community entrepreneurship in action.

Human Capital

As we have noted elsewhere (Dupuis *et al.*, 2000), human capital theory is a fundamental theory in economics aimed at explaining individual differences and social inequalities, turning on the idea that individuals vary in the extent of human capital they possess. Put another way, individuals vary in the abilities and qualities they possess which, in turn, affects how productive and successful they will be in the labour market (Becker, 1964; Shanahan and Tuma, 1994). The concept of human capital is generally understood as an amalgam of all the abilities and traits possessed by individuals that make them economically productive in society. It is considered that human capital includes both innate qualities like intelligence, health, personality, attractiveness and so on, as well as acquired skills that come from education, training and work experience. While work experience cannot be taught, people can certainly invest in education and training (or, as is often the case, in their children's education and training), in order to increase their human capital. Human capital theory therefore, refers to 'an individual's investment in personal productivity' (Light and Karageorgis, 1994: 658).

Human capital theory generally underpins employment creation schemes. Similarly, it informs the kind of compensatory education and training programmes that are aimed at redistributing resources. There is a widespread acceptance therefore, that a lack of human capital is the key cause of individuals being disadvantaged in the labour market. Put simply, lack of education and training lies at the core of unemployment. The theory also takes a macro focus to encompass the effects of education on aggregate output and productivity for national economies (Rubinson and Browne, 1994).

The notion of community entrepreneurship as developed in this chapter, can be seen as a critique of orthodox approaches to employment creation that focus largely on an individual's acquisition of labour market skills. While we are not disputing that higher education levels and the acquisition of formally recognized labour market skills will undoubtedly open up greater employment opportunities for labour market disadvantaged ethnic minorities, we do maintain that the basic focus on the individual inherent within orthodox human capital theory, can be too narrow. It fails to recognize the social nature of human beings, the way they are located within specific contexts and their propensity to operate within social networks. In other words, it fails to take into account the fact that individuals are embedded within the context in which they operate. We argue that rather than ignore this facet of human action, be that social or economic, it can be drawn upon to become the basis for entrepreneurial activity. It is particularly relevant when considering education and training and employment creation for groups of people who hold a strong collectivist, rather than an individualistic orientation. Our argument here is that the concept of community entrepreneurship extends the orthodox view of human capital and offers a perspective on employment creation which recognizes the multi-faceted nature of human capital and, for some situations and in some circumstances, the need for a broader, collectivist orientated approach to employment creation.

Development of the Concept

In its original conception, community entrepreneurship was developed by the authors (de Bruin and Dupuis, 1995a, 1995b) while working on a feasibility study of a grassroots urban tourism project in an ethnically diverse, low socio-economic area of Auckland, New Zealand's largest city. The project itself was aimed at addressing the problem of ethnic unemployment in a labour market disadvantaged community, which had been severely impacted upon by restructuring and closures of local manufacturing plants, and downsizing within such public sector areas as the railways and forestry. Community entrepreneurship was seen as a possible answer to both an initial lack of individual entrepreneurial skills and employment opportunities for this community. Crucial to its development, however, was our awareness ·that many of the unemployed with whom we were working had remarkable talents and skills based on their deep cultural knowledges which permeated all facets of their lives. Unfortunately, they were not the talents and skills deemed necessary in the market place of the new global age.

By way of background that contextually locates the development of the concept of community entrepreneurship, we focus on two considerations: first, the wider economic conditions as played out in the New Zealand context that led to high rates of local ethnic unemployment; and second, the theoretical catalyst for the concept's development, namely Schumpeterian and neo-Schumpeterian ideas on entrepreneurship. The latter are delineated and extended to examine their contemporary relevance.

Political and Economic Change

From 1984 onwards, New Zealand's political economy underwent a range of sweeping reforms (Bollard and Buckle, 1987), which were:

> Driven by the imperative created by a rapidly declining economic performance and shaped by the particular economic philosophy adopted by successive governments to respond to that decline (Davidson, 1995: 99).

The reforms were of such a magnitude that they were described as marking a revolutionary change to New Zealand's political economy (Roper, 1991). Characterized as 'the New Zealand experiment', the fundamentals of the reform programme can be summed up as market liberalization, free trade, a move to more limited government, narrow monetarist policies, a deregulated market and fiscal restraint (Kelsey, 1995: 1-2). Early in the reform period monetary, fiscal and regulative reforms were introduced, intended to reduce inflation and overseas debt, increase private sector productivity and public sector efficiency. Driven by the notion of competition being the catalyst for higher productivity and greater efficiency, the intention was to create a 'level playing field' where true competition would thrive. This was to be achieved through the reduction or elimination of tariffs, subsidies, import licensing and tax concessions. In addition, labour markets became increasingly deregulated and New Zealand's long established system of national wage awards and collective bargaining was replaced by one of individually negotiated contracts, covering both public and private sectors.

The reforms outlined had substantial impacts in the areas of work and employment. In the years since 1984, there has been an increase in service sector employment and a decline in the primary, secondary and public sectors of New Zealand's economy. Part-time employment has increased rapidly, reflecting an increasing number of women in the paid work force, young people combining work and study, and the increasing necessity for more than one income to sustain a family. Flexible work patterns, such as casual and temporary work, flexitime, shift work, job sharing and weekend work have also grown in scope (Davidson and Bray, 1994; Davidson, 1995; Perry *et al.*, 1995).

By far the most immediate and apparent impact of the reforms, however, was the rapid rise in unemployment, to reach a peak of 11.1 per cent in 1992. While the rise in unemployment affected all New Zealand ethnic groups, it had a disproportionate impact on Maori and Pacific Island people. For example, between 1986 and 1991 the unemployment rate for Maori increased from 14.9 per cent to 24.2 per cent. Over the same period the rate for non-Maori increased from 5.8 per cent to 9 per cent. Much of this growth was due to increased unemployment among Maori men, especially in the late 1980s, as a result of substantial job losses in the manufacturing sector (Department of Statistics, 1993). While the year 1993 marked the beginning of strong employment growth and a significant decline in unemployment, there were still striking differences in the rates of unemployment between those in the European ethnic group and Maori and Pacific Island people. The Household Labour Force Survey which provides employment data on a quarterly basis, showed that for the December 1997 quarter the national seasonally adjusted unemployment rate was 6.7 per cent. However, while the European rate was 4.5 per cent, the Maori rate was 16.8 per cent and the Pacific Island rate 13.7 per cent (Statistics New Zealand, 1997). Unemployment rates for the March 2002 quarter exhibit a similar ethnic differential, with the European rate at 4.2 per cent, the Maori rate at 10.8 per cent and the Pacific Island rate at 9.7 per cent (Statistics New Zealand, 2002). In part, it was the implication of how local communities were being affected by these high ethnic unemployment rates that provided the impetus for the development of the concept of community entrepreneurship.

Theoretical Underpinnings

In the Introduction to this text, we discussed in some detail our overall approach to entrepreneurship. In this section we focus on the development of the concept of entrepreneurship in the work of Schumpeter, and others who followed in similar vein and whose work provides the theoretical underpinning for the concept of community entrepreneurship. Schumpeter, in highlighting the role of the entrepreneur in the stimulation of dynamic growth, saw the entrepreneur as the key agent of change whose function is, 'the doing of new things or the doing of things that are already being done in a new way (innovation)' (1991: 412). Thus the entrepreneur is depicted as the individual who 'gets things done' (1991: 413). Schumpeter saw entrepreneurial profit as being derived from new forms of production, ways of organization, or new ways of combining commercial activity. In this schema the entrepreneur perceives opportunity, namely the possibilities for making profit, and uses new technology and inventions for this purpose. In fact Schumpeter saw the entrepreneur as propelling technological progress.

Similarly, Schmookler concluded that the stimulus for inventions 'was the recognition of a costly problem to be solved or a potentially profitable opportunity to be seized; in short, a technical problem or opportunity evaluated in economic terms' (Schmookler, 1966: 199). Without entrepreneurship, therefore, profit making potential would not be exploited and scientific inventions and other discoveries would not be harnessed to create employment opportunities. Leibenstein too, saw the entrepreneur as part of the growth process and describing the entrepreneur as 'a gap-filler and input-completer [who] is probably the prime mover of the capacity creation part of these elements of the growth process' (Leibenstein, 1968: 73).

In his consideration of economic growth, Schumpeter (1961) developed the idea taken from Kondratiev, that long waves of economic growth, were related to inventions and innovations. Within this framework he distinguished between structural economic change which her termed 'development', and economic growth. His notion of 'creative destruction' as a cause of development, involved waves of innovation in different industries across different periods. He argued that historically, creative destruction is clustered in a few activities during any one period of time, where basic innovations lead to a series of secondary innovations, which in turn would yield higher entrepreneurial profit, thus providing the catalyst for launching a long wave. His view therefore, was that entrepreneurial innovation comes in 'swarms', gathers momentum, is imitated and is then followed by stagnation until entrepreneurs again emerge and a new series of innovations starts a new round of technical progress. Capitalist economies thus move through cycles or long waves.

Later in his career Schumpeter identified the 'creative response' in business activity with entrepreneurship. This he defined as a reaction 'outside the range of existing practice' and contrasted it with an 'adaptive response', which is an adaptation to change by an expansion or contraction within existing practice. Creative responses are apparent during transition periods and are 'an essential element in the historical process' (Schumpeter, 1991: 412). This latter point is worth noting because, as has so often been highlighted in the chapters in this book, the current era may be characterized as one of transition between one distinct phase of capitalism and another, with elements of the new epoch evolving.

Following a similar type of argument Leibenstein distinguishes between two broad types of entrepreneurship, routine entrepreneurship and 'new type' or 'N-entrepreneurship'. Routine entrepreneurship involves the activities of co-ordinating and operating a firmly established enterprise in known and well defined markets, whereas N-entrepreneurship involves creating or carrying on an enterprise 'where not all the markets are well established or clearly defined and/or in which the relevant parts of the production function are not completely known' (Leibenstein, 1968: 73). This chapter assumes that both types of entrepreneurship are prerequisites for aggregate economic growth, though it is suggested that at the local level N-entrepreneurship (or the creative response) is far more important. This is especially so in the case where in order to create jobs in labour market disadvantaged communities, new products and activities that build on existing resources, such as the cultural and ethnic riches of the community may have to be developed.

Neo-Schumpeterians, (for example Freeman *et al.*, 1982; Perez, 1983, 1985, 1986; Freeman and Perez, 1988; Tylecote, 1991), highlight current developments in information and communication technology to argue that they are all the harbinger of a new technology style which is information and knowledge intensive. As we have discussed in the Introduction to this text, it is clear that the new technology style is a major catalyst for the movement to a new era in capitalist development, characterized by heightened globalization, in which entrepreneurship becomes vital if economies and communities are to operate successfully.

Community Entrepreneurship: The Concept

The framework for community entrepreneurship we develop in this chapter is made up of a number of elements. In some instances of community entrepreneurship in action, some elements may take on greater significance than others, or one or other element may not necessarily be present. However, in its broadest conceptualization the framework for community entrepreneurship comprises the following elements; a community focus, community initiatives, partnerships, social energy, the investment of cultural capital, a market-leading orientation, empowerment, and leadership.

First, community entrepreneurship entails innovative community effort as a catalyst for the growth of local employment opportunities. While it could possibly complement the role of individual entrepreneurship in stimulating change and creating employment at a local level, it moves away markedly from the model of entrepreneurship as emanating from the individual. It is decidedly community focused and envisages the community supplying initiative and enterprise for the creation, transformation and expansion of employment creating ventures. Thus it is seen as a possible response to high rates of unemployment in labour market disadvantaged communities and within disadvantaged ethnic minority groups (de Bruin and Dupuis, 1995a, 1995b).

Next, the concept of community entrepreneurship recognizes the importance of partnerships in local employment creation. It therefore sits well with current international approaches to employment creation. For example, the OECD describes partnerships in local employment creation as the 'key to job creation' (OECD, 1993). The types of participation involved in community entrepreneurship entail partnerships between local community groups, local and central government agencies, private development companies, existing local businesses and other 'honest brokers'. Such partnerships take a proactive role to stimulate economic activity within a community. The role of private firms in community enterprises, while relatively new, is on the increase, as more and more firms come to recognize that a community conscience and other social responsibilities, complement other commercial goals. The concept of community entrepreneurship thus fits within a broader move in business that focuses not just on the bottom line of profit, but the triple bottom line that incorporates profit with positive environmental and social outcomes. It is expected therefore, that business support for local initiatives will rise. Thus for businesses, community entrepreneurship can be an expression of ethical practice. The recent call for corporate social innovation (CSI) and socially innovative corporate social responsibility (CSR) projects which demonstrate *real* CSR and commitment to local communities is particularly encouraging. CSI as the next phase of the CSR agenda involving 'more systematic and positive engagement' (Jupp, 2002: 11) is a trend that augurs well for the strengthening of partnership aspects of community entrepreneurship.

Building further on the Schumpeterian inspired basic framework, we draw on work of the development economist Hirschman (1984) and add the element of 'social energy'. We propose that community entrepreneurship would release social energy to provide development and employment at a grass roots level. Social energy has been conceptualized as a renewable motivation, which induces participation in a group movement, or co-operative activities, which occur despite of, or on account of hardship, disadvantage and even in the face of failure (Hirschman, 1984: 42-57).

Further, and of relevance to ethnic communities where unemployment is high, community entrepreneurship could build upon cultural strengths and ethnic identity. Thus cultural strengths becomes the next element in the community entrepreneurship framework. Like Kleymeyer, we see that 'cultural expression, in all its richness and variety', will become 'a major means of generating and focusing a vital social force that can be called *cultural energy*. This force is a prime source of motivation that inspires people to confront problems, identify solutions, and participate in carrying them out' (Kleymeyer, 1994: 4). Cultural energy would thus augment social energy, especially in the type of community referred to earlier by Hirschman. The combination of social energy and cultural energy has been termed 'community energy' (de Bruin, Power and Toko, 2001). Drawing together the key features of social and cultural energy, community energy can be defined as an energy which, in the face of hardship or even failure, integrates a renewable motivation for participation in co-operative activities that draws on shared identity to undertake bottom-up, grassroots community development.

In the initial conceptualization of community entrepreneurship, an important consideration was a recognition that cultural capital is inherent in many ethnic communities (de Bruin and Dupuis, 1995a, 1995b; de Bruin, 1999). Our argument is that community entrepreneurship can invest and thus profit from cultural capital. The term cultural capital signifies particular kinds of knowledge and social styles (Codd *et al.*, 1985: 12). It can be thought of as savvy or proficiency within a particular milieu, and involves ease and familiarity with the language, life style, and accepted ways of being that are embodied within particular groups. Bourdieu (1984: 13) also refers to a 'cultural competence', which may be manifested in the nature and the way cultural goods (like food, clothing and music) are consumed. Importantly, these vary among groups and are differentially consumed. Within the concept of community entrepreneurship, the cultural competence of otherwise disadvantaged groups, is recognized as a form of cultural capital that has value in itself. It thus becomes differentiated from the cultural capital of the dominant group and not viewed as inferior, but as an important resource in its own right. It can therefore be tapped into and converted into economic capital by being utilized to provide employment through innovative community initiatives (see also Chapter 4, 'Entrepreneurial Capital' for a discussion of convertibility).

The next element to be added to the community entrepreneurship framework is that of 'market-leading'. We contend that community entrepreneurship can open new horizons through market-leading activity. Market-leading is described as a deliberately staged affair which manages change to create demand and employment growth which would not otherwise have occurred. Market-leading may be likened to the Schumpeterian 'creative response' mentioned earlier, or Leibenstein's N-entrepreneurship, since it engages in the creation and operation of ventures where the production function is not completely known. Market-following on the other hand, is more in line with an 'adaptive response' or routine entrepreneurship. Market-leading, in the context of community entrepreneurship, has a community-base bias. Community co-operation and innovative exploitation of the community's social, cultural and other resources, nurtures and expands a market for the goods and services produced at the local level.

The process by which community energy is harnessed is one of empowerment, the next element within the framework. The concept of empowerment is important in relation to specific disadvantaged communities and therefore, at this point, it is useful to elaborate on the term. There are varied definitions of empowerment (Rappaport *et al.*, 1984), but common themes run through these definitions. These are that empowerment: is the goal and the means of community organization and action (Minkler, 1997); relates to the enhancement of the individual and collective capacity to take and re-gain control over the conditions determining well-being (Henderson and Thomas, 1987); and involves the on-going enabling of individuals and groups of individuals to participate in collective action (Daly and Cobb, 1994).

Collective mobilization of resources and the active exploration of ways to involve local populations in ownership and control of their own economic destiny is fundamental to community entrepreneurship. This cannot, however, be achieved without effective leadership, the final element of the framework. Leaders form an integral aspect of the entrepreneurship which develops and turns vision into the reality of viable, commercially sustainable ventures to provide jobs at the local level. Such leadership may come from a variety of sources. It may emanate from 'outsiders' who are the 'honest brokers', or be provided by the more educated, already successful professional who wants to give something 'back' to his/her community and drives a project to fruition, or from group leadership within the community, from, for example, some members of a trust or enterprise board. This leadership will provide the motivating force to harness and build on the existing resources as well as draw in additional resources to the community venture.

Strong, initial resistance to change is possible at the community level and particularly where smaller communities are involved. Yet as Schumpeter highlighted, entrepreneurship involves, on the one hand, the ability to identify new opportunities that are unproven and take action on them, 'and, on the other hand, willpower adequate to breaking down the resistance that the social environment offers to change' (1991: 417). Therefore, if innovative ideas for local job creation are to be acted on, leadership is necessary to draw in and maintain community support for such new ventures. The measure of the success of this leadership would be the extent of change that takes place within the community (see for example Heifetz, 1994).

This section has described the concept of community entrepreneurship and set in place the various elements that together make up the concept; community, community initiatives, partnerships, social energy, cultural capital, market-leading, empowerment and leadership. In the following section we provide examples of community entrepreneurship in action which highlight these elements.

Community Entrepreneurship in Action

Whale Watch Kaikoura

An eco-tourism whale watching company provides the first example of community entrepreneurship in action. This venture, Whale Watch, operates from Kaikoura (translated from the Maori as 'meal of lobster'), a small town on the east coast of New Zealand's South Island. At the last Census (2001), the town itself had a population of 2,106, of whom 16.2 per cent were Maori. Income data show that only 18.5 per cent of people in the Kaikoura Township earn over $30,000, compared with 30.7 per cent of people in New Zealand (Statistics New Zealand, 2002). While Kaikoura is clearly not an affluent town, if the Whale Watch venture had not been established the impacts of economic reform would have been highly damaging.

Until the mid 1980s employment in Kaikoura, like many other small towns in New Zealand, relied strongly on central government. The town's biggest employer in the post-WW2 decades was the New Zealand Railways, which at its peak supported about 200 local Kaikoura families. Other government departments, among them the Post Office and the Ministry of Works, were also major employers of the local population. The reforms of the 1980s, and their accompanying programmes of rationalization and privatization, impacted severely on Kaikoura, at the same time as the major areas of private sector employment, farming and fishing were also undergoing adjustments. As a consequence, unemployment rates rose rapidly and many families left the area (Riordan, 2001: A15).

Whale Watch, as an example of community entrepreneurship in action, can be viewed as a locally based project aimed at addressing these wider economic and political circumstances. It arose as a response to local disadvantaged conditions and clearly demonstrates both the community orientation and the effort required for community entrepreneurship. Moreover, it has drawn on the culture and heritage of local Maori. It has been successful in providing local employment, strengthening the town's economy and adding to general social cohesion and well-being. While the project itself has directly provided jobs for local Maori, the huge increase in tourism has had spin-off effects for employment for a variety of local enterprises. Over the years many other tourism-related businesses which appeal to a similar client group have been created, including dolphin encounters, helicopter and fixed-wing whale watching and sea kayaking. In addition, other businesses to service the needs of tourists with regard to food, accommodation and entertainment have flourished. The spin-off effects are obvious, given that it is estimated that annual visitor numbers are expected to reach one million by 2003 and an estimated annual growth in tourist numbers of 8 per cent. Based on taxation data it is also estimated that tourist operations bring into the township annually some $40 million (*Whale Watch News*, n.d.; Riordan, 2001).

Whale Watch was started by local Maori in 1987 and from very modest beginnings is now a multi-million dollar business which has accrued considerable assets in the form of boats, buildings, buses and harbour facilities. Given the history of railway employment in the area, there is a certain irony to the fact that Whale Watch Kaikoura runs its operation from what was once the town's railway station. Now termed the Whaleway Station, the old building has been renovated and refitted to a very high standard. As a result of its growth, Whale Watch Kaikoura has become the single largest employer in the town. In peak season the company employs up to 70 people, most of whom are Maori, and supports many Maori extended families. Moreover, dividends are set aside to provide education and training for adults and young people (*Whale Watch News*, n.d.).

Whale Watch Kaikoura Limited is a community trust owned and operated by Maori in Kaikoura (the sub-tribe of Kati Kuri) in partnership with Ngai Tahu, their affiliated tribal people. Energy and commitment at the local level provided the catalyst for Whale Watch. A small group of local Maori who were concerned with the town's declining economic situation and extremely high rate of youth unemployment (90 per cent) developed the vision for the project, consistent with their oral history which told of their ancestor, Paikea, who arrived in Aotearoa (New Zealand) riding on the back of a whale. The vision was based on the fact that a number of different whale varieties abound off the Kaikoura Coast. These include great sperm, right, blue, orca and the humpback whale, all of which can be readily seen feeding and playing. Hectors and dusky dolphins are also plentiful. Both types of animals are attracted by the specific sea conditions. The water around Kaikoura is a place where the cooler ocean currents from the south meet the warmer currents from the north, creating a nutrient-rich area where many forms of marine life, from krill to the giant squid, thrive and provide a fine feeding ground for sea mammals.

Originally called Kaikoura Tours, the initial venture began in a small way in 1987. Funding the vision was decidedly difficult as no banks would lend money for the venture. This set-back was overcome initially when the group raised $35,000 from personal savings and such activities as bingo. To run their first boat, a small rubber dinghy that would take 10 people, four families mortgaged their houses. However, others could see the value of the vision and provided financial help or other aid. A retired banker from the nearby city of Christchurch offered his services and a marketing lecturer from the Christchurch Polytechnic and his students exchanged a whale watch holiday in return for a marketing plan. Other early funding came from a $100,000 Maori agency venture capital loan (*Whale Watch News*, n.d.).

While the enterprise is run in a way consistent with Maori principles and practices, an important component of its success has been its ability to ensure it retains a monopoly. When a competitor was granted a permit to begin a similar enterprise, Ngai Tahu challenged the decision. The Court of Appeal decided that the government's obligations to the Treaty of Waitangi (the founding document between Maori and Pakeha which was signed in 1840), ensured that tribal interests were protected and that Ngai Tahu were entitled to a 'reasonable degree of preference' (*Whale Watch News*, n.d.: 10/14). The Court also noted that the company's use of coastal waters for whale watching was in keeping with historical practices of fishing and shore-based whaling. Also, a common role for indigenous people had been to guide visitors to see the natural resources of the country. This recognition demonstrates the extent to which the venture had been able to draw on longstanding cultural practices and knowledge.

Whale Watch Kaikoura is not the only whale watch company in the world. Nor was it the first. However, with respect to market-leading, it was the first whale watching venture in New Zealand and the first in the world that was owned and operated by indigenous people. The breathtaking nature of the activity itself, plus the authenticity of the Maori experience, have led many tourists to describe their whale watching trip as a spiritual experience.

Empowerment for the community has come in a number of ways. Initially the venture was seen as a way of getting local people out of unemployment and into work. The training involved in this has been vital to the success of the venture. The Kaikoura Centre for Continuing Education gets paid by Whale Watch Kaikoura to provide courses and train staff in the marine tourism business. There have been significant benefits to the wider community as well. The explosion of tourists to the area have ensured a range of other ventures have been set up for their entertainment and accommodation. These too bring necessary revenue into the community.

The importance of leadership has been highlighted in this venture. While Whale Watch is really a community enterprise, the leadership role of long time Chief Executive Wally Stone requires comment. Stone has been described as having the leadership qualities of drive, vision and a way of incorporating others into the plan, all qualities that fed into the eventual success of Whale Watch. A few years ago when Stone was appointed to the New Zealand Tourism Board he was recognized as 'one of the country's outstanding entrepreneurial businessmen'. Such an accolade is even more meritorious when it is known that earlier in his life Stone had been a street kid with a number of convictions. It has been suggested that the catalyst for Stone's transformation to an important Ngai Tahu business leader was the impact of these early experiences on his life (Aldridge, 1999). In itself Stone's personal story provides both a catalyst and a model for the venture's success.

The advantages derived by the local community from this business are obvious. However, this venture has also made its mark internationally. The success and recognition of this venture can be seen in that within a decade of operation Whale

Watch Kaikoura received three international awards: in 1995 it was presented with a British Airways Award for the world's best eco-tourism venture; later, in Berlin, it received the Green Globe Achievement Award for distinction in tourism; finally a Pacific Asia Travel Association gold award was won for excellence in the cultural and heritage category. The venture aims to add to the knowledge of sea life in the area and the group involved have worked with marine researchers from the Smithsonian Museum of Natural History in Washington DC seeking information on marine life, especially the elusive giant squid in the Kaikoura Canyon, a deep offshore trench. Whale Watch has detailed database information on the whale's social, feeding and responsive behaviour. The material compiled is being used for the development of environmental and conservation plans in the company's area. Politically the company supports marine conservation practices. In particular it supports the international fight to protect whales against commercial whaling. Fundamental to this eco-tourism project is a view that it must be economically and environmentally sustainable and culturally authentic, the latter a feature of the venture to which all staff are committed. Most importantly, however, the commercial nature of the venture has been maintained with integrity, and in a way that builds on and continues the community's history and culture.

Youth Grow: A Community Employment Project for Disadvantaged Youth

Youth Grow is a community project for young people who are aged between 16 and 24 and who are disadvantaged in the urban labour market of Dunedin, a South Island city in New Zealand. The impetus for the Youth Grow project came from the observations of staff at Presbyterian Support Otago's food bank, that they were seeing a lot of young people who were not connected to their families, were not working, or in training or study, and who seemed to be drifting. Research was done to identify their needs, especially the needs of those who were suffering from mental illness. A partnership was set up between two local Presbyterian parishes, also concerned about the high levels of local youth unemployment. A feasibility study was then commissioned on possible job creation programmes and it was decided that a land based industry would be most appropriate given the job intensive nature of such work (Employment Matters, 2002: 11).

A seeding grant of $300,000 was provided by the British based Council for World Mission. This was used to buy a nursery and lease some adjacent land on which to grow saffron and arnica for the export market, evidence of a market-leading approach. Further support and advice came from the Community Employment Group (CEG), the central government's major funder of community based employment initiatives, the Health Funding Authority and the Department of Work and Income. The partnership model in this venture is clearly evident.

The Director of Family and Community Services of Presbyterian Support Otago, has indicated in its first year Youth Grow intends to employ 12 young people, and up to 24 in the second year. The Project is particularly focused on employing young people with poor mental health or those who have been involved with the welfare or justice systems. The first young people have been employed already and are working in the retail side of the nursery, in propagation and contract work and planting a hillside in arnica plants. The project also involves developing a worm farm and an off-site contracting business. It is intended that for the first two years, until the export crops come on stream, the focus will be on development work.

The community, through Presbyterian support has made a major commitment to the project and its long-term development. The partnership with the parishes has provided the community basis. Finally, it is evident that the young people involved find working in the supportive environment an rewarding experience.

A Business High School: Entrepreneurship at School

The next example we offer for community entrepreneurship is a little different in that the employment creation is essentially indirect and through the human capital development of the individual. Nevertheless, the example can still be regarded as community entrepreneurship. with a number of elements of the framework in evidence.

The catalyst for New Zealand's first business high school, came as an intersection of coincidences. Late in 2001, a New Zealand entrepreneur, Tony Falkenstein, who was taking a sabbatical in Britain at the time, was reading on-line, the New Zealand Herald, Auckland's daily newspaper, and saw an article discussing the Global Entrepreneurship Monitor (GEM) report which had just been published (see also Chapter 12, 'Youth Entrepreneurship' for further reference to this report). The article noted that New Zealand ranked second only to Mexico in a 29 country entrepreneurship table. It also pointed to an interesting problem when it posed the question of why was it, given New Zealanders had been shown to be amongst the most entrepreneurial people in the world, that New Zealand was gradually declining in position among the world's developed countries? The article offered the response of inadequate business education. It claimed that New Zealand schools were below the global average for their teaching about the market economy and entrepreneurship and that management education was close to the bottom in the 29 countries surveyed.

Coincidentally, at the same time, Britain's Prime Minister Tony Blair was on a campaign to turn several of Britain's schools into technical centres. Reflecting on his own experiences as a late starter in coming to understand the possibilities of entrepreneurship, Falkenstein decided to begin a similar initiative in New Zealand. Six months later, with Falkenstein back in New Zealand, the country's first business high school, Onehunga High School in Auckland, is planning to teach business classes at the beginning of the new school year, early in 2003. It is no coincidence, however, that Falkenstein is an ex-student of Onehunga High.

It is intended that Onehunga High School will offer business courses to students from around the Auckland Region, international fee paying students and adults. School students too, in their final four years of high school education, will attend courses covering international and entrepreneurial business skills. In the final two years it is expected that students will take tertiary level papers including commercial law, marketing, management studies and economics. Initially some 100 students can be catered for in the programme (Hendery, 2002: C1).

How can this business high school initiative be analyzed in terms of the community entrepreneurship framework? The programme is definitely community focused and located in a local Auckland high school. It is aimed at producing students who have a strongly developed appreciation of entrepreneurship. In this sense it is also about employment creation. It is market-leading in that it is the first programme of its type in a New Zealand high school. In addition, the partnership element is very clear. Finally, leadership is obvious. Driven strongly by Falkenstein, the vision was also picked up by members of the school community. These leaders in the field of entrepreneurship in schools, with a small number of others, are part of the programme's foundation board. Apart from the underwriting of the programme with up to NZ$300,000 over two years by the corporation Falkenstein heads, the board has also been able to secure funding of NZ$386,000 from Industry New Zealand's Enterprise Culture and Skills Activities Fund, so government has entered the partnership.

Regional Revival: The Waitaki District and Waitaki Valley

The final example of community entrepreneurship describes a regional revival project. The Waitaki District and Waitaki Valley is in New Zealand's South Island and comprises several small towns, little townships and communities centred around the Waitaki River. The District is strongly associated with New Zealand's pioneering past and is a place of outstanding natural beauty. The region is promoted as 'Whitestone Waitaki' after the locally quarried limestone and the historic landmark buildings which are constructed from whitestone. The main town centre of the District is Oamaru, which grew around the harbour serving the area and its rich farming hinterland. Several of the communities in the Valley were also formed around the construction of a hydro-electric dam system. Otematata was based on the Benmore Dam and Kurow was associated with the Waitaki Dam. With construction companies moving out, coupled with general rural population decline, the survival of small towns and employment creation in the area could no longer rely on the stimulatory impact of aggregate demand growth. Community action and group entrepreneurial activity became vital for the prosperity of small rural communities such as those in the Waitaki Valley.

Several linked entrepreneurial initiatives, with a co-operative community approach to managing economic revival, characterizes the action of three small Waitaki Valley communities (Otematata, Kurow and Duntroon), to keep their region economically viable. These initiatives are mainly associated with heritage and eco-tourism (Employment Matters, 2001a, 2001b). Taken together these projects are a concerted market-leading activity which can provide a 'Big Push' for rural revival in the region.

We now showcase one of the Waitaki Valley ventures – a community owned business, *Vanished World* based in Duntroon. *Vanished World – Fossils on a Whitestone Trail* in North Otago opens up to public viewing 25-30 million year old marine mammal fossils sites. One site has such an abundance of fossils embedded in the limestone rocks that it has been give the name, Valley of the Whales. The vision of Dr Helen Brookes, formerly a researcher and teacher at Otago University, has been responsible for the project getting underway. Dr Brookes recognizing the tourism fossil resource, worked in conjunction with University of Otago geology Associate Professor Ewan Fordyce, a fossil expert who knew the local landowners well, to garner support for the project. There is now strong landowner support, CEG funding and close advice from the field worker, together with broad support from Tourism Waitaki, the tourism promotional arm of the Waitaki Development Board and even the Prime Minister, Helen Clark as a patron, all of which gives the venture a springboard for success. The first site on the trail where the public can view fossils in their natural surroundings is now ready. A protective case has been placed over exposed ancient baleen whale bones at an excavation site, providing viewing without exposure to the elements or any danger of vandalism (Anonymous, n.d.). An interesting facet of the project is the 'town-gown' partnership which has become more possible in recent years as universities have changed their policies to ensure science is taken out to communities. With reference to the university connection, Dr Brookes is quoted as saying, 'They have a sense of responsibility to community that they didn't have 10 years ago' (Employment Matters, 2001b: 7).

Conclusion

The supply of entrepreneurship is a vital element in the process of employment creation in the new global age of capitalist development. More so than during previous periods, it is reasonable to argue that entrepreneurship assumes greater importance as a stimulant of dynamic economic growth. Yet in this era of heightened globalization and competition, regional and ethnic disparities in employment levels have emerged as a major socio-economic problem. In relation to this problem, therefore, the argument offered in this chapter is that attention should be paid to the supply of entrepreneurship at the community level.

The concept of community entrepreneurship was developed to widen conventional thinking on entrepreneurship and act as the catalyst for job creation at the grassroots community level. The concept is put forward to provide a solution to an initial shortage of entrepreneurial talents at an individual level and act as the catalyst for the creation of employment opportunities which would not otherwise eventuate. It offers a framework through which current community employment creation initiatives can be analyzed, while also providing a conceptual rationale to drive new community-based entrepreneurial ventures.

In New Zealand, local initiatives for employment creation are vital for the mitigation of high unemployment levels of Maori and Pacific Island ethnic minorities and of regional disadvantage. Special locality based efforts become necessary for employment generation, especially in communities where the majority of individuals lack human capital in the orthodox sense, manifested in the form of formal educational qualifications and skills compatible with the new technology style of the current global era. The development of community entrepreneurship is a viable means of harnessing social and cultural energy – channelling community energy, into sustainable employment, especially through the partnership model. Market-leading community entrepreneurship, in particular, could be instrumental in the creation of jobs, on a much larger scale than would be the outcome of the normal aggregate growth of the economy. For those groups, communities and regions that are unlikely to benefit from this growth it would provide a way of empowering communities to create new economic opportunities, as well as take advantage of existing opportunities, and to address poverty issues. It could also be the catalyst for local and regional revival and reaffirm the cultural heritages of a multi-ethnic society.

References

Albrow, M. (1996), *The Global Age: State and Society Beyond Modernity*, Polity Press, Cambridge.

Aldridge, V. (1999), 'Strangers Smile that Turned Life Around', *The Dominion*, Wellington, 11 May.

Amin, A. (1995), *Post-Fordism: A Reader*, Blackwell, Oxford, Cambridge, MA.

Anonymous (n.d.), http://www.tourismwaitaki.co.nz/index.cfm/news/Vanished/ (accessed 2 June, 2002).

Becker, G. (1964), *Human Capital: A Theoretical and Empirical Analysis with Special Reference to Education*, National Bureau of Economic Research, New York.

Bell, D. (1974), *The Coming of Post-Industrial Society*, Heineman, London.

Best, S. and Kellner, D. (1997), *The Postmodern Turn*, Guilford Press, New York.

Bollard, A. and Buckle, R. (1987), *Economic Liberalisation in New Zealand*, Allen and Unwin, Wellington.

Bourdieu, P. (1984), *Distinction: A Social Critique of the Judgement of Taste*, Harvard University Press, Cambridge, MA.

Castells, M. (2000a), *End Of Millennium*, Blackwell Publishers, Oxford and Malden, MA.

Castells, M. (2000b), *The Rise of the Network Society* (2nd Edition), Blackwell Publishers, Malden, MA.

Codd, J., Harker, R. and Nash, R. (1985), 'Introduction: Education, Politics and the Economic Crisis', in J. Codd, R. Harker and R. Nash (eds), *Political Issues in New Zealand Education*, The Dunmore Press, Palmerston North.

Daly, H. and Cobb, J. (1994), *For the Common Good: Redirecting the Economy Toward Community, the Environment, and a Sustainable Future*, Beacon Press, Boston.

Davidson, C. (1995), 'Employment in New Zealand after the "Revolution": The Outcome of Restructuring', *British Review of New Zealand Studies (BRONZS)*, No. 8, pp. 99-115.

Davidson, C. and Bray, M. (1994), *Women and Part Time Work in New Zealand*, New Zealand Institute for Social Research and Development (SR&D), Christchurch.

de Bruin, A. (1998), 'Entrepreneurship in a New Phase of Capitalist Development', *The Journal of Interdisciplinary Economics*, Vol. 9, pp. 185-200.

de Bruin, A. (1999), 'Cultural Capital', in P. O'Hara (ed.), *Encyclopedia of Political Economy*, Routledge, London and New York, pp. 169-171.

de Bruin, A and Dupuis, A. (1995a), 'A Closer Look at New Zealand's Superior Economic Performance: Ethnic Employment Issues', *British Review of New Zealand Studies*, No. 8, pp. 85-97.

de Bruin, A. and Dupuis, A. (1995b), *Feasibility of Otara as a Desirable Tourist Destination, Final Report to Enterprise Otara*, Enterprise Otara, Auckland.

de Bruin, A., Power, G. and Toko, S. (2001), 'The Role of Community Employment Creation: Lessons and Challenges for a New Era', in P. Morrison (ed.) *Labour Employment and Work in New Zealand: Proceedings of the Ninth Conference*, Victoria University of Wellington, Wellington, pp. 156-163.

Department of Statistics (1993), *New Zealand Social Trends: Work*, Department of Statistics, Wellington.

Dicken, P. (1998), *Global Shift: Transforming the World Economy* (3rd Edition), Chapman, London.

Dupuis, A., de Bruin, A. and Firkin, P. (2000), 'Human Capital Acquisition: Constrained Choice in a Regional Labour Market', *Access: Critical Perspectives on Cultural and Policy Studies in Education*, Vol. 19(1), pp. 57-78.

Employment Matters (2001a), 'Power to the People', *Employment Matters*, Vol. 12(8), p.5

Employment Matters (2001b), 'Vanished World Brought to Life', *Employment Matters*, Vol. 12(7), pp.1, 7.

Employment Matters (2002), 'Youth Grow', *Employment Matters*, Vol. 13(1), p. 11.

Felstead, A. and Jewson, N. (1999), *Global Trends in Flexible Labour*, Macmillan Business, Basingstoke.

Freeman, C., Clark, J. and Soete, L. (1982), *Unemployment and Technical Innovation*, Frances Pinter, London.

Freeman, C. and Perez, C. (1988), 'Structural Crises of Adjustment, Business Cycles and Investment Behaviour', in G. Dosi, C. Freeman, R. Nelson, G. Silverberg and L. Soete (eds), *Technical Change and Economic Theory*, Pinter, London.

Heifetz, R. (1994), *Leadership without Easy Answers*, Belknap Press of Harvard University Press, Cambridge, MA.

Held, D., McGrew, A., Goldblatt, D. and Perraton, J. (1999), *Global Transformations: Politics, Economics and Culture*, Polity Press, Cambridge.

Henderson, P. and Thomas, D. (1987), *Skills in Neighbourhood Work* (2nd Edition), Routledge, London and New York.

Hendery, S. (2002), 'Building an Enterprise Culture', *The New Zealand Herald*, 25-26 May, p. C1.

Hirschman, A. (1984), *Getting Ahead Collectively*, Pergamon Press, New York.

Jupp, R (2002), 'Getting Down to Business: A New Agenda for Corporate Social Innovation', Demos, London, http://www.demos.co.uk/ (accessed 3 August, 2002).

Kelsey, J. (1995), *The New Zealand Experiment: A World Model for Structural Adjustment?*, Auckland University Press with Bridget Williams Books, Auckland.

Kleymeyer, C. (1994), 'Introduction', in C. Kleymeyer (ed.), *Cultural Expression and Grassroots Development*, Lynne Rienner Publishers, Boulder, CO.

Leibenstein, H. (1968), 'Entrepreneurship and Development', *American Economic Review*, Vol. 58(2), pp. 72-75.

Light, I. and Karageorgis. S. (1994), 'The Ethnic Economy', in N. Smelser and R. Swedberg (eds), *The Handbook of Economic Sociology*, Princeton University Press, Princeton, NJ and Russell Sage Foundation, New York, pp. 647-671.

McLennan, G. (1995), *Pluralism*, University of Minnesota Press, Minneapolis, MN.

Minkler, M. (ed.) (1997), *Community Organizing and Community Building for Health*, Rutgers University Press, New Brunswick.

OECD (1990), *Labour Market Policies for the 1990s*, Organisation for Economic Co-operation and Development, Paris.

OECD (1993), *Partnerships: The Key to Employment Creation*, Organisation for Economic Co-operation and Development, Paris.

Perez, C. (1983), 'Structural Change and Assimilation of New Technologies in the Economic and Social Systems', *Futures*, October, pp. 357-375.

Perez, C. (1985), 'Microelectronics, Long Waves and World Structural Change: New Perspectives for Developing Countries', *World Development*, Vol. 13(3), pp. 441-463.

Perez, C. (1986), 'Structural Change and Assimilation of New Technologies in the Economic and Social System', in C. Freeman (ed.), *Design, Innovation and Long Cycles in Economic Development*, Frances Pinter, London.

Perry, M., Davidson, C. and Hill, R. (1995), *Reform at Work: Workplace Change and the New Industrial Order*, Longman Paul, Auckland.

Rappaport, J., Swift, C. and Hess, R. (eds) (1984), *Studies in Empowerment: Steps Toward Understanding and Action*, Haworth Press, New York.

Riordan, D. (2001), 'Old Town's Having a Whale of a Time', *The New Zealand Herald*, 27 December, 2001, p. A16.

Roper, B. (1991), 'From the Welfare State to the Free Market: Explaining the Transition. Part 2 Crisis, Class, Ideology and State', *New Zealand Sociology*, Vol. 6(2), pp. 135-176.

Rubinson, R. and Browne, I. (1994), 'Education and the Economy', in N. Smelser and R. Swedberg (eds), *The Handbook of Economic Sociology*, Princeton University Press, Princeton, NJ, and Russell Sage Foundation, New York, pp. 581-599.

Schmookler, J. (1966), *Invention and Economic Growth*, Harvard University Press, Cambridge, MA.

Schumpeter, J. (1961), *The Theory of Economic Development*, Oxford University Press, New York.

Schumpeter, J. (1991), 'Comments on a Plan for the Study of Entrepreneurship', in R. Swedberg (ed.), *The Economics and Sociology of Capitalism/Joseph A. Schumpeter*, Princeton University Press, Princeton, NJ.

Seidman, S. (1994), *The Postmodern Turn: New Perspectives On Social Theory*, Cambridge University Press, Cambridge and New York.

Shanahan, S. and Tuma, N. (1994), 'The Sociology of Distribution and Redistribution', in N. Smelser and R. Swedberg (eds), *The Handbook of Economic Sociology*, Princeton University Press, Princeton, NJ and Russell Sage Foundation, New York.

Statistics New Zealand (1997), *Household Labour Force Survey*, Statistics New Zealand, Wellington.

Statistics New Zealand (2002), http://www.statistics.govt.nz (accessed 10 May, 2002).

Tylecote, A. (1991), *The Long Wave in the World Economy*, Routledge, London and New York.

Whale Watch News (n.d.), 'History of Whale Watch', http://www.whalewatch.co.nz (accessed 14 May, 2002).

Wilson, H. (1999), 'The Information Age: Economy, Society and Culture', *Journal of Sociology*, Vol. 35(3), pp. 375-378.

Chapter 8

Municipal-Community Entrepreneurship

Ann Dupuis, Anne de Bruin and Rolf D. Cremer

Introduction

In the Introduction to this book we noted that our sub-title locates entrepreneurship in a global age. We qualified that, however, by observing that the global age focus is not meant to situate the discussion of entrepreneurship as a mainly global activity, but rather is intended to highlight the possibilities and opportunities for entrepreneurship that the global age creates. The topic of this chapter, municipal-community entrepreneurship, extends our discussion of community entrepreneurship in the previous chapter and offers an analysis of a further form of entrepreneurship that has emerged within the context of the global age. Like community entrepreneurship, municipal-community entrepreneurship is also a type of locally-based entrepreneurship that arose as a response to the economic and political changes that characterize the global era. Furthermore, as in the previous chapter, this chapter, too, engages with a major theme of the book – that entrepreneurship and entrepreneurial activity is increasingly common, and even necessary, as a collective enterprise, rather than simply an individual activity. The key site of entrepreneurial activity highlighted in this chapter is the public sector at the municipality, city or regional level.

Municipal-community entrepreneurship, while not solely an urban phenomenon, is nevertheless most clearly evident in cities. A major emphasis within contemporary urban studies has been on the global processes that have shaped the roles of global cities in the new global economy (Sassen, 1991, 1996). Three of these cities, London, Tokyo and New York, termed world cities by Short (1996), have been identified as now sitting 'atop the global urban hierarchy', operating as command centres of the global economy and world business (Short, 1996: 70) and as being the most unequal cities (Sassen, 1991). Short also identifies other types of cities; the Keynesian city, which had its heyday in the 1960s and 1970s, in which the booms and slumps of capitalism were modified by government intervention and the comparatively recent post-Fordist city, which is characterized by a 'reregulated state in which welfare provisions are reduced, public services are underfunded, and the dominant shift is towards various forms of privatization' (Short, 1996: 80).

While cities are linked to a dynamic and changing global economy it is unwise to view global changes and patterns as determining, particularly in light of the countervailing trend which focuses on the significance of the local, tracing 'urban diversity to internal force and the tactics used by local actors' (Fainstein, 1996: 170). By posing these tendencies as counterbalancing, we have no wish to imply a simple global-local divide. Quite the contrary. Rather our aim here, as in other chapters, is to stress the interplay between the global and the local and the possibilities and opportunities for entrepreneurship that have thus emerged.

This chapter, therefore, seeks to explore the entrepreneurial lead role of urban organizations and local government bodies, especially as they pertain to the post-Fordist city, and the various ways they stimulate and promote economic activity, employment and the general well-being for residents. This chapter, therefore, engages with questions and issues around the nature and extent of entrepreneurship at the level of the municipality. The analytical framework we offer for this purpose is the concept of 'municipal-community entrepreneurship' (Cremer, de Bruin and Dupuis, 2001). Posing the question, 'Can city governments become strategic brokers that influence their city's ... position in the global hierarchy?', the 2000 *World Development Report* answers in the affirmative, with the caveat that appropriate planning and support is required (World Bank, 2000: 136). We contend that municipal-community entrepreneurship is a crucial facet of such urban entrepreneurial strategies.

Fundamental to the concept of municipal-community entrepreneurship is the idea that, at the municipal level, opportunities are created and responded to by municipal governments through opportunity-related strategic behaviour. The stress on entrepreneurialism as opportunity, as opposed to risk taking, is an important component of our position. We agree with Osborne and Gaebler (1993: xx) who note that in the context of public entrepreneurship it is more appropriate to highlight opportunity, for 'who wants bureaucrats taking risks with their hard-earned tax dollars?'. The tension between risk and opportunity and the debate this has engendered is a key theme of the chapter.

The next section of the chapter provides a contextual backdrop to the development of the concept of municipal-community entrepreneurship by examining the broader issue of the rise of 'entrepreneurial government' at the local level in many municipalities, cities and regions. The concept of municipal-community entrepreneurship is then outlined and followed by examples of municipal-community entrepreneurship in action. The first example incorporates the international sister-cities movement into the concept of municipal-community entrepreneurship. The remaining examples, which provide further elaboration of the concept, highlight municipal economic development strategies.

The Movement to Public Entrepreneurship

The concept of municipal-community entrepreneurship sits well within the wider view of governments as entrepreneurs, which is seen increasingly as a new model for central, municipal and city governments across the western world. Variously described as 'entrepreneurial government', 'city governments as strategic brokers', 'the reinvention movement' or 'public entrepreneurship' (Osborne and Gaebler, 1993; Osborne and Plastrik, 1997; Cohen *et al.*, 1999; World Bank, 2000), the movement towards governments as entrepreneurs must be viewed as a response to the rhetoric of the neo-liberal shift of the 1980s and beyond, which stressed less and cheaper government at whatever level. Associated with the Thatcher years in the United Kingdom, the Reagan government of the United States and the Douglas influence in New Zealand's fourth Labour Government, the neo-liberal shift was based on a perception of the poor results of many government programmes and the perceived contrast between the inefficient workings of public sector bureaucracies with private sector efficiency (Cohen *et al.*, 1999: 5). The result was that many governments not only advocated privatization of previously government run agencies and services in order to cut costs and achieve the goal of efficiency, but went well down the route of implementing such policies. As noted in the previous chapter on 'Community Entrepreneurship', a frequent outcome of the phenomenon of 'rolling back the state' (Kelsey, 1993) was increased rates of unemployment. This factor, together with the recognition that less government did not result in benefits to disadvantaged groups, provided the context for the reinvention movement, advocating a different emphasis within governments.

The entrepreneurial government response did not dispute that typically, government bureaucracies of the post-World War Two era were characterized by inefficiencies and were far from ideal in the political and economic climate of the late twentieth century. However, rather than support the privatization principle, the argument was made that both private and public sectors are equally subject to inefficiencies and therefore privatization will not of itself provide a better alternative (Cohen *et al.*, 1999). Instead, public entrepreneurship was signalled as the form reinvention should take and thus as the best option for the way forward.

In a cogent argument that hits at the very heart of orthodox Weberian, or the later neo-Weberian, urban managerialist views of rationality and efficiency in modernist, bureaucratic governmental settings (see, for example, Pahl, 1975), Osborne and Gaebler claim that orthodox bureaucracies are no longer the best way of organizing large scale operations in contemporary societies. Further, they point out that this new trend towards public sector entrepreneurship is compatible with private sector changes observed over the last decade such as 'decentralizing authority, flattening hierarchies, focusing on quality, getting close to customers – all in an effort to remain competitive in the new global marketplace' (1993: 12). Osborne and Gaebler elaborate on their thesis as follows:

The kinds of governments that developed during the industrial era, with their sluggish, centralized bureaucracies, their preoccupation with rules and regulations, and their hierarchical chains of command, no longer work very well. ... Gradually, new kinds of public institutions are taking their place (1993: 12).

Central to their argument is a recognition of the capacity and abilities of entrepreneurs in a range of public sector contexts. Working on an early definition of the entrepreneur, put forward in about 1800 by the French economist J.B. Say, Osborne and Gaebler define the entrepreneur as someone who 'uses resources in new ways to maximize productivity and effectiveness' (1993: xix). In addition, they maintain that this definition applies equally well to the public sector and the voluntary, or third sector as it does to the private sector.

There are ten features which characterize the new form of entrepreneurial government set out by Osborne and Gaebler. These are: the promotion of competition; the empowerment of citizens; measuring performance through outcomes; being driven by goals; the redefinition of clients as customers; the prevention of problems rather than offering services later; putting energies into earning money rather than simply spending; participatory management; the preference of market over bureaucratic mechanisms; and the focus on catalyzing all sectors into solving a community's problems. A number of these features will be highlighted in subsequent sections that deal with the concept of municipal-community entrepreneurship and offer examples of this concept in operation. Underpinning their argument about the shift in forms of governance in all three sectors, however, is the idea of partnerships aimed at creating institutions that are 'more flexible, more innovative, and more entrepreneurial' (ibid).

Municipal-Community Entrepreneurship

A common trend in local government in developed countries, particularly since the 1980s, has been greater activism in promoting local economic development and employment growth. The catalyst for such activism is the concern that incomes, employment and quality of life are not being adequately catered for by the market. The local emphasis requires that local resources are used, whether that refers to people, material or physical resources. Thus local and regional development is based on promoting local approaches to local conditions. In practice, there is no single blueprint for local initiatives. Instead, a key feature of this type of local development is flexibility, which entails matching the right programmes to the right locality.

We term this phenomenon of local government intervention in local development and employment growth, municipal-community entrepreneurship. This form of entrepreneurship focuses on the way in which the forces of localization, decentralization and devolution have shifted numerous roles and responsibilities from central government to regional and local government level and the form of local level entrepreneurship that has developed in response. However, our use in the next section of the example of sister-cities, which is inherently international in nature, demonstrates that this form of entrepreneurship can also involve innovative action that transcends the local, to take advantage of opportunities that present globally, albeit forging urban links between cities across nations.

Municipal entrepreneurship has been widely recognized as a necessary feature of any city strategy for economic growth and development. In particular, it is necessary to reap and grow agglomeration economies, which are acknowledged as an important 'source of urban efficiency' (World Bank, 2000: 126). The term agglomeration economies refers to the positive overflow effects that occur when organizations and industries of a similar nature benefit from being located close to one another (see, for example, Ingram and Inman, 1996; Porter, 1998). These benefits are described as 'localization economies' (World Bank, 2000: 127). At the city and regional levels, agglomeration economies include not only localization economies, but also 'urbanization economies', referring to the 'benefits that derive from proximity to many different economic actors' (World Bank, 2000: 127). Agglomeration in large urban areas can also result in a diversified economic base that can act as a buffer against economic fluctuations. For example, employment can flow relatively easily between and within different sectors and industries, thus ensuring that unemployment rates will be only minimally affected by downturns in any one specific sector or industry. The World Bank (2000: 127) also identifies the benefits of agglomeration for consumers brought about by the concentration of specific activities within cities. Furthermore, agglomeration economies offer economic benefits and incentives to firms to operate locally as clusters, as against the costs of operating elsewhere, where cluster development has not developed or been encouraged. Thus, higher productivity is ensured. This facet of municipal-community entrepreneurship is demonstrated later in the chapter through the Waitakere City example.

Elsewhere in our work the concept of 'community entrepreneurship' was developed and New Zealand applications provided by way of illustration (de Bruin and Dupuis, 1995; de Bruin, 1998; see also Chapter 7, 'Community Entrepreneurship'). In its original formulation, community entrepreneurship was depicted as complementing the role of individual entrepreneurs in stimulating change and creating employment at a local level. It envisaged the community supplying initiative and enterprise for the creation, transformation and expansion of employment creating ventures and was seen as a possible answer to both an initial lack of individual entrepreneurial skills and employment opportunities in labour market disadvantaged communities and for ethnic minority groups. It entailed innovative community efforts as a catalyst for the growth of local employment opportunities, particularly for ethnic minorities with low levels of human capital.

However this formulation of entrepreneurship did not adequately convey the wider partnership element that municipal-community entrepreneurship emphasizes.

As previously discussed, with the shift from managerialist type local government regime, to a more entrepreneurial orientation (Harvey, 1989a, 1989b), local governments have increasingly become involved in enterprise initiatives and the searching out of other proactive means to promote their particular cities or regions as desirable locations for economic and social activity. An important element of this new locally based entrepreneurialism is that of 'public-private partnerships'. According to Harvey (1989b: 11), these partnerships work 'to lure highly mobile and flexible production, financial and consumption flows into its space'. New Zealand has been no exception in this regard (Lancaster, 1993) and in a later section we highlight New Zealand examples that illustrate this aspect of municipal-community entrepreneurship.

In further refining the concept of municipal-community entrepreneurship for this chapter we feel it is necessary to comment on the chosen terminology. We deliberately chose both terms, 'municipal' and 'community', as we consider they effectively communicate the need for active community participation, together with explicit and leading support provided at the local, rather than the central, governmental level. While we agree with Glaeser that local governments are 'crucial to the fate of cities' (1998: 141), we also contend that local governments, as entrepreneurs, do best when they develop partnerships. Our concept of municipal-community entrepreneurship effectively captures this partnership element and can be applied as readily to regional governments as to local governments, and to the variety of communities these levels of governments engage with. Specifically, the concept of municipal-community entrepreneurship can be used as a means by which the effectiveness of current local public sector entrepreneurial activities can be analyzed and as a model to guide the development of new, local level opportunities, pursued to benefit the local community.

As with community entrepreneurship, municipal-community entrepreneurship can also open new horizons through 'market-leading' activity. As described in Chapter 7, market-leading is deliberate, building on an intentional strategy to bring about and manage change by the creation of demand. It is often visionary in nature, and closely linked to a goal of employment growth at the urban or regional level. As noted in Chapter 7, market-leading can be likened to the Schumpeterian 'creative response' and market leading community entrepreneurship (or with respect to the current chapter municipal-community entrepreneurship), is akin to Leibenstein's N-entrepreneurship, since it engages in the creation and operation of ventures where the production function is not completely known (de Bruin, 1998).

Before examining examples of municipal-community entrepreneurship in action, it is necessary, however, to recognize the debate around the ethics of local and municipal entrepreneurship (Cohen and Eimicke, 1995; Cohen *et al.*, 1999). The importance of ethics in local government entrepreneurship became a major issue in the United States with the bankruptcy of Orange County, California in 1994. In this highly publicized case, the Orange County Treasurer was sentenced to one year's gaol and fined $100,000 stemming from the County's declaration of bankruptcy in the face of $1.7 billion in losses sustained by the investment pool he managed (Cohen *et al.*, 1999: 5). Specifically, what the case demonstrated so strikingly was the tension for governments between operating innovatively on the one hand, and on the other, operating ethically, transparently and with integrity.

Frederickson (cited in Cohen *et al.*, 1999) has used the Orange County example as the basis for his argument against public entrepreneurship, pointing to two issues to support his position: first, the impropriety of governments taking risks with public money; and second, the incompatibility of the profit making objective of entrepreneurs with the public good objective of governments. Such a view, however, is underpinned by a specific perspective on entrepreneurship that is not universally shared and certainly not shared by the authors.

Entrepreneurship, in Frederickson's opinion, is associated with risk taking. This has significant ethical implications, given that at the local government level it could mean that taxpayer funds might be at risk. However, keeping in mind Say's definition of the entrepreneur, we would argue that public entrepreneurship, defined as the use of resources in new ways to maximize productivity and effectiveness, does not require risk taking. In fact, we would go further and maintain that it should not require risk taking, but instead should focus on opportunity. This view accords with that of Drucker, the respected management theorist, who sees the successful entrepreneur as someone who attempts to define the risks that have to be taken and then 'confine them', or minimize them as much as possible. In Drucker's view, the extent of success lies in the entrepreneur's ability to take advantage of opportunity, or as he states, to 'systematically analyze the sources of innovative opportunity, then pinpoint the opportunity and exploit it' (Drucker, 1985: 139). The focus on entrepreneurship as exploiting opportunities allows Drucker to move even further away from the view of the entrepreneurial personality, to claim that almost anyone can be an entrepreneur if the organization they work within is structured in such a way that entrepreneurship is encouraged. This observation clearly has implications not only for the way local governments are organized, but also for the legislative frameworks within which local governments operate.

The emphasis on entrepreneurship as exploiting opportunity rather than risk taking does not, however, preclude a concern with ethics. In exploiting opportunities, local government actors must always be mindful of the need for ethical behaviour. Of value here are the five principles developed by Cohen *et al.* (1999: 14-17) that offer ethical guidelines to public entrepreneurs. We suggest these could be incorporated as a useful minimum framework from which to guide and evaluate all municipal-community entrepreneurial activity. These principles are: first, obeying the law, which is more than merely sticking to the law, but also implies good faith and trustworthiness; second, serving the public interest, which suggests assessing the opportunity objectively, without consideration for the personal interest of the decision making public entrepreneur or the political interests of those to whom the individual is accountable; third, ensuring thorough analysis of the opportunities that are presented, highlights the need for competent and well trained decision makers; fourth, acting with compassion and empathy for all those who may be affected by the policy implications of local government entrepreneurial decisions; and fifth, the requirement that public decision makers take personal responsibility for the decisions they make and the impacts that may result from such decisions. This fifth principle is facilitated through the development of partnerships, the participation of those in the community being served and ensuring the widest promulgation of information to the public regarding possible entrepreneurial activities.

Municipal-community Entrepreneurship in Action

The Example of Sister-Cities

In previous work we developed the concept of municipal-community entrepreneurship to draw attention to and describe the simultaneously operating multi-level entrepreneurial partnerships necessary to sustain active, international, sister-city relationships (Cremer *et al.*, 2001). Using the sister-city example we demonstrated that while the setting up of the overall institutional framework for the twinning pact is an initial first step, to carry the agreement forward requires commitment and proactive nurturing by local government officials to build trust, co-operation and yield tangible, as well as less tangible and measurable, economic and social benefits. The distinguishing feature for the viability and success of the arrangement, however, is that it also requires significant community activism. It is this partnership mix of community and municipal level action to tap into the opportunities that the sister-city arrangement presents for the mutual advantage of economic and social actors in both cities, that we conceived as 'municipal-community entrepreneurship'. The notion of entrepreneurship used was a simple one, conveying the specific, proactive steps to organize, establish, maintain and foster, at the various levels, relationships and opportunities, that directly or indirectly present within the sister-city arrangement. The combination of all these actions are entrepreneurial, in that they are taken in order to avail of opportunities afforded by the sister-city arrangement.

Before discussing sister-cities as an example of municipal-community entrepreneurship, it is in order to describe in more detail the sister-city programme. The roots of sister-city affiliations can be traced back to the aftermath of the Second World War and the help British cities gave European cities devastated by the conflict. However, the popular literature largely credits sister-city development to an American initiative supported by President Dwight D. Eisenhower (Hepler, 1994: 22) intended to 'involve individuals and organized groups at all levels of society in citizen diplomacy, with the hope that personal relationships, fostered through sister-city, county and state affiliations, would lessen the chance of future world conflicts' (Sister Cities International, 1999). The purpose of the movement was 'to increase international understanding and foster world peace by furthering international communication and exchange at the person-to-person level through city-to-city affiliations' (Sister Cities New Zealand Inc., n.d.).

Sister-city relationships relationships are distinguished by five unique features. First, the signing of a formal agreement by each city's key dignitaries – usually the mayors or equivalent, embeds the relationship. Second, it is intended that agreements last indefinitely. Third, because the relationship is an ongoing one, it is not limited to one single project, but covers a range of shared activities such as: school exchanges of all sorts, friendship visits, reciprocal council staff visits, celebrations of the sister-city's culture and the exchange of trade, research and technology. Fourth, despite city officials being crucial in instituting and providing underpinning support to the arrangement, the majority of those involved in sister-city activities are unpaid volunteers. Fifth, these relationships are carried out largely at a grassroots and local body level and do not rely on the support or patronage of national governments. Lastly, there is an implicit understanding that sister-city relationships should be characterized by 'genuine reciprocity of effort and benefit, with neither community profiting at the expense of the other' (Zelinsky, 1991: 3).

The choice of a sister-city is not random but based on such criteria as 'historical connections, shared economic, cultural, recreational and ideological concerns, similar or identical place names, and, to a certain extent, the friction of distance' (Zelinsky, 1991: 1). Often too, persoanl contacts and private initiatives contribute to the formation and sustainability of city connections. In the United States, the implementation of sister-cities programmes has been seen as a support for democratic principles and some American cities have adopted partnerships as a way of expressing disapproval of, and resistance to, official American policies. This observation helps explain for example, the very high number of sister-city relationships (91 in 1990) with Nicaraguan cities (*The Economist*, 1989; Zelinsky, 1990).

The early phase of the sister-city movement was dominated by the idea of international friendship through the understanding of the culture of others (Ramasamy and Cremer, 1998: 449). O'Toole (1999: 2) termed this 'the associative phase', aimed at developing international friendship, cultural exchange and a general international awareness. More recently sister-city relationships have entered a commercial phase where issues of commerce and economic development have become increasingly important, reflecting greater pressure for local governments to act as economic developers (O'Toole, 1999). This does not mean abandoning municipal friendships, but rather is an attempt to take act entrepreneurially to further local economic aims at the same time as maintaining friendship links and supporting the goal of deeper cultural understandings. This facet of the sister-city relationship was strongly recognized by Ramasamy and Cremer (1998: 449-540) when they acknowledged the reciprocal relationship that exists between commerce and culture and the necessity for these two facets of the sister-city relationship to remain closely interwoven. Their argument was that understanding another culture contributes to trade and investment, while engaging in business provides cultural understandings with a reliable and lasting base. An overemphasis on either the cultural or the economic aspect of the relationship is not likely to result in successful sister-city relationships. They termed this two way relationship to the support and maintenance of sister-city relationships, the integrative approach (Cremer, Gounder and Ramasamy, 1996; Ramasamy and Cremer, 1998).

Inherent in the Cremer *et al.* (1996) argument is an understanding that formal sister- city projects are akin to a rediscovery of one of the original roles of cities as meeting places between different people and cultures through which comes the creation of a market (or in earlier times an actual market place) where economic and business activities can be undertaken. The integrative approach, however, goes far beyond a simple blending together of culture and economics when it insists on outcomes that are of benefit to both the partners involved. As Cremer *et al.* (1996: 12) state, the integrated approach 'strives for a balance of cultural, political, social, and economic development for both cities, and insists on tangible results in all of those priority areas' Elsewhere it is described as combining 'trade and cultural initiatives, strategic planning, leadership from the top, the involvement of community and the media and committing resources rather than "relying on the efforts of a few individuals"' (Cremer, quoted in *Sister Cities New Zealand*, 1999: 5). These elements are similarly fundamental to municipal-community entrepreneurship.

In keeping with the theme of embeddedness that runs through this book, we argue that implicit within the integrated approach are assumptions about human nature that support a critique of the self-interested, utility maximizing actor, or *homo economicus*, the central figure of the economic orthodoxy. It is clear from the integrative approach that sister-city programmes will not operate effectively when those involved act only in terms of their immediate economic self interest in a separative or atomized way (Granovetter, 1985; England, 1993). The profit motive, while important, is nevertheless penetrated with sociability and the desire to know and connect with others at the human level. In other words, the integrative approach also acknowledges elements crucial to the notion of embeddedness, such as the frequent demonstration of altruism and trust and the intertwining of non-economic goals with economic goals.

As has already been suggested both theoretically and practically, the integrative approach has much in common with municipal-community entrepreneurship. In fact Cremer *et al.* (1996: 12) recognized the fundamental role of entrepreneurial activity in sister-city relationships when they argued that paying insufficient attention to, or not taking account of the economic dimension of sister-city relationships, and the contribution that commerce can make to the sustainability of relationships is 'expensive romanticism'. They also claimed that the most reliable and strongest drivers for international understanding and exchange are economic and business links and work opportunities. This should not be interpreted, however, as meaning that sister-city relationships driven solely by economic interests will be successful. Within the accepted agreement frameworks it is cultural exchanges and the development of greater cross-cultural understandings that are the prime motivations for the grass roots involvement necessary to sustain sister-city relationships. Moreover, it is grassroot contacts and the cultural understandings that are built up over time through such contacts that provide the positive environment that reduces risks involved in such enterprises as trade, tourism and investment.

We now turn to an analysis of New Zealand sister-city relationships through which we can provide concrete examples of municipal-community entrepreneurship in action. In New Zealand the location of cities chosen for sister-city relationships has shown an interesting shift over time. As of 1998, of the 83 sister-city affiliations with Australian, European and North American cities, only two have been cemented since 1990 (Cremer *et al.*, 2001). Since 1990 the majority of new affiliations have been forged with Japanese cities, but currently Chinese cities are making a concerted push to intensify their links with New Zealand cities (and cities in other countries too) and formal sister-city relationships with Chinese cities are steadily increasing. This has coincided with China's broader economic development strategies which have seen a considerable opening of the economy to competition, foreign investment and tourism.

An analysis of Chinese-New Zealand sister-city relationships helps strengthen the understanding of the concept of municipal-community entrepreneurship. In the first instance we cannot avoid exploring the idea of why it is that Chinese city officials are so enthusiastic about developing sister-city relationships with New Zealand cities. An immediate, and superficial response, might be that Chinese city officials see New Zealand as being able to provide them with two necessary commodities: firstly, investment in their economy in terms of both economic investment and 'know how', and secondly, proficiency in English language skills. With regard to the latter, it is clear that New Zealand's clean, green image and relatively low educational fees make New Zealand a desirable destination for English language students. However, to focus only on these criteria as motivation for Chinese approaches for sister-city relationships is much too limited. The history of sister-city links with Chinese cities has demonstrated that when affiliations are formed there must be a mutual understanding that they must be accompanied by motives other than economic profit. It is here that we turn to the idea of the interpenetration of the cultural with the economic, in order to understand how links are established and sustained between cities in the two nations. As Cross (2000: 2) has noted, Chinese people take a very long term view of their international relationships and, as such, take time to develop friendships. Added to this is the controlled and formal nature of Chinese life, which requires that any contacts, other than those between individuals, must be made through official channels. As a consequence, the roles of urban officials, and the formal and ceremonious procedures with which they involve themselves, become vital to the acceptance and success of sister-city relationships. The commitment to such formality is a crucial element in establishing partnerships at all levels. It is also valuable in developing and sustaining not only the required friendship and trust necessary as a basis for economic enterprises, but also in order to decrease the risks these might otherwise entail.

Elements of municipal-community entrepreneurship are clearly evident in existing Chinese sister-city affiliations. Municipal partnerships are particularly necessary in the early phases of the relationship when, as indicated above, the commitment of mayors and city councillors to formality and protocol is vital in sending appropriate cultural messages. Without visible and active support from the mayor and city councillors and other leading local personalities, initiatives and activities in China lack credibility and clout. Pragmatically, building a good relationship between the two respective city mayors is seen as a signal that any possible administrative or bureaucratic obstacles could be overcome smoothly and that any specific requirement, procedures or formalities could be dealt with adequately. Such activities and attitudes need also be perceived as appropriate for chief executive officers when working on business ventures with representatives of Chinese enterprises. The cultural background to this is that Chinese tend to emphasize individual authority, integrity and personal links more than written procedures and contracts with organizations. In addition, the importance within the Chinese ethos of 'face' and 'giving face to somebody' provides further reason for the involvement of city dignitaries in sister-city activities whenever possible (Cremer *et al.*, 1996).

The remainder of this section draws on a well established and successful sister-city relationship, that of the city of Hastings, New Zealand with Guilin in China. This example of a sister-city relationship in operation was selected as it highlights elements of successful sister-city relationship which also often correspond to municipal-community entrepreneurship. These elements are: people-to-people links; strong involvement of city officials, particularly the Mayor; strong community support; a well developed strategic plan; a highly organized governance structure; and adequate economic support.

The relationship between Hastings and Guilin developed from a personal link the late Dr Don McKenzie, a research scientist and New Zealand leader in the pipfruit industry, had established in Guilin, China. He identified common areas of interest between the two cities, particularly horticulture, and developed a range of contacts. Dr McKenzie first broached the idea of a sister-city arrangement with city officials in 1978. Following reciprocal visits between the cities, the sister-city protocol was signed in 1981. The agreement also set out that friendship would be developed by 'an interchange of all information in the fields of industry, agriculture, science and technology, city management and development, tourism, culture, education and trade' (Hastings-Guilin Sister City Strategic Plan, 1999: 3). The Mayoral support so necessary for these programmes to flourish, was initially strong and is still highly visible today, with Hastings' ex-Mayor also being the president of Sister Cities New Zealand Inc. (Sister Cities New Zealand, n.d.). Similarly, the dedication of Dr McKenzie illustrates the importance of individual ties and common interests. Upon his death in 1988, he was described in the Guilin newspaper as 'the friendship messenger' (Hastings-Guilin Sister City Strategic Plan, 1999: 2).

The Hastings City Council provides modest but adequate financial support and more importantly, personnel support for its sister-city programme. Hastings' strategic plan sets out plainly the mission statement and the objectives of the relationship. The latter include: educational development aimed primarily at children, students and professionals, through exchanges and curriculum programmes; cultural development, to be achieved in its broadest sense through people to people exchanges of all kinds; business links aimed at the facilitation of quality data, contacts, identification of opportunities and business links; and local government exchanges and information sharing. The plan includes three specialist link groups to strategically organize educational, business and cultural links between the two cities.

To conclude this section we need to make the point that the Hastings-Guilin relationship emerged before the spate of more recent sister-city affiliations with Chinese cities in the 1990s. It demonstrates how local actors fostered the creation and nurturing of ties, which now can be described as firmly embedded. It also amply illustrates the operation of vertical and horizontal multi-level ties. The dynamic flow of the vertical line of partnership incorporates, in a non-hierarchical fashion, the Guilin Community Forum, the Sister City Board of Directors, specialist link groups and the Hastings District Council. The imagery of the horizontal flow is apt, in that it symbolizes the international outreach between the two cities. At each and every level of partnership there is evidence of aspects of the operation of municipal-community entrepreneurship. While this form of entrepreneurship can be applied beyond the confines of the sister-city programme, this example has highlighted that municipal-community entrepreneurship can involve innovative action that transcends the local, to take advantage of opportunities opened up in a global age.

An Urban Growth Strategy: the Example of Waitakere City

This section offers an example of the concept of municipal-community entrepreneurship in action, drawn from the development strategies set in place by Waitakere City and its economic development agency, Enterprise Waitakere. Waitakere City is one of the four cities that is part of the Auckland Region, New Zealand's most populous region.[1] It has a land area of 367 square kilometers, a population of 168,750. The majority of the population are of European ethnicity, although significant groups identify their ethnicity as Maori, Pacific Island or Asian. Waitakere City has 11,054 businesses. Most jobs in the City are provided by the service sector, although construction and manufacturing are also significant (Waitakere City Council, n.d.).

Waitakere City is widely recognized as an eco-city. In the early 1990s, the Waitakere City Council prepared its Greenprint, the guiding document for Waitakere City's eco-city vision. It is based on Agenda 21, which takes an holistic approach to sustainable development, recognizing the interrelationship between people, the economy and the environment, encouraging a cautious and long-term view on future development, thus eschewing any notions of municipal risk taking. In keeping with Agenda 21, the Greenprint provides a framework for integrated municipal decision making, involving community led initiatives, in the areas of economic and social development, and environmental protection. The Greenprint is structured around seven key areas: community empowerment as a means of improving social, environmental and economic well-being; urban consolidation to accommodate future population growth within the current urban area, especially around commercial and town centres, and transport corridors; a strategy aimed at involving local people in protecting and restoring their environment and appreciating the nature, history and heritage of their City; an holistic approach to health and safety based on a recognition of the natural, social and economic environments that underpin health and safety issues; the development of a city where the need to travel is reduced and public transport, cycling and walking is encouraged; the adoption of an holistic approach to resource use, aimed at using less energy, generating energy from renewable resources, the careful use of resources and less waste production; greater economic independence gained through targeting and attracting economic activity building on Waitakere's strengths, while simultaneously working with existing businesses to encourage more sustainable practices (Waitakere City Council, n.d.). This latter point, in particular, signals the entrepreneurial role of the local state, while retaining the principles of sustainability, compatible with the eco-city perspective.

In keeping with the philosophy of promoting local approaches to local conditions, Waitakere City's approach to economic development included taking account of the limited business base of the City. Waitakere businesses are predominantly small, with 88 per cent employing fewer than 6 people and 93 per cent with fewer than 9 employees. In addition, the quality and productivity of jobs is not high. As a result there is a lack of local job opportunities in Waitakere City with many people travelling outside the city for employment (Rogers, 2002).

The Waitakere City Council has used a number of tools in its approach to development. It has promoted policies that support: broader regional town centre development and transport strategies; various kinds of economic and social partnerships; the development of schools, leisure, library and hospital facilities; and the establishment of a trading enterprise to invest in residential housing projects which have contributed to land value increases, increased local shopping and act as a demonstration of sustainable development ideas.

In the context of rapidly changing markets and technologies, Waitakere City Council has recognized that the success of local business depends on the quality of the local environment, the physical infrastructure and the business support and educational services available. With these considerations in mind, the Council has developed strategies that build on local resources business and encourage networks through focused cluster·initiatives. It has also attempted to build on the skills and productivity of local people, in order to develop a sound bed of locally-based entrepreneurs.

A key aspect to Waitakere City's local development strategy has been the setting up of Enterprise Waitakere. This is the City's primary economic development arm which supports enterprise facilitation, training, tourism and cluster development. Enterprise Waitakere was established as an independent and commercially relevant organization. It has developed as an organization which focuses on partnerships and which develops strong stakeholder linkages so it can mediate between the Council and the business community. The Enterprise has been set up to be transparent and accountable and to ensure that the relationships it develops are 'arms length' relationships, which are on the one hand flexible and responsive to the market, and on the other, able to act in a confidential, independent and impartial manner. Important too, for the operation of Enterprise Waitakere, is its ability to tap into central government funds. Enterprise Waitakere adheres to best practice in engaging the economy by ensuring it attends to the triple bottom line of sustainable development through seeking economic, social and environmental objectives. It also acknowledges a fourth component, that of cultural diversity, thus effectively recognizing a quadruple bottom line. It is the integration of these four components that produces a comprehensive and holistic framework for underpinning economic development (Rogers, 2002).

In addition to assisting business in general, Enterprise Waitakere supports specific industry clusters in the areas of tourism, film, marine and wine. It facilitates the establishment of sustainable tourism businesses within Waitakere City and assists with new tourism product or service development and new venture. Frequent meetings among tourism industry entrepreneurs are facilitated by the Enterprise, at which business networking and industry knowledge are promoted and marketing initiatives discussed. The stark beauty of Waitakere City's beaches and lushness of the forested Waitakere Ranges provide stunning film locations and filming is actively encouraged in the city. Enterprise Waitakere acts as a resource and information provider for the film and television industries and has developed a simple activities approval process that allows for location issues to be dealt with quickly and efficiently. The marine cluster is a network of boat building and marine related businesses, working collaboratively to promote growth. Some twenty wineries are located within Waitakere City. Their economic importance is significant in terms of income and employment. There are also increasing benefits from ventures associated with the wine industry such as wine tourism (Waitakere City Council, n.d.). Enterprise Waitakere has also recently become involved in supporting a business incubator in partnership with a local tertiary institution, UNITEC and Industry New Zealand, a central government agency. In keeping with the character of the city, plans for the incubator also include an eco-tech focus (Enterprise Waitakere, 2002).

To finish this section it is worth mentioning that an important commercial connection has been forged between Waitakere City and its sister-city of Ningbo, the second largest trading port in China. Although initially it might not appear that there are similarities between the two cities, Ningbo city officials especially, saw themselves as facing similar problems to those of Waitakere City. The desire to know more about sustainability issues, particularly those relating to sustainable building and sustainable technology prompted the initiation of the sister-city relationship.

The E-centre at Massey University, Albany

A further illustration of municipal-community entrepreneurship in action is drawn from the university where the authors are employed. Massey University's Albany Campus 'e-centre' (Enterprise Centre) was opened in March 2001. A tripartite initiative with partners North Shore City Council and the Tindall Foundation, the e-centre is New Zealand's first purpose-built and envisioned, business incubator to nurture and build the capability of growth-focused 'knowledge economy' companies. The idea for a science and technology park intended to grow and commercialize products from waste materials of the primary sector, was put forward at Massey University, Palmerston North in the 1970s. However, it was not until the late 1990s that a confluence of local factors gave birth to the e-centre. These included: a vibrant, expanding new campus at Albany, Auckland, keen to establish tangible business links to better serve both its students and the local community; a burgeoning Albany business district which the local City Council envisaged as a technology hub for North Shore City; and the commitment of The Tindall Foundation (supported by a local entrepreneur Stephen Tindall and his family), to support family, employment and the environment in New Zealand.

The financial viability of the centre rests on a three tier mix of tenants ranging from anchor tenant SOFT TECH, a leading edge, award winning, industrial software company, through to fledgling companies and new start-ups like IOSIS, the newly formed software company of four Massey University information technology students. An important element to ensure success for the companies involved, is the business-networking environment offered by the centre itself and the expansion of the knowledge and resource base of the companies through their link to Massey University.

Collective mobilization of resources and the active exploration of ways to involve local populations in ownership and control of their own economic destiny are key elements of municipal-community entrepreneurship. All this cannot, however, be achieved without effective leadership, an inherent element of municipal-community entrepreneurship. Leaders form an integral aspect of the entrepreneurship which develops and turns vision into the reality of viable, commercially sustainable initiatives to create wealth and provide employment. Such leadership is often group leadership, in the same way that the entrepreneurship notion is a collaborative and collective one. Group leadership provides the motivating force to harness and build on existing resources, as well as draw in additional resources to the venture. Thus, in the case of the e-centre, leadership from Massey University involved the visionary input of the Principal of the Albany Campus, Professor Ian Watson, drawing also on his earlier Palmerston North Campus experiences; and the drive and energy of the Director of Research Services, Dr Chris Kirk and the Business Development Manager, Dr Brian Chrystall. Stephen Tindall of the Tindall Foundation, also added to this initial leadership pool. Currently the group leadership dynamic comprises the centre's Board of Management and the centre manager.

As Schumpeter highlights, entrepreneurship involves, on the one hand, the ability to identify new opportunities that are unproven and take action on them, 'and, on the other hand, willpower adequate to breaking down the resistance that the social environment offers to change' (1991: 417). If innovative ideas for local job creation are to be acted on, leadership is necessary to draw in and maintain community support for such new ventures. The measure of the success of this leadership would be the extent of change that takes place within the community (see, for example, Heifetz, 1994). As this example indicates, municipal-community entrepreneurship and the leadership that accompanies it, can be an integral part of this change and a vital catalyst for sustainable employment generation and socially responsible wealth creation.

Conclusion

A major response to the neo-liberal shift of the 1980s across the western world has been the movement towards governments as entrepreneurs. The focus of this chapter has been entrepreneurship at a municipal level. It is widely recognized that local government entrepreneurship, while operating strategically and taking advantage of local conditions and possibilities, need not (in fact many people argue should not), be risk taking. The concept of municipal-community entrepreneurship has been developed to capture both this aspect of entrepreneurship and the wider partnerships, especially the public-private partnerships involved.

The examples presented demonstrate the concept of municipal-community entrepreneurship has wide applicability. The sister-city movement may be viewed as an unheralded, yet potentially powerful element of the '"quiet revolution" in local governance' (World Bank, 2000: 154-5). Successful sister-city relationships embody a partnership that allows 'synergy and the combining of resources among the public sector, international organizations, the voluntary and community sector, individuals and households' (World Bank, 2000: 155), and symbolize the benefits that can accrue from bridging the global-local divide. The example of Waitakere City and its business development arm Enterprise Waitakere, provides an illustration of municipal-community entrepreneurship that not only encourages the development of agglomeration economies through industry clustering in various areas, supports new business start ups, the strengthening of existing businesses and a range of employment training initiatives, but does so while strongly adhering to the local eco-city principles of integrated decision making, an holistic approach and sustainability. Partnerships once again become the focus, in the example of a university's enterprise centre, where the partners include a university, the local city council and a trust headed by a well known entrepreneur.

Current urban, political landscapes, focusing as they do on decentralization and the rethinking of the role of local government, are increasingly highlighting the importance of multi-level partnerships for economic, social, environmental and cultural development. For the new global age we have entered, we can foresee the value and strength of the concept of municipal-community entrepreneurship as an explanatory tool for analyzing the current urban condition. When operationalized, its potential for reaping agglomeration economies, developing partnerships and encouraging social, environmental and cultural well-being, and hence enhancing the sustainability of cities, should not be underestimated. It represents a crucial catalyst in the facilitation of urban well-being in the 21st century.

Note

1. Auckland Region is made up of four cities (Auckland City, North Shore City, Manukau City and Waitakere City), collectively referred to as Auckland, plus three districts (Rodney, Papakura and part of Franklin District). The region is the home to 1.2 million people, which represents approximately 31 per cent of the total population of New Zealand (Statistics New Zealand, 2001).

References

Cohen, S. and Eimicke, W. (1995), 'Ethics and the Public Administrator', *The Annals of the American Academy of Political and Social Sciences*, No. 537 (January), pp. 96-108.

Cohen, S., Eimicke, W. and Salazar, M. (1999), 'Public Ethics and Public Entrepreneurship', paper presented to the Annual Research Meeting of the Association of Public Policy Analysis and Management, Washington D.C., November 4-6, pp. 1-22.

Cremer, R.D., de Bruin, A. and Dupuis, A. (2001), 'International Sister-Cities: Bridging the Global-Local Divide', *The American Journal of Economics and Sociology*, Vol. 60(1), January, pp. 377-402.

Cremer, R., Gounder, R. and Ramasamy, B. (1996), 'Guidelines for New Zealand-Asia Sister City Relationships: Economic Rationale for an Integrated Approach', Department of Economics, Massey University, Palmerston North.

Cross, B. (2000), *Council Relations with China*, Porirua City Council Paper, Porirua, New Zealand.

de Bruin, A. (1998) 'Entrepreneurship in a New Phase of Capitalist Development', *The Journal of Interdisciplinary Economics*, Vol. 9, pp. 185-200.

de Bruin, A and Dupuis, A. (1995), 'A Closer Look at New Zealand's Superior Economic Performance: Ethnic Employment Issues', *British Review of New Zealand Studies*, No. 8, pp. 85-97.

Drucker, P. (1985), *Innovation and Entrepreneurship: Practice and Principles*, Harper and Row, New York.

England, P. (1993), 'The Separative Self: Androcentric Bias in Neoclassical Assumptions', in M. Ferber and J. Nelson (eds), *Beyond Economic Man: Feminist Theory and Economics*, University of Chicago Press, Chicago.

Enterprise Waitakere (2002), http://www.enterprisewaitakere.co.nz/index.

Fainstein, S. (1996), 'The Changing Economy and Urban Restructuring', in S. Fainstein and S. Campbell (eds), *Readings in Urban Theory*, Blackwell, Cambridge, MA.

Glaeser, E. (1998), 'Are Cities Dying?', *Journal of Economic Perspectives*, Vol. 12(2), pp. 139-160.

Granovetter, M. (1985), 'Economic Action and Social Structure: The Problem of Embeddedness', *American Journal of Sociology*, Vol. 91 (3), pp. 481-510.

Harvey, D. (1989a), 'From Managerialism to Entrepreneurialism: The Transformation of Urban Governance in Late Capitalism', *Geografiska Annaler*, Vol. 71B(1), pp. 3-17.

Harvey, D. (1989b), *The Urban Experience*, Basil Blackwell, Oxford.

Hastings-Guilin Sister City Strategic Plan (1999), Hastings City Council, Hastings, New Zealand.

Heifetz, R. (1994), *Leadership without Easy Answers*, Belknap Press of Harvard University Press, Cambridge MA.

Hepler, H. (1994), 'Sister Cities Program Links Cultures, Businesses', *American City and Country*, September, p. 22.

Ingram, P. and Inman, C. (1996), 'Institutions, Intergroup Competition, and the Evolution of Hotel Populations around Niagara Falls, *Administrative Science Quarterly*, Vol. 41, pp. 629-59.

Kelsey, J. (1993), *Rolling Back the State: Privatisation of Power in Aotearoa/New Zealand*, Bridget Williams Books, Wellington.

Lancaster, S. (1993), *Taking the Initiative: Local Government Employment and Economic Development Initiatives*, Local Government Association, Wellington.

OECD (2001), *Cities and Regions in the New Learning Economy*, OECD, Paris.

Osborne, D. and Gaebler, T. (1993), *Reinventing Government: How the Entrepreneurial Spirit is Transforming the Public Sector*, Plume, New York, N.Y.

Osborne, D. and Plastrik, P. (1997), *Banishing Bureaucracy: The Five Strategies for Reinventing Government*, Addison Wesley, Reading, MA.

O'Toole, K. (1999), *Sister Cities in Australia: A Survey Report*, Centre for Regional Development, Deakin University, Melbourne.

Pahl, R. (1975), *Whose City?*, (2nd Edition) Penguin, Harmondsworth.

Porter, M. (1998), 'The Adam Smith Address: Location, Clusters, and the "New" Microeconomics of Competition', *Business Economics*, Vol. 33, pp. 7-14.

Ramasamy, B. and Cremer, R. (1998), 'Cities, Commerce and Culture: The Economic Role of International Sister-City Relationships between New Zealand and Asia', *Journal of the Asia Pacific Economy*, Vol. 3(3), pp. 446-461.

Rogers, C. (2002), 'Regional Development: The Role of Local Government', seminar presentation in the course entitled Public Policy and Local Government in New Zealand, Massey University, Auckland, April.

Sassen, S. (1991), *The Global City: New York, London and Tokyo*, Princeton University Press, Princeton, NJ.

Sassen, S. (1996), 'The Global City', in S. Fainstein and S. Campbell (eds), *Readings in Urban Theory*, Blackwell, Cambridge, MA.

Schumpeter, J. (1991), 'Comments on a Plan for the Study of Entrepreneurship', in R. Swedberg (ed.), *Joseph A. Schumpeter*, Princeton University Press, Princeton, NJ.

Short, J.R. (1996), *The Urban Order: An Introduction to Cities, Culture and Power*, Blackwell, Cambridge, MA.

Sister Cities International (1999), 'About SCI: History', http://www.sister-cities.org/go/wego.pa (accessed 24 January, 2000).

Sister Cities New Zealand (n.d.), http://www.sistercities.org.nz/ (accessed June, 28 2002).

Sister Cities New Zealand (1999), *Sister Cities- A Strategy for Success*, Sister Cities New Zealand, May, p. 5.

Sister Cities New Zealand Inc. (n.d.), *Guidelines for Developing a Sister Cities Programme*, Sister Cities New Zealand, Whakatane.

Statistics New Zealand (2001) http://www.statistics.govt.nz/ (accessed December 14, 2001).

The Economist (1989), 'Sister Sandinist', *The Economist*, Vol. 312, pp. 28-29.

Waitakere City Council (n.d.), http://www.waitakere.govt.nz/ (accessed June 12, 2002).

World Bank (2000), *World Development Report, 1999/2000: Entering the 21st Century*. Oxford University Press, New York.

Zelinsky, W. (1990), 'Sister City Alliance', *American Demographics*, Vol. 12(6), pp. 42-45.

Zelinsky, W. (1991), 'The Twinning of the World: Sister Cities in Geographic and Historical Perspective', *Annals of the Association of American Geographers*, Vol. 81(1), pp. 1-31.

Chapter 9

State Entrepreneurship

Anne de Bruin

Introduction

The global age is based on different economic and societal principles and an altered role of the state. This chapter provides a global perspective on the changes that have taken place in the role of the state. It is situated sequentially as the third chapter (following on from Chapters 7, 'Community Entrepreneurship' and 8, 'Municipal-Community Entrepreneurship') dealing with a general premise of the book which views the rising prevalence of more collective forms of entrepreneurship that focus on broader community action and outcomes, as a response to the economic, social and political changes that characterize the global age. It has a strong synergy with Chapter 8, which emphasized the context and regional development agenda of public entrepreneurship at the local government or municipal level. The differentiation in this chapter is the spotlight on entrepreneurship at the central government driven and national policy-making level. As with the earlier two chapters, this chapter serves to illustrate the point made by Schumpeter, when he updated his earlier theory of the entrepreneur in the 1940s, that the 'entrepreneurial function need not be embodied in a physical person and in particular in a single physical person. Every social environment has its own way of filling the entrepreneurial function' (Schumpeter, cited in Swedberg, 1991: 173).

In the developed Western economies, the modern welfare state and its progression was an integral component of the previous era. The term welfare state is used here in a wide sense to encompass the nature of the function, policy and degree of state involvement. It is presented as the state form that characterized a particular phase of capitalist development. It is argued that the regression and transformation of the welfare state has been underpinned by change at an overarching global level and marks the transition to the new global era.

This chapter tracks the implications of the global age for the structure and changing nature of the state. The discussion is illuminated mainly by the New Zealand experience, though other international experiences such as the South Korean model of technology support are also cited. An examination of the state owned enterprise (SOE) sector, as an aspect of profit-making state entrepreneurship is also provided.

Highlighting the need to re-conceptualize the role and responsibilities of the state, it is argued that the term welfare state is not an appropriate descriptor and does not convey the current realities of the function of the state in the global age. Alternative terminology is explored and the new concept of 'strategic state' to substitute for welfare state and embody entrepreneurial behaviour at the central government level, is suggested. The strategic state is itself entrepreneurial in its policy making and interventions for economic development, including regional development. Aspects of the strategic state are delineated.

The Evolution of State Forms

An Overview of the Welfare State

There is no unambiguous definition of the 'welfare state'. Writing in the heyday of the welfare state, Titmuss referred to it as an 'indefinable abstraction' with which he was 'no more enamored today' than he had been two decades earlier (1968: 124). Barr points out that 'the welfare state is one of those concepts that defies precise definition ... the boundaries of the welfare state are not well defined' (1993: 2, 3).

The term welfare state is thought to have been coined by William Temple, the Archbishop of York, when he distinguished between the 'welfare state' serving the common interests of citizens and the 'power state' which serves the interests of tyrants as in Nazi Germany (Temple, 1941, cited in Barr and Whynes, 1993: 6). Losing its original religious and moralistic overtones, the term became popularized in Britain after the Second World War and its use spread to other developed capitalist economies. It came to be used as a convenient way of referring to the economic and social policy changes that were taking place at the time. These policy changes had three broad strands: the introduction and extension of state provision of social security, health, education, housing, employment and other welfare services; the maintenance of full employment; and a programme of nationalization. Together these strands constituted the welfare state (Johnson, 1987: 3).

Often, the term welfare state is used generically to refer to public programmes, chiefly in the areas of income maintenance, health, education, training, social welfare services and housing. These programmes are, however, only the more obvious manifestation of the principle of the modern Western welfare state, which is, that the state has the ultimate responsibility to ensure that the material well-being of any of its citizens does not fall too far below that of the average citizen. There can, nevertheless, be varied normative interpretations of what this minimum level of well-being should be. In New Zealand, the 1972 Royal Commission on Social Security (RCSS) formalized this minimum level in terms of the state ensuring a standard of living that would allow *participation in and belonging to the community*' (RCSS, 1972: 65, original's italics).

The sustained prosperity of the developed capitalist countries during the post-war period to around the mid 1970s, has been described as the 'golden age of capitalism' (see, for example, Lipietz, 1992: 1). Since Keynesian economics was the dominant economic paradigm of the time, the progression of the modern welfare state may be viewed as a corollary of Keynesian economics. Keynesian thought underpinned the social alliance and national consensus on economic and social goals and policies that emerged in the post-war period and the welfare state form that characterized this time may therefore be differentiated as the 'Keynesian Welfare State' (KWS).

An important aspect of the KWS was the unity of the capital-labour relation that prevailed. Though this capital-labour relation model had many national brands, it typically comprised four major strands: large scale division of labour; specialization and mechanization of manufacturing; mass production of standardized goods, and rather strong unions (Boyer, 1995: 23-24). These gave rise to increases in productivity and a compromise on productivity sharing which influenced wage formation. Thus:

> Conceptually, after the Second World War the wage was no longer a pure market variable since it took into account a minimum standard of living. Second, this wage was then raised according to the general advances in productivity (Boyer, 1995: 25).[1]

The KWS was part of the 'mode of regulation'[2] or the socio-institutional framework of the post-war golden age. It was characterized by policy commitment to the full employment, seemingly made possible by the pursuit of Keynesian economic management. The San Francisco United Nations Charter, drawn up at the close of the Second World War, had included the clause under Article 55 that 'the United Nations shall promote: higher standards of living, full employment and conditions of social progress and development'. The enactment of the Employment Act of 1945, which established a Department of National Employment Service charged with promotion and maintenance of full employment, was New Zealand's response to the Charter. Even in West Germany, where much emphasis was placed on price stability, the goal of full employment was explicitly declared in the Stabilization Law of 1967, at quasi-constitutional level.

The KWS was also based upon the stable nuclear and patriarchal family form. Perhaps nowhere is this made clearer than in the pursuit of housing policy in New Zealand. Housing was an important facet of New Zealand's KWS and historically the main focus of housing policy in New Zealand has been ongoing encouragement for home ownership for nuclear families on low and modest incomes. Thus for instance, the centrality of the nuclear family to housing policy, reinforced by a national ideological preference for home ownership and the low labour market status of women, instituted a housing sector which marginalized many women in non-nuclear households (de Bruin and Dupuis, 1995a).

The Changing Nature and Role of State

There is extensive debate on the appropriate role for the state in the new epoch of globalization. The erosion of state autonomy in the face of global forces, is argued as a contemporary reality. The continuation of traditional social democratic economic policy, namely Keynesian style policy, was contended to be less feasible, if not impossible, as new forces of globalization and increased international competition took hold after the end of the post-war long cycle of world economic growth which followed the oil crisis of 1973 (Scharpf, 1991).

It cannot be denied that the growth and re-ordering of the global trading system and increased capital mobility constrain the capacity of governments, particularly of small open economies such as New Zealand, to pursue independent economic policies. The capitalist 'world hegemony', according to Cox (1987), entails 'the internationalizing of the state' to meet and complement the needs of the global production and distribution system. Furthermore, globalization has forced convergence in economic policy which breaks down impediments to the operation of the free market (Kurzer, 1991; Notermans, 1993). Globalization and the importance of international competitiveness to national economies, has reduced the scope for Keynesian discretionary economic policies. As Drache observes:

> What is irrefutable is that the structure of local, national and international markets has always shaped state policy and civil society in modern times. In no era is this more apparent than the present. As capital becomes increasingly mobile, the investment characteristics of capital flows reflect increasingly the pressures of the global market over local markets. The aggressive pursuit of these heightened investment and trade opportunities by business and government is changing the structure of the modern state (1996: 32).

Neoclassical, monetarist and public choice economic theory provided an academic rationale and the stagflation of the post oil shock world economy supported a new direction in economic and social policy (often collectively referred to as New Right or neo-liberal policy) and the demise of Keynesian type stabilization and regulation of the market economy. By the mid 1980s, the notion of 'crisis' of the welfare state, was widely accepted. This view received prominence in the literature (see, for example, OECD, 1981; Mishra, 1984). According to Galbraith, the discarding of the KWS was cemented by 'A Contented Electoral Majority' or a 'Culture of Contentment' and its line of economic thought (Galbraith, 1992). Serving this contentment are three basic requirements: limited government intervention, social justification for the uninhibited pursuit of wealth, and a reduced sense of public responsibility for the poor (Galbraith, 1992: 96, 97). Changing family forms, also contributed to the erosion of the foundations of the KWS.

By the mid 1990s, however, the implication that globalization necessarily rules out effective economic management and state intervention has been challenged

(Boyer, 1996; Binefeld, 1996). Boyer, for example, stresses that it is 'still the epoch of the nation-state', and points out that:

> To be efficient market mechanisms would have to be embedded in adequate institutions governing money, labour and relations with nature ...the next century will still be the era of nation-states in charge of disciplining and taming the markets, but the contours of this involvement are still largely unknown (Boyer, 1996: 110, 111).

In the political arena, rather than a consolidation of Galbraith's culture of the contented electoral majority, referred to earlier, there has been a growing tendency toward what may be termed an 'uneasy majority' that has questioned the need for minimum state intervention and reduced public social responsibility, and has eroded acquiescence for the untrammeled pursuit of business profits. The entry of Centre-Left political parties to the ranks of Government (for example, the Blair (United Kingdom), Schroeder (Germany) and Clark (New Zealand) governments) and their desire to offer an alternative rationale for their politics, has been accompanied by Third Way thinking (see, for example, Blair, 1994, 1998; Blair and Schroeder, 1999; Giddens, 1998, 2000, 2001) to replace the New Right agenda underpinned by the 'Washington Consensus' formula of the 1980s.

A recent *World Development Report* dedicated to examining the role of the state in a changing world, stressed that the minimalist state is not the ideal state (World Bank, 1997). As the Staff Director of the Report aptly put it: '[A] minimalist state would do no harm, but neither could it do much good' (Chhibber, 1997: 17). The state has a key role to play in economic and social development as a partner, catalyst and facilitator and an effective rather that minimalist state is needed (Chhibber, 1997: 17). While Keynesian aggregate demand management may be incompatible with the contemporary world, and the interventionist style that characterized the old industrial economy a thing of the past, I would argue that the state has a fundamental role in the new knowledge economy. Different state forms and policies can, however, emerge in response to the demands of the new global era, with political factors ultimately also playing a crucial role in their determination.

Towards New Terminology

It is clear that there is a need for new terminology to be developed to better convey the nature of the state and conceptualize the reconfiguration of the role of the state in this new era. The 'welfare state' descriptor is now outmoded. Moreover, today the term 'welfare' has a popular connotation of something quite different from its initial meaning. Welfare, once synonymous with well-being, is now perceived as ill-being. Illustrative of this perception in New Zealand, is an initiative of the government's Department of Social Welfare – *'From Welfare to Well-Being'* with the aim of 'rehabilitating welfare's image and seeking greater community buy-in to the longer term goals of ensuring that all citizens are able to contribute positively to society' (Player, 1994: 77).

There have been a number of attempts to provide new terminology to reflect the shifting nature of state action. For instance, Jessop argues that 'a Schumpeterian workfare state is more suited in form and function to an emerging post-Fordism' (1994a: 251). The crisis of Fordism, the success of the post-Fordist economies of East Asia with their type of effective Schumpeterian workfare state regimes and the growing importance of structural competitiveness suggests that 'we will witness the continuing consolidation of the 'hollowed-out Schumpeterian workfare state' in successful capitalist economies' (Jessop, 1994b: 36). Distinctive objectives of this state form are promotion of innovation in open economies to strengthen structural competitiveness of the national economy through supply side intervention, and subordination of social policy to labour market flexibility and/or the constraints of global competition (Jessop, 1994a: 263). These economic and social objectives represent a firm break with the KWS tradition, since now, international competitiveness of the economy takes precedence over domestic full employment and a 'productivist reordering of social policy' is given a higher priority than redistributive welfare rights (ibid).

The Schumpeterian workfare state can take different forms according to the strategies adopted – neo-liberal, neo-corporatist and neo-statist forms, with a mixture of these also possible (Jessop, 1994a). Neo-liberal strategies provide for a market-based transition to the new economic regime, similar to Thatcherism in the United Kingdom and Reaganism in the United States. Public sector restructuring takes place with privatization and the application of commercial principles to the remaining state sector. Deregulation of the economy, and an enabling legal and political framework, supports the market operations of the private sector and a flexible labour market. Favoured economic activities often receive subsidies and incentives through the tax system. Social partnership arrangements are rejected. The free play of market forces and internationalization are accorded primacy and innovation is expected to spontaneously follow on from this.

In contrast to the neo-liberal regime, neo-corporatist arrangements arise out of advance planning and concertation of economic decisions and activities by economic agents in order to further their own economic ends. Unlike under the KWS, where corporatist strategies aimed at the maintenance of full employment or stemmed from concerns about stagflation, neo-corporatist arrangements of the Schumpeterian workfare state are linked to the desire to promote innovation and structural competitiveness. There is also a movement away from macro level corporatist arrangements, as, for example, between the broad organizations of capital and labour, toward more selective, micro arrangements between, for instance, functionally distinct policy communities, such as health and education. Neo-statist strategies involve active intervention by the state to promote the structural competitiveness of the economy. Thus, the state, in its own right and as an economic actor among others, acts to ensure dynamic efficiency of the industrial core, particularly by overseeing the restructuring of declining industries and through microeconomic targeting of policies toward particular sectors, chiefly in the high technology arena. Reskilling of the labour force is given high priority, as is the stimulation of innovation.

While the Schumpeterian workfare state and its variants have merit, in that it conveys the changed focus of the state, it is hard to see it as substitute terminology with similar comparable appeal to the popularized welfare state concept. The following section therefore, offers the concept of the strategic state as a better alternative and one which also fits with the entrepreneurship perspective of the global age, which as Audretsch and Thurik (1999) observe, has changed from the 'managerial economy' of the previous industrial era to a knowledge-based 'entrepreneurial economy'.

The Strategic State

In Chapter 8 it was noted that the question posed in the 1999/2000 *World Development Report* – 'Can city governments become strategic brokers that influence their city's ... position in the global urban hierarchy?' (World Bank, 2000: 136), was answered in the affirmative, with the caveat that there must be appropriate planning and support. This question can be re-framed: 'Can national governments become strategic brokers that influence their nation's competitive position in the global economy?' This question may also be answered in the affirmative, when there is a strategic state – a proactive state that acts entrepreneurially and exhibits opportunity related strategic behaviour.

The Hébert and Link (1989: 47) definition of the entrepreneur as 'someone who specializes in taking responsibility for and making judgmental decisions that affect the location, form and the use of goods, resources and institutions', was drawn attention to in the introductory chapter of this text. This definition clearly can apply to the state that makes deliberate decisions to influence the employment and access to resources at national and regional levels. Similarly, using the definition of the entrepreneur put forward by economist J.B Say around 1800, as one who 'shifts economic resources out of one area of lower into an area of higher productivity and greater yield', as Osborne and Gaebler[3] rightly point out, 'Say's definition applies equally to the private sector, to the public sector, and to the voluntary, or third, sector' (1993: xix). In light of the state entrepreneurship, according to the aforementioned definitions, and with the state acting as the key driver and/or the catalyst in the effective mobilization, utilization and movement of the nation's resources and defining the productivity of the nation in the current phase of capitalist development, the state is a strategic state.

The strategic state concept strongly parallels the notion of 'entrepreneurial state' that has been associated with economic development activities of government[4] in the developed economies (see, for example, Eisinger, 1988) and more recently been coupled with the Asian newly industrializing economies (see, for example, Yu, 1997). Eisinger (1988) distinguishes between supply-side and demand-side approaches to economic development. With the latter approach, state and local governments become entrepreneurial. This demand-side approach to economic development is, in fact, compatible with the market-leading perspective outlined as an element of community entrepreneurship in chapter 7. Unlike the supply-side approach where government enters the picture '... after an opportunity has been identified by an investor or firm' (Eisinger, 1988: 228), the demand-side approach features government taking an active role at a much earlier stage. Opportunity creation, identification, and encouragement and enabling of opportunity to be availed of, for instance through matching of skills and resources, together with recognition of the importance of small businesses, characterizes this approach. Although some of the instruments of the supply-side approach, such as low interest loans and tax credits, are common to both approaches, the demand-side use of these devices has them aimed at targeted firms or sectors. Similar to the demand-side approach of the entrepreneurial state, an opportunity focused, strategic targeting approach to economic development is a core aspect of the strategic state.

The moot question then is: Why not use the entrepreneurial state concept instead of opting for the new strategic state descriptor? The reason for preference for the latter is due to pre-existing connotations of the entrepreneurial state terminology, especially in explaining the role of the state in developing economies. Political scientists, notably Duvall and Freeman (1983), have used the idea of the entrepreneurial state to understand the process of development in dependent industrializing economies such as Brazil, with state entrepreneurship used as a lever to promote the interests of the so called technobureaucratic elite. The entrepreneurial state notion is also often associated more with direct entrepreneurial activity of the state (see, for example, Davis and Ward, 1990), whereas the strategic state concept I suggest, has wider nuances. It encompasses both the pursuit of chosen social goals and other newer systemic functions (the systemic failure argument for state intervention is discussed later in this section), as well as profit-related public entrepreneurship and the entrepreneurship – economic development nexus characterizing the entrepreneurial state.

Yu (2001) stresses the implied link between entrepreneurship and strategic planning and the need for strategic planning at the national level in order to build competitive advantage. In his model of the entrepreneurial state, based on Schutz's theory of human action, he highlights that 'entrepreneurial intervention' of government involves the selection of strategies and a vision of future outcomes which results in a successful economy which outperforms its competitors (Yu, 2001). According to Yu, movement from opportunity identification to implementation of opportunity ideas by public sector agents, involves a continuous process of learning, experimentation and plan revision. There are conscious actions towards selected goals and purposes oriented to the future. Although Yu views these objectives as essentially economic ones that affect the competitive advantage, the strategic state concept, as mentioned previously, can include social goals as well. Economic adjustment to the forces of globalization, can have detrimental social implications, such as increasing inequality of wages and earnings that has accompanied increased labour market flexibility and labour market disadvantage of ethnic minorities and regions (de Bruin and Dupuis, 1995b; de Bruin, 2002; Sarfati, 2002). It is important, therefore, that strategic planning takes account of potential negative aspects of the adjustment process, so that individual well-being outcomes may be maintained and improved. In the twenty-first century, social protection systems need to adjust to a new world of work with 'non-linear employment tracks' and a need for lifelong learning (Sarfati and Bonoli, 2002: 4). Under these circumstances, the strategic state becomes the principal actor in laying the foundations for building a strong, socially inclusive economy within the globally connected world.

Innovation is often seen as an integral aspect of entrepreneurship and was an important feature of Schumpeter's (1934) highly influential discourse on entrepreneurship. Sustaining an innovative edge is crucial to both the continued success of entrepreneurs (Glancey and McQuaid, 2000) and the competitive advantage of the nation. In this new global era, however, innovation does not revolve on the activity of a single firm, but requires an active search for new knowledge and technology involving various actors – firms and institutions (OECD 1999a; 1999b). The strategic state is a key driver of innovation in the national economy and is seen as an important actor within the National Innovation Systems (NIS) framework. There is also growing awareness of the role of industrial clusters (see, for example, Porter, 1990, 1998) and clusters 'can be interpreted as reduced scale national innovation systems' (Guinet, 1999: 8). Strategic alliances, networks and partnerships appear to be becoming a feature of this new era of capitalist development, with the phrase 'alliance capitalism' (Dunning, 1997), being proffered to describe this form of market-based capitalism. The strategic state has a vital role as a facilitator of such networking, including cluster development, and as a catalyst in the creation of favourable systemic conditions for knowledge creation and regional systems of innovation.

The new role of government in the global age involves a variety of policy responses to reduce systemic imperfections, such as 'removing informational failures by providing strategic information' and 'removing institutional mismatches and organisational failures within systems of innovation' (Roelandt and Hertog, 1999: 18). This rationale for government intervention, based on the systemic imperfections argument, is broader than the standard market failure argument for intervention. Under the innovation systems approach, 'the goal of governments is to remove systemic imperfections in their innovation systems' (Roelandt and Hertog, 1999: 17), and this approach underpins the entrepreneurial role of the state in the innovation process. The strategic state can exert a powerful influence on the 'national innovative capacity' (Furman *et al.*, 2002).

Alertness to hitherto unnoticed opportunities for profit is often associated with entrepreneurship (Kirzner, 1973) and the profit motive is often cited as a vital characteristic of entrepreneurship (see, for example, Schumpeter, 1962 [1939]: 83).

There is room for the strategic state to be a profit-seeking entrepreneur in its own right or through its state owned enterprises (SOEs) – public corporations owned and operated by central government. Illustrative of state entrepreneurship primarily motivated by profit, is Singapore's regional industrial parks programme (Perry and Yeoh, 2000). During the 1980s, with rising wages and labour shortages in Singapore (Okposin 1999: 12) and lower operating costs in other Asian-Pacific economies, several multinational corporations sought to relocate their operations in these countries. The Singapore government, perceiving an opportunity for profit, decided to supply industrial infrastructure and administration for multinational corporations by establishing self-contained industrial estates and offering 'ready-built factories' in selected locations in the Asia Pacific region (Perry and Yeoh, 2000). Similarly, with reform and restructuring of the SOE sector, which has been a feature of the roll-back of the state in the last two decades in a large number of countries, there are many entrepreneurial profit-making success stories in this sector.

Though concerned with the viability of the welfare state, the challenge, as Rodrik (1997: 85) sees it, is 'to engineer a new balance between market and society, one that will continue to unleash the creative energies of private entrepreneurship without eroding the basis of cooperation'. It could be argued that engineering of an appropriate state-market-civil society mix encompasses the entrepreneurial element of state action. The outcome of meeting this challenge is the development of an environment that harnesses and builds on the resources, including cultural capital, of the nation and mitigates the risks of the global 'invisible hand', yet allows its citizens access to the opportunities opened up by globalization. The policy making and changing processes of the strategic state are thus geared toward enhancing the capacity of its economy and capabilities of its people through targeted intervention, within the context of the imperatives of the new global age.

Toward a Strategic State in New Zealand

Examining New Zealand's welfare state I have previously highlighted its foundations – the synergy between full employment (of the adult male) and a state-capital-labour relationship that gave rise to a fair living wage (see this chapter end note 1), with the nuclear family as its core, and argued that with the collapse of these foundations, coupled with the change in its guiding principles, policies and theoretical underpinnings, there has been a demise of the welfare state and the emergence of a new state form (de Bruin, 1997, 1999a, 1999b, 2000).

There is no shortage of literature on the altered welfare state principles and policy directions of the 'New Zealand reform model' (see, for example, Bollard *et al.*, 1996; Quiggin, 1998; Cremer, 1999 and Galt, 2000 provides a good summary). Summarizing the phasing of the reforms, Cremer (1999) notes three major strands in an on-going process which transformed an overly regulated, inward-looking, protective and public sector dominated economy, into a highly deregulated, liberalized and competitive one. Public sector reform with corporatization and privatization, reform of the social welfare and taxation systems, coupled with labour market reform, and competition policy, comprise these strands. The changed role of government in the welfare provision has resulted in an altered welfare mix, away from a predominance of state provision toward a concept which seeks to direct and/or enable the procurement of welfare through market means, namely through labour market participation in a deregulated labour market (de Bruin, 1997; 1999a).

Since 1999, with the first Labour-led centre left Coalition Government, New Zealand began another era in policy reconfiguration. There has been a firm move away from the earlier hands-off industry policy. Active industry policy and dedicated regional development is now firmly on the agenda and this may be viewed as a characteristic of a strategic state. After the 1984-1989 reforms, and in the face of rising unemployment, regional development polices in the 1989-1993 period had been essentially a response to unemployment and were focused on employment creation through self-employment. Regional Development Councils (later renamed Business Development Boards), together with a focus on community employment creation through the funding of micro scale local initiatives administered by the Community Employment Development Unit (subsequently renamed the Community Employment Group), comprised a programme of low cost support for employment creation at the local level through small and medium enterprises (SMEs) (see, for example, Massey *et al.*, 2001). The establishment of the BIZ programme in 1998, designed to improve SME management through training and information, saw continued recognition of SMEs, but it is only in the post 1999 period that a heightened focus on regional development is evident. The establishment of a new Crown economic development agency – Industry New Zealand (INZ), together with a reconstituted government Department – the Ministry of Economic Development, has been the key institutional infrastructure for implementing industry and regional policy.

Planning and partnership forms the core of industry and regional development practice and policy. All regions in New Zealand now have formulated development strategies and partnership agreements are in place. INZ's Regional Partnerships Programme identifies partners and supports and funds regional projects, chiefly involving tertiary research and training partnerships. INZ has also become the major catalyst for attracting foreign investment to peripheral geographic regions and targeted high value added industries. Thus, for example, INZ has been the catalyst in attracting a world-class wood processing plant to be built in Gisborne, on the East Coast of New Zealand's North Island, by a Malaysian-owned company. This venture has been acclaimed as the agency's biggest success (Taylor, 2002). The plant is part of the government's efforts to move New Zealand up the value chain in the forestry and wood industry. A further example of the targeted assistance for this industry is the government support received by the National

Centre of Excellence for Wood Processing Education and Training, which involves partnership with an Institute of Technology, a University, and the Forest Industries Training and Education Council, and is designed to overcome the industry's skill shortage.

In February 2002, the government announced a policy framework, *Growing an Innovative New Zealand* (Clark, 2002a), to systematically bring New Zealand back into the top ranks of the OECD group of countries. Initiatives in four key areas are being promoted to achieve a significant change in New Zealand's rate of economic growth: 1. Developing Skills and Talent; 2. Enhancing New Zealand's innovation system; 3. Increasing New Zealand's global connectedness; 4. Focusing Government's resources. The growth and innovation framework identifies three key industry sectors – Information and Communications Technology (ICT), biotechnology and creative industries, to strategically focus government resources and help raise New Zealand's international competitiveness. Industry Taskforces will map out strategies to overcome bottlenecks and tap the potential of these sectors. The broad initiatives designed to enhance global connectedness are the attraction of quality foreign direct investment, aggressive export promotion, and improved national branding. The latter seeks to re-brand New Zealand as technologically advanced, innovative, creative and successful, including leveraging off key events such as the release the movie Lord of the Rings, which was filmed in New Zealand and made by New Zealanders, and New Zealand's second defence of the America's Cup yachting trophy (Clark, 2002b). Enhancing the innovation system initiatives build on an earlier increase in state research and development spending, support for business incubators and cluster development and the Venture Investment Fund, set up in 2001, for government investment of NZ$100million in innovative businesses, over three years. A new Tertiary Education Strategy, and the newly established Tertiary Education Commission, will oversee better alignment between tertiary education and New Zealand's development goals. In summary, the current policy framework sees the state assuming leadership in strategies for economic development that are based on fostering an effective innovation culture.

Market-driven, profit-seeking activity of the New Zealand state is evident in its SOE sector. The legislative architecture to support efficient functioning of the sector was put in place in the latter half of the 1980s and formed the basis for reform of the public sector. The State-Owned Enterprises Act 1986, provided for corporatization of public trading enterprises, so that SOEs were required to run as profit making, efficient, commercial enterprises, similar to their private sector counterparts. The Act also paved the way for privatization. The State Sector Act 1988 imposed the requirement of clarity of objectives and improved accountability for the core public service (i.e. the service with no trading activities), and the Public Finance Act 1989, specified a changed focus of state sector financial management from inputs, to measurable outputs and outcomes (Boston *et al.*, 1991).[5] Currently New Zealand's SOE sector provides a range of services and products including electricity generation and transmission, postal services, air traffic control, and public broadcasting, and provides a useful supplement to government revenue. 'SOEs paid $688 million in dividends and tax in the 2000/01 year. These companies make a significant contribution to the New Zealand economy and they continue to trade successfully and profitably. Many companies have demonstrated that they are innovative and have world-class skills and technology' (Burton, 2002).

New Zealand Post (NZP) illustrates the response of a SOE to changed market conditions and demonstrates an active approach to seizing opportunity in the global arena. NZP's international consultancy arm, Transend (formerly New Zealand Post International Limited), has provided consultancy services on postal service restructuring and reform offshore and even acquired a partial stake in Maltapost. The pursuit of opportunities through international partnerships and alliances – 'alliance capitalism' (Dunning, 1997) mentioned previously, applies to successful SOEs. Thus, for instance, Airways Corporation, has joined forces with Lockheed Martin Air Traffic Management, to win profitable international contracts. In the case of NZP, however, analyses indicate (Evans and de Boer, 2000), that NZP's reaction to deregulation of the mail delivery market in April 1998 was significant; suggesting that market competition was the catalyst for NZP's entrepreneurial activity. NZP also faces growing competition in its traditional mail delivery market from electronic communications. Diversification into new areas, such as courier parcels and international consultancy, may therefore be viewed from a market survival perspective.

At this point it is worthwhile emphasizing that profit motivated state entrepreneurship is not as straightforward as profit-driven private entrepreneurship. How SOEs should balance their profit-making focus with other social policy requirements of government, and the need for reconciliation of issues, such as Parliamentary scrutiny of state enterprises and accountability to taxpayers and the commercial confidentiality requirements of successful business operation, are just some of the considerations that enter the picture in this connection.

The Recent Korean Experience

The strategically focused state industry and innovation policy of South Korea is worth drawing attention to since it epitomizes how '[A] society can do much to stimulate or inhibit the development of entrepreneurship. Government policy can do much to create opportunity' (Stevenson and Gumpert, 1985: 93). In 1998, in the wake of the Asian financial crisis, the economy shrank by 6.7 per cent and large numbers of employees, who had previously counted on lifelong job security, were made redundant as Korea's huge conglomerates, or chaebol, were forced to rationalize their operations. Unemployment peaked in early 1999 at 8.4 per cent. Since then, however, Korea's economic performance has improved markedly. The 2000 Global Entrepreneurship Monitor indicated Koreans have a leading propensity towards entrepreneurial activity, with 9 per cent of all 18-64 year old Koreans, reporting operating a new business, more than double that of the second ranking U.S.A. (Reynolds *et al.* 2000: 7). Information technology (IT) is playing an ever-increasing role in Korean economy. By recent estimates IT contributed close to 10 per cent of GDP, with this figure expected to rise to 20 per cent by 2010 (Bremner and Ihlwan, 2000) and there has been creation of a profusion of new IT and technology-based firms, well positioned to take advantage of the global marketplace. For instance, in one area of Seoul known as Teheran Valley, over 1,500 technology-based ventures have sprung up since 1997. While the sharp increase in technology-based venture firms is partly rooted in the chaebol restructuring efforts of 1997 and 1998, three key government policies have combined to create an environment in which new science and technology ventures can flourish.

First is the government's concerted financial and infrastructural support of advanced science and technology research. Since the 1960s, when the first government research institute (GRI) was established, government policy has focused on strengthening the country's research capacity, in a manner consistent with the requirements of Korean industry. In addition to creating several industry-specific GRIs throughout the 1970s and 1980s, recent policy has been to locate GRIs within science parks, so as to increase knowledge-transfer and the creation of spin-off ventures. In 1978, GRIs began to relocate to the country's leading science park, Taedok Science Town, which now boasts 70 research centres (GRIs and private institutions) and five universities. Several venture companies are also located there, most of them direct spin-offs of Taedok's research institutes and universities. Secondly, government policy has shifted so as to acknowledge the important role of venture businesses in driving Korea's competitiveness. In 1994, a system of Technology Business Incubators (TBIs) was launched to provide technological and management expertise to SMEs. TBI's are housed in GRIs and there are currently around 40 such incubators. Previously stringent restrictions on foreign investment in venture businesses have been abolished and recently, the government has pledged matching funds to assist newly created investment companies to invest in targeted venture businesses. Thirdly, recent government measures have seen changes to intellectual property laws enabling researchers to collect royalties from their discoveries, rather than royalties automatically being passed to the chaebol (Engardio and Ihlwan, 2000). This has created real incentives for individual researchers to drive the innovation process.

Sustained government efforts to advance the country's science and technology capacity, through a network of GRIs and the establishment of science parks, have also supplied a highly developed science-based workforce. When placed in this context, recent policy changes to promote innovation, such as increased government contributions to the funding of venture businesses and royalty-based incentives for researchers, have created a fertile environment for the success of technology-based Korean venture businesses (de Bruin and Dupuis, 2001). The Korean state has demonstrated active facilitation of the NIS and been instrumental in reducing systemic imperfections (the new view on justifying state intervention, as discussed earlier) – it has taken strategic steps to position the nation for success in the knowledge-intensive global age, though the lack of technologically agile SMEs is a bottleneck in the NIS that needs policy attention (Suh 2000).

Concluding Comments

This chapter examined the changing contours in the landscape of state action, form and function. The welfare state was presented within an historical perspective and its incompatibility in the context of the emergence of a new phase of capitalist development was emphasized. Thus, the emergence of alternative state forms, in line with the demands of the global era was discussed and the notion of the strategic state put forward. Within the context of the new entrepreneurial economy that characterizes the twenty-first century, when strategic decision/policy-making and leadership at the central governmental level becomes a central factor in innovation, opportunity-seeking/generating/seizing and the mobilization/shifting and effective utilization of the nation's resources, the state form tends toward that of a strategic state. A strategic state, must also actively determine social policy and a social protection agenda that takes into account the demands and features of the global age.

The clear policy direction to build opportunity for New Zealand and New Zealanders, within a growth and innovation framework and 'global connectedness' (Clark, 2002a), characterizes New Zealand's strategic state and state entrepreneurialism. Strategic steps to position the nation for technology and innovation based success in the global marketplace, as in the case of South Korea, is a crucial element of a strategic state.

In conceptualizing the role of the state in the global age, it is useful to acknowledge where the broad policy stance of national governments sits within general politics and political science discourse that are current. Thus, understanding for instance, the link between social democratic policy and the Third Way debate (see, for example, Giddens, 1998, 2000, 2001; Scanlon, 2001) is pertinent. Taking New Zealand as a case in point, the underlying principles of recent policies have much in common with the Third Way ideology. For instance, partnership with the community, is one of the themes that runs strongly through political statements and policy of the Blair/Schroeder/Clark governments. Equality of opportunity and human capital enhancement are also important policy strands. It is important, however, that the 'Third Way' be built on to suit the context of particular nations. For New Zealand the challenge is to find:

> ...Another path, a 'Fourth Way', perhaps, that builds on the proposition that economy and society cannot and should not be disentangled; that the processes of economic activity are as important as the outcomes; indeed, really *are* the outcomes? I think we

should, but I would not call it the Fourth Way, even though the new economic ideas underpinning it do have some universal validity. Rather, I suggest that we struggle to find 'Our Way' a path that suits us, in Aotearoa/New Zealand (Hazledine, 1999: 23).

In designing 'Our Way' – a strategic state model that is not based on a minimal, but rather a proactive state that takes into consideration the nation's development and social protection needs within the overarching constraints and opportunities afforded by the global age, is an optimum way forward.

In the search for 'Our Way' for New Zealand, or any other nation, further analysis of different strategic and entrepreneurial aspects of state action is necessary. Thus, for example, considerations such as the risk society perspective could inform additional elaboration on the role of a strategic state. As Taylor-Gooby *et al.* (1999) point out, the British welfare state developed as a state focused response to the problem of the dealing with risks met in a typical life-course. The value placed on security, or in other words, protection from risk, lay at the core of the New Zealand welfare state. For the New Zealand state in the twenty-first century, it is now necessary that the state is strategic, in the sense of recognizing and perceiving the risk definitions of households and business. To use the words of Beck, 'risk definitions do not deprive us, but rather make political decisions *possible* ... political action gains influence in parallel to the *detection* and *perception* of risk potential' (1992: 227). National governments have a strategic role in helping their constituents cope in a changing risk environment of heightened global competition.

As the current era of heightened globalization evolves, state forms defining the contours of state involvement too will evolve. These state forms, however, do not necessarily have to converge across developed economies. The time frame of adaptation may vary from country to country and the ultimate form of the state, be it a strategic state or some other form, will also depend upon the political culture, socio-institutional framework and the degree of capital-labour accord. With regard to 'the entrepreneurial function', as Schumpeter highlighted, this may be 'filled cooperatively' (Schumpeter, cited in Swedberg, 1991: 173). At the more overarching national and regional level, this would no doubt involve the state working in partnership with other actors.

Notes

1. In New Zealand this gave rise to a wage level which, buttressed by full employment, guaranteed the male breadwinner the ability to comfortably maintain himself, a wife and three children.
2. The regulation approach proffers a theoretical framework to explain the prolonged economic growth of the developed capitalist countries during the post-war period to around the mid 1970s and the subsequent 'crisis' which emerged. Regulationists usually distinguish three core aspects of the Fordist model where the term Fordism, is derived from the techniques of production pioneered in the American auto assembly factories of Henry Ford in the early 1900s. Firstly, mass production and mechanization in

accordance with 'Taylorism' is the distinctive form of labour organization or 'labour process model', technological or industrial paradigm, with separation between the mental and manual aspects of production. Thus the tasks of the organizers of the production process, such as engineers and managers, were distinct from the repetitive tasks of the semi-skilled manual workers performing one narrowly-defined operation on the assembly line. The second aspect – the 'regime of accumulation', is 'the set of regularities at the level of the whole economy, enabling a more or less coherent process of capital accumulation' (Nielsen, 1991: 22). Thirdly, the 'mode of regulation', or social and economic regulation, involves the mechanisms, including institutional structures, whereby the behaviour of individuals adjusts to the regime of accumulation. The separation of ownership and control in large corporations, social legislation like minimum wage laws and award wages, trade union activity and collective bargaining, progressive taxation and an advanced social security system, the money supply and credit policy are all facets of the mode of regulation (Jessop 1991: 136-137, Lipietz 1992: 1-7). The functionality of the welfare state (see, for example, Pfaller *et al.*, 1991: 2), is also a distinctive feature, with different types of welfare state emerging in different national contexts. Interestingly, Lipietz argues that regulatory institutions arose out of national social pressures, and the theorising of a few like Beveridge in Great Britain and Pierre Masse or Bloch-Laine in France, 'within the wider context of a fierce world-wide contest with Fascist and Stalinist models' (1992: 9). This, accordingly, helps explain the differences in the regulatory mechanisms of different countries and why, for example, the social security system in the United States differed from that of Northern Europe.

3. Citing Osborne and Gaebler whose book was important to popularizing the re-inventing government movement (see, for example, Moe, 1994; Kobrak, 1996), which is essentially underpinned by the economic theory rationale of public choice theory and is associated with tax and spending limits and downsizing of government, is by no means to suggest that the strategic state notion is based on similar rationale and the re-inventing government exercise.

4. The term 'development state' has been used by political scientists to describe the state that actively targets economic development (see, for example, Johnson, 1982; Wade, 1990), but while this term may be suited to classify states in developing countries, it is not appropriate for the developed Western economies.

5. For a good overview of New Zealand's current Crown Company legislation and the monitoring framework see CCMAU, 2002, pp. 7-25.

References

Audretsch, D. and Thurik, R. (1999), 'Capitalism and Democracy the 21st Century: From the Managed to the Entrepreneurial Economy', *Journal of Evolutionary Economics*, Vol. 10, pp. 17-34.

Barr, N. (1993), *The Economics of the Welfare State* (2nd Edition), Weidenfeld and Nicholson, London.

Barr, N. and Whynes, D. (1993), 'Introductory Issues', in N. Barr and D. Whynes (eds), *Current Issues in the Economics of Welfare*, Macmillan, Houndmills and London. pp. 1-19.

Beck, U. (1992), *Risk Society: Towards a New Modernity*, Sage Publications, London.

Binefeld, M. (1996), 'Is a Strong National Economy a Utopian Goal at the End of the Twentieth Century?', in R. Boyer, and D. Drache (eds), *States Against Markets: The Limits of Globalization*, Routledge, London and New York, pp. 415-440.

Blair, T. (1994), 'Socialism', Fabian Pamphlet 565, Fabian Society, London.

Blair, T. (1998), 'The Third Way', Fabian Pamphlet 588, Fabian Society, London.

Blair, T. and Schroeder, G. (1999), *The Third Way/Die Neue Mitte*, British Labour Party, London.

Bollard, A., Lattimore, R. and Silverstone, B. (eds), (1996), *A Study of Economic Reform: The Case of New Zealand*, North Holland, Amsterdam.

Boston, J., Martin, J., Pallot, J. and P. Walsh (eds) (1991), *Reshaping the State: New Zealand's Bureaucratic Revolution*, Oxford University Press, Auckland.

Boyer, R. (1995), 'Capital-Labour Relations in OECD Countries: From the Fordist Golden Age to Contrasted National Trajectories', in J. Schor and J. You (eds), *Capital, the State and Labour: A Global Perspective*, Edward Elgar, Aldershot and United Nations University Press, Tokyo, pp. 18-69.

Boyer, R. (1996), 'State and Market: A New Engagement for the Twenty-First Century?', in R. Boyer, and D. Drache (eds), *States Against Markets: The Limits of Globalization*, Routledge, London and New York, pp. 84-114.

Bremner, B. and Ihlwan, M. (2000), 'Korea's Digital Quest', *Business Week*, September 25, The McGraw-Hill Companies, pp. 68-76.

Burton, M. (2002), 'SOEs Briefing to Incoming Minister', Media Statement, 4 September.

CCMAU – Crown Company Monitoring Advisory Unit (2002), *Briefing to Incoming Minister for State Owned Enterprises*, www.ccmau.govt.nz (accessed 5 September, 2002).

Chhibber, A. (1997), 'The State in a Changing World', *Finance & Development*, Vol. 34(3), pp. 17-20.

Clark, H. (2002a), *Growing an Innovative New Zealand*, http://www.executive. govt.nz/minister/clark/innovate/innovative.pdf (accessed 11 August, 2002).

Clark, H. (2002b), Prime Minister's Address to the London School of Economics, Speech 21/2/2002, http://www.executive.govt.nz/speech.cfm?speechralph=37394&SR =1 (accessed 26 March, 2002).

Cox, R. (1987), *Production, Power and World Order*, Columbia University Press, New York.

Cremer R. (1999), 'Relying on Market Forces: Is New Zealand's Economic Policy a Model for Others? – An Insider's View' *Wirtschaftpolitische Blaetter*, Vol 3, pp. 251-257.

Davis, D. and Ward, M. (1990), 'The Entrepreneurial State: Evidence from Taiwan', *Comparative Political Studies*, Vol. 23(3), pp. 314-331.

de Bruin, A. (1997), *The New Zealand Welfare State: With Special Reference to Employment*, Unpublished PhD Thesis, Massey University, Albany.

de Bruin, A. (1999a), 'The Welfare State in a Global Age', in A. de Bruin (ed.) *Proceedings of the 'The Global Society: Issues and Challenges for New Zealand' Symposium*, Massey University, Albany, February, pp. 69-79.

de Bruin, A. (1999b) 'Transformation of the Welfare State in New Zealand', Department of Commerce, Massey University, Albany, *Working Paper Series*, No. 99.11, April.

de Bruin, A. (2000), 'The Welfare State in a Global Age: The New Zealand Experience', Paper presented at the Society for the Advancement of Socio-Economics Conference, London School of Economics, July.

de Bruin, A. (2002), 'The New Zealand Reforms Outcomes and New Policy Directions', in H. Sarfati and G. Bonoli (eds), *Labour Market and Social Protection Reforms in International Perspective: Parallel or Converging Tracks?*, Ashgate, Aldershot. pp. 221-225.

de Bruin, A. and Dupuis, A. (1995a), 'The Implications of Housing Policy for New Zealand Women in Non-Nuclear Families', Paper Presented at the 50th Anniversary Conference of the New Zealand Geographic Society, University of Canterbury, August.

de Bruin, A. and Dupuis, A. (1995b), 'A Closer Look at New Zealand's Superior Economic Performance: Ethnic Employment Issues', *British Review of New Zealand Studies (BRONZS)*, No. 8, pp. 85-98.

de Bruin, A. and Dupuis, J. (2001), 'Learning from South Korea', *Venture: The Industry New Zealand Magazine that Celebrates Initiative*, Issue No. 6, September, pp.17-18.

Drache, D. (1996), 'From Keynes to K-Mart: Competitiveness in a Corporate Age', in R. Boyer, and D. Drache (eds), *States Against Markets: The Limits of Globalization*, Routledge, London and New York, pp. 31-61.

Dunning, J. (1997), *Alliance Capitalism and Global Business*, Routledge, London.

Duvall, R. and Freeman, J. (1983), 'The Technobureaucratic Elite and the Entrepreneurial State in Dependent Industrialization', *American Political Science Review*, Vol. 77, pp. 569-587.

Eisinger, P. (1988), *The Rise of the Entrepreneurial State: State and Local Economic Development Policy in the United States*, University of Wisconsin Press, Madison.

Engardio, P. and Ihlwan, M. (2000), 'Beyond the Lab', *Business Week*, November 27, The McGraw-Hill Companies, pp. 136-139.

Evans, L. and de Boer, D. (2000), 'The Economic Performance of Five State Owned Enterprises 1989 to 1998', New Zealand Institute for the Study of Competition and Regulation – ISCR, http://www.treasury.govt.nz/soes/econperf/soes-iscr.pdf (accessed 22 April, 2002).

Furman, J., Porter, M. and Stern, S. (2002), 'The Determinants of National Innovative Capacity', *Research Policy*, Vol. 31(6), pp. 899-933.

Galbraith, J. (1992), *The Culture of Contentment*, Houghton Mifflin, New York.

Galt, D. (2000), 'New Zealand's Economic Growth', *Treasury Working Paper*, 00/09. http://www.treasury.govt.nz/workingpapers (accessed 31 August, 2000).

Giddens, A. (1998) *The Third Way: The Renewal of Social Democracy*, Polity Press, Cambridge.

Giddens, A. (2000), *The Third Way and its Critics*, Polity Press, Cambridge.

Giddens, A. (ed.) (2001), *The Global Third Way Debate*, Polity Press, Cambridge.

Glancey, K. and McQuaid, R. (2000), *Entrepreneurial Economics*, MacMillan, London.

Guinet, J. (1999), 'Introduction', in OECD (1999), *Managing Innovation Systems*, Organisation for Economic Co-operation and Development, Paris, pp.7-8.

Hazledine, T. (1999), 'Third Way, Fourth Way, Our Way!' in A. de Bruin (ed.) *Proceedings of the 'The Global Society: Issues and Challenges for New Zealand' Symposium*, Massey University, Albany, February, pp. 17-24.

Hébert, R. and Link, R. (1989), 'In Search of the Meaning of Entrepreneurship', *Small Business Economics*, No. 1, pp. 39-49.

Jessop, B. (1991), 'Thatcherism and Flexibility: the White Heat of a Post-Fordist Revolution', in B. Jessop, H. Kastendiek, K. Nielsen and O. Pedersen (eds) *The Politics of Flexibility*, Edward Elgar, Aldershot, pp. 135-161.

Jessop, B. (1994a), 'Post-Fordism and the State', in A. Amin (ed.) *Post-Fordism*, Blackwell, Oxford.

Jessop, B. (1994b), 'The Transition to Post-Fordism the Schumpeterian Workfare State', in R. Burrows and B. Loader (eds) *Towards a Post-Fordist Welfare State?*, Routledge, London and NY. pp. 13-37.

Johnson, C. (1982), *MITI and the Japanese Miracle*, Stanford University Press, Stanford, CA.

Johnson, N. (1987), *The Welfare State in Transition*, Harvester Wheatsheaf, London.

Kirzner, I. (1973), *Competition and Entrepreneurship*, University of Chicago Press, Chicago.

Kobrak, P. (1996), 'The Social Responsibilities of a Public Entrepreneur', *Administration and Society*, Vol. 28(2), pp. 205-238.

Kurzer, P. (1991), 'Unemployment in Open Economies: The Impact of Trade, Finance and European Integration', *Comparative Political Studies*, Vol 24, pp. 3-30.

Lipietz, A (1992), *Towards a New Economic Order* (English Translation), Polity Press, Cambridge.

Massey, C., Cameron, A. and Tweed, D. (2001), 'The New Zealand Experiment & Its Impact on Entrepreneurship', in RENT XV Research in Entrepreneurship and Small Business 15th Workshop, November 22-23, 2001 Turku, Finland Conference Proceedings, Small Business Institute, Turku School of Economics and Business Administration, pp. 236-248.

Mishra, R. (1984), *The Welfare State in Crisis*, Brighton, Harvester Press.

Moe, R. (1994), 'The "Reinventing Government" Exercise: Misinterpreting the Problem, Misjudging the Consequences', *Public Administration Review*, 54(2), pp. 111-122.

Nielsen, K. (1991), 'Towards a Flexible Future – Theories and Politics', in B. Jessop, H. Kastendiek, K. Nielsen, and O. Pedersen (eds), *The Politics of Flexibility*, Edward Elgar, Aldershot, pp. 3-30.

Notermans, T. (1993), 'The Abdication of National Policy Autonomy: Why the Macroeconomic Policy Regime has Become so Unfavorable to Labor', *Politics and Society*, 21(June), pp. 133-67.

OECD (1981), *The Welfare State in Crisis*, Organisation for Economic Co-operation and Development, Paris.

OECD (1999a), *Managing Innovation Systems*, Organisation for Economic Co-operation and Development, Paris.

OECD (1999b), *Boosting Innovation: The Cluster Approach*, Organisation for Economic Co-operation and Development, Paris.

Okposin, S. (1999), *The Extent Of Singapore's Investments Abroad*, Ashgate, Aldershot.

Osborne, D. and Gaebler, T. (1993), *Reinventing Government: How the Entrepreneurial Spirit isTtransforming the Public Sector* Plume, New York.

Perry, M. and C. Yeoh (2000), 'Singapore's Overseas Industrial Parks', *Regional Studies*, 34(2), pp. 199-206.

Pfaller, A., Gough, I. and Therborn, G. (eds) (1991), *Can the Welfare State Compete?*, Macmillan, Houndmills and London.

Player, M. (1994), '"From Welfare to Well-Being" – Communicating a Vision', *Social Policy Journal of New Zealand*, Vol.3, pp.77-81.

Porter, M. (1990), *The Competitive Advantage of Nations*, Free Press, New York.

Porter, M. (1998), 'The Adam Smith Address: Location, Clusters, and the "New" Microeconomics of Competition', *Business Economics*, Vol. 33, pp. 7-14.

Quiggin, J. (1998), 'Social Democracy and Market Reform in Australia and New Zealand', *Oxford Review of Economic Policy*, Vol. 14(1), pp. 76-95.

RCSS – Royal Commission on Social Security (1972), *Social Security in New Zealand*, Government Printer, Wellington.

Reynolds, P., Hay, M. Bygrave, W., Camp, S., and Autio, E. (2001), *Global Entrepreneurship Monitor: 2000 Executive Report*, Babson College, Babson, MA.

Rodrik, D. (1997), *Has Globalization Gone Too Far?*, Institute for International Economics, Washington, D.C.

Roelandt, T. and den Hertog, P. (1999), 'Cluster Analysis and Cluster-Based Policy Making in OECD Countries: An Introduction to the Theme', in OECD, *Boosting Innovation: The Cluster Approach*, Organisation for Economic Co-operation and Development, Paris, pp. 9-23.

Sarfati, H. (2002), 'Labour Market and Social Protection Policies: Linkages and Interactions', H. Sarfati and G. Bonoli (eds), *Labour Market and Social Protection Reforms in International Perspective: Parallel or Converging Tracks?*, Ashgate, Aldershot, pp.11-57.

Sarfati, H. and Bonoli, G. (2002), 'Introduction – Tight Constraints, New Demands and Enduring Needs: Addressing the Labour Market versus Social Protection Challenge', in H. Sarfati and G. Bonoli (eds), *Labour Market and Social Protection Reforms in International Perspective: Parallel or Converging Tracks?*, Ashgate, Aldershot, pp.1-10.

Scanlon, C. (2001), 'A Step to the Left? Or Just a Jump to the Right? Making Sense of the Third Way on Government and Governance', *Australian Journal of Political Science*, 36(3), pp. 481-498.

Scharpf, F. (1991), *Crisis and Choice in European Social Democracy*, Cornell University Press, Ithaca.

Schumpeter, J. (1934), *The Theory of Economic Development*, Harvard University Press, Cambridge, MA.

Schumpeter, J. (1962 [1939]) *The Theory of Economic Development*, Oxford University Press, New York.

Stevenson, H. and Gumpert, D. (1985), 'The Heart of Entrepreneurship', *Harvard Business Review*, March-April, pp. 85-94.

Suh, J. (2000), 'Korea's Innovation System: Challenges and New Policy Agenda', *UNU/INTECH Discussion Papers*, 2000-4, The United Nations University, Institute for New Technologies, Maastricht, The Netherlands.

Swedberg, R. (1991), *Joseph A. Schumpeter: His Life and Work*, Polity Press, Cambridge.

Taylor, K. (2002), 'Secretive Firm Invests $100 million', *NZ Herald*, July 5, p. C1.

Taylor-Gooby, P. Dean, H., Munro, M. and Parker, G. (1999), 'Risk and the Welfare State', *British Journal of Sociology*, vol. 50(2), pp.177-95.

Titmuss, R. (1968), *Commitment to Welfare*, Allen & Unwin, London.

Wade, R. (1990), *Governing the Market*, Princeton University Press, Princeton, NJ.

World Bank (1997), *The State in a Changing World*, Oxford University Press, New York.

World Bank (2000), *World Development Report, 1999/2000: Entering the 21st Century*, Oxford University Press, New York.

Yu, T. F-L (1997), 'Entrepreneurial States: the Role of Government in the Economic Development of the Asian Newly Industrialising Economies', *Development Policy Review*, Vol. 15(1), pp. 47-64.

Yu, T. F-L (2001), 'Towards a Theory of the Entrepreneurial State', *International Journal of Social Economics*, Vol. 28(9), pp. 752-766.

Chapter 10

Indigenous Entrepreneurship

Anne de Bruin and Peter Mataira

Introduction

The relatively low socio-economic status of indigenous peoples in developed countries is a matter of significant concern. In Australasia, the lesser economic status of indigenous Australians – Aboriginal and Torres Strait Islander people, and of Maori, the indigenous people of New Zealand, is well documented (see for example Taylor and Hunter, 1998; Altman, 2000; Te Puni Kokiri, 2000; ATSIC, 2002). Indicative of the relative poverty of First Nations people of Canada is the statistic that over 60 per cent of these people in the Saskatchewan Province are classified as living in poverty – 'roughly four times the average found in non-Aboriginal communities' (Peters, 1996: 8, cited in Anderson, 1997). In the United States, American Indians living on reservations are among the poorest in the world (Cornell and Kalt, 1992; Duffy and Stubben, 1998).

The capacity of indigenous communities to improve their state of health and well-being will be dependent upon their abilities to foster and generate their own sources of revenue and sustainable economic wealth. This chapter contends that entrepreneurial activity, at multiple levels, is a crucial element of any action package to enhance the self-sustaining economic development of indigenous peoples. At the more overarching level, the notion of 'heritage entrepreneurship' is put forward and argued to be necessary to acquire and secure their cultural heritage resources. At the next more macro level, effective tribal entrepreneurship is argued as a prerequisite for deriving commercial value from tribally owned resources. Tribal entrepreneurship includes indigenous enterprises at the larger community, reservation based and regional levels. Finally at the micro level of the individual and family, entrepreneurship, normally equated with self-employment, is also necessary to provide greater employment opportunities.

The organization of the main discussion in the chapter follows the tri-levels of entrepreneurial activity. Firstly, the concept of heritage entrepreneurship is explained and mainly illustrated by drawing on the study of recent claims made by Maori, under the Treaty of Waitangi, an 1840 agreement between several Maori tribes and the British Crown, upon which the colonization of New Zealand was based. Following on from here, the next level of tribal entrepreneurship is delineated with the principal elements for the success of this model drawn out. The importance of leadership is also highlighted. Joint ventures and partnerships and connectedness with the global economy are asserted to be increasingly important for the dynamism of tribal entrepreneurship. At the third level of entrepreneurship discussed – indigenous self-employment, the supporting role of government assistance is drawn attention to and an associated definition of commercial viability set out. The broad notion of advancing indigenous economic development is fundamentally linked to indigenous peoples' efforts to reduce their reliance on government benefits and to reassert their sovereign claims.

At the outset it must be mentioned, however, that a rigid separation into distinct levels of entrepreneurship is not the intention. There could well be overlap. For example the micro level of indigenous self-employment, especially indigenous-owned small businesses, may be linked to the wider community or regional level of entrepreneurial endeavours that is included under tribal entrepreneurship.

In exploring the entrepreneurial capacity of indigenous peoples, this chapter implicitly adopts a Resource-Based Theory framework. Entrepreneurship is viewed as the mobilization of resources (Oinas, 2001) and the harnessing of 'entrepreneurial value' from the 'entrepreneurial capital' base which comprises all forms of capital – economic, human, physical, social and cultural (see Chapter 4, 'Entrepreneurial Capital', and Firkin, 2001). In keeping with the embeddedness theme of the book, it is also pointed out that cultural imperatives and kinship play a role in the exercise of indigenous entrepreneurship. This discussion also complements the approach in Chapter 6, 'Familial Entrepreneurship'.

Heritage Entrepreneurship

In this section the concept of 'heritage entrepreneurship'[1] is put forward to offer a novel interpretation of the entrepreneurship at a more overarching level, that avails itself of opportunities to acquire and/or safeguard customary, heritage based resources. In particular this concept views the resource claims of indigenous peoples and action to protect their intellectual and cultural property rights (also termed 'Indigenous Heritage Rights'), as entrepreneurial behaviour. The understanding of heritage is a broad one where:

> Heritage consists of the intangible and tangible aspects of the whole body of cultural practices, resources and knowledge systems developed, nurtured and refined by Indigenous people and passed on by them as part of expressing their cultural identity (Janke, 1998: Executive Summary).

Through the exercise of heritage entrepreneurship, which includes processes of settlement negotiation with government and the securing of rights through legislation, the economic capital base of indigenous people is expanded.

Heritage entrepreneurship in action is well illustrated by Maori activities at this macro-level, particularly after 1975. Maori are tangata whenua or 'people of the land'. At New Zealand's most recent Census, of the 3,737,277 usual residents, 14.7 per cent reported Maori ethnicity, compared with 80 per cent European ethnicity (Statistics New Zealand, 2001). Maori were guaranteed, under Article II of the Treaty of Waitangi full, exclusive and undisturbed rights to their land, forests and fisheries and other properties, and under Article III to equal citizenship rights. Both before, and immediately following the signing of the Treaty, Maori engaged in significant entrepreneurial activity. They were active traders in fish, agricultural produce and pigs, owned flour mills and trading vessels that sailed frequently for commercial purposes to Australia (Waitangi Tribunal, 1988: 44-66). Merrill (1954) provides an interesting discussion which affirms private (individual) entrepreneurship as practice encouraged by Maori hapu (sub-tribal) groups in the 1800s and thought to be uncharacteristic behaviour for a society that was essentially communal. The Land Wars of the 1860s, however, resulted in the confiscation of large scale tracts of prime Maori land and the dispossession of Maori land continued with illegal purchases, conversion from customary to individual title and other forms of expropriation such as leases (with limits on rents) in perpetuity sold to settlers (Waitangi Tribunal, 1996). This dramatic erosion of the resource base of the Maori underpinned their economic deprivation.

As Maori renaissance and activism focusing on Treaty of Waitangi grievances grew in the 1960s and 1970s, the Waitangi Tribunal was established by the Treaty of Waitangi Act, 1975. Under the Act any Maori or Maori group can lodge a claim with the Tribunal, a permanent commission of inquiry, whose role is to make recommendations on claims brought by Maori relating to the practical application of the Treaty and to determine whether certain matters are inconsistent with the principles of the Treaty. This has provided the legal foundations for restoring resources for Maori.

The concept of heritage entrepreneurship explicitly recognizes the implicit acknowledgment of entrepreneurship inherent in the process of reaching asset settlement:

> Grievances under the Treaty since 1975 have been directed through the Treaty of Waitangi Act and the Tribunal, they have also been the source of direct negotiations with the Crown for the reason that Maori entrepreneurial activity has often been linked to litigation with the Crown, direct negotiations and achievement of settlement of Maori assets (Matiara, 2000: 216).

The whole process of negotiation of Maori claims to commercial fisheries is an example, *par excellence*, of heritage entrepreneurship in action. After the chief claimants gave leadership mandates to the main Maori negotiators (Sir Graham Latimer, Sir Robert Mahuta, Sir Tipene O'Reagan and Matiu Rata), in lengthy negotiations and with considerable entrepreneurial ability they were able to secure a commercial fishing rights deal. Initially Maori were awarded 10 per cent of the fishing quota under the 1989 Maori Fisheries Act, with an additional $10 million to form a commercial fishing company. This was supplemented when the

Government provided Maori with a 50 per cent share in Sealord Products Limited, the largest fishing and fish processing company in New Zealand and a 20 per cent share of new species quota (Durie, 1998:159). These negotiations culminated in the Treaty of Waitangi (Fisheries Claim) Settlement Act 1993. It should be noted, however, that the settlement also meant renouncement of any further rights to commercial fisheries and the Fisheries Claim has been the subject of much Maori dissension. In particular pan-tribal focused urban Maori interests complicate the allocation of these assets (see for example Mataira, 2000: 233-236, for a discussion of Maori fisheries issues). Nevertheless, Maori now own nearly 60 per cent of the allowable commercial fish catch which is a significant asset base to grow business activity (Sullivan and Margaritis, 2000).

Action to fast-track settlement claims by stake-holders can also be viewed as entrepreneurial behaviour. Early settlement means that the use of these resources to further self-determined indigenous development ends, is similarly fast-tracked. For example, it is expected that the NZ$500 million Treaty of Waitangi claim for the central North Island forests will be settled years earlier than expected (O'Sullivan and Collins, 2002). A multiplicity of competing claims for Treaty settlements are a constant source of conflict and delay. Formation of the Volcanic Interior Plateau group to give concerted voice to several of the major Maori claimants has speeded the process. The facilitative role of social networks in the process, while important, can also be the source of tensions (see for example Collins, 2002).

Another instance of heritage entrepreneurship is the development of a Maori-made trademark. This trademark, 'toi iho' is an icon that represents protective hands cupped around the Maori community, was created to identify Maori art, but will be more widely used to brand Maori products and services (Milne, 2002). The development and administration of the trademark by Creative New Zealand, a government agency, also illustrates that government sponsored bodies can be integral to the exercise of heritage entrepreneurship. Thus for example in Australia, the Aboriginal and Torres Strait Islander Commission (ATSIC) has an important role in engaging in, or acting as a catalyst for heritage entrepreneurship. Hence heritage entrepreneurship can be an aspect of state entrepreneurship which is discussed in Chapter 9 of this book.

The use of the mainstream legal framework, as well as the development of innovative alternative approaches to help establish and protect indigenous culture and intellectual property rights (IPR) (see for example Riley and Moran, 2001), will provide mounting evidence of the significance of heritage entrepreneurship, in an age marked by the resurgence of self-determination by indigenous groups and increasing world-wide awareness of indigenous claims to land, cultural resources, and intellectual property. Perhaps the IPR area will be the domain of greatest conflict and a need for heightened heritage entrepreneurship. As Solomon and Watson (2001) emphasize, the Western IPR model is based on private economic rights, but the indigenous system is collectively based and not only considers the right of use but also regards as equally important the obligations to, and respect for, these natural resources. The effective exercise of heritage entrepreneurship, albeit in all likelihood hand-in-hand with controversy, is certainly vital to laying a resource foundation for entrepreneurship, particularly at the tribal level.[2]

Tribal Entrepreneurship

The strategic utilization of the indigenous resource base, the growing of this base, and taking advantage of opportunity,[3] for the development of the indigenous community e.g. tribe or American Indian reservation, through tribally (collectively) owned enterprises and/or joint ventures and business alliances, is what we classify as tribal entrepreneurship. The exercise of sovereignty – tribal self-determination and control of its own affairs, is a key aspect of this entrepreneurship model.

Mataira (2000: 14) provides a framework and schematic view of the core determinants of Maori tribal entrepreneurship. He asserts as an enterprise determinant: 'A knowledge that the core of tribal entrepreneurship is spiritual and embedded in the ethical dimensions of tikanga',[4] and identifies the following twelve variables related to 'Maori-driven entrepreneurial intent':

(i) The planning, goal setting and decision-making as the step-by-step pathway to change (ii) the necessity for personal revitalisation as a key to growth and means to maintaining "passion" commitment and enthusiasm (iii) the need to strengthen responsible communities and accountable organisations that serve the need of those who live and work in communities themselves (iv) the need to appreciate learning as necessity to remaining at the cutting edge of innovation (v) the need for advisors as sounding boards who have access to up-to-date information (vi) the ability to take action – good intention has little meaning without decisive planned action (vii) the need to address conflict and tension with a positive frame of mind and to manage change effectively (viii) the building of unity between heart and mind (between intelligence and emotion – matauranga and hinengaro)[5] as the key to entrepreneurial wisdom (ix) creating a collective vision for a desired future for self, family and community (x) a collective shared experience and leadership (xi) knowing processes of evaluation as actions require understanding of what, where and how developments are going (xii) the ability to network and form alliances ... .

The development of culturally appropriate institutional frameworks and sound organizational and governance structures, (which can be said to be encompassed in Mataira's variable (iii) above), is an essential accompaniment for enterprise development (Cornell and Kalt, 1992; Rose *et al.*, 1997; Matiara, 2000). The commercial operations of Ngai Tahu, a New Zealand South Island Maori tribe, demonstrate that vital to the success of tribal entrepreneurship is the separation of commercial from tribal development activity and political decision-making (see de Bruin *et al.*, 2001; http://www.ngaitahu.iwi.nz/). As Parata (1995) draws attention to, this is one of the first lessons to be learned for Maori tribal-based business investment. The need for tribally owned enterprises to be insulated from politics is also emphasized by Cornell and Kalt (1992), who show vastly improved profitability of American Indian tribal enterprises with independent, rather than council controlled management.

Competent leadership is also a prerequisite if tribal entrepreneurship is to make a visible difference to economic development. As Cornell and Kalt highlight:

> While basic management skills are certainly necessary, the success of tribal development activities depends also upon the *strategic* skills of decision makers. Picking "winners" is crucially dependent on these skills. The heart of the strategic problem is the appropriate matching of particular development activities and projects to the governance capabilities, asset endowments, and cultural attributes of the tribe (Cornell and Kalt, 1992: 38).

For the Mississippi Band of Choctaw Indians (MBCI) the able leadership and determination of Chief Phillip Martin, who returned to the reservation in 1955, has been invaluable. The tribe has moved from being 'the poorest tribe in the poorest county of the poorest state' (Anonymous, 2001), with an unemployment rate of almost 80 per cent in the late 1950s, to self-reliance and a current unemployment rate of between 3-4 per cent. The tribe is one of the state's largest employers. Tribal enterprises make a significant contribution to Mississippi State in state income tax and state and local sales tax (USM, 1999). Aided by United State tax laws and no levies of property tax on reservation-based businesses, and entrepreneurial moves such as building a 32ha industrial park in the early 1970s, MCBI has attracted a variety of corporate partners in the manufacturing sector. Competitive pressures and lower cost imperatives of the global economy have also now led to offshore business expansion. The tribe's automotive wiring harness business, Chahta Enterprise, opened an automotive wiring harness facility in an industrial park in the city of Guyamas in the state of Senora, Mexico in 1999. The facility currently employs approximately 1,700 people (MBCI, 2002). Other tribal businesses – Choctaw Electronics and First American Plastics, now have operations in Mexico too. Although the morality of gambling ventures has been questioned in some quarters, MBCI also operates Silver Star, the state's second biggest casino.

Joint ventures and partnerships with other non-indigenous stakeholders can be instrumental for the convertibility of existing capital of indigenous peoples into entrepreneurial capital. Partnerships enable extraction of entrepreneurial value from capital, which otherwise would be underutilized or not harnessed, for entrepreneurial purposes. While it is acknowledged that the possibility exists for the returns from such partnerships and joint ventures to be skewed in favour of the non-indigenous partner (see, for example, Jaimes, 1992),[6] the focus here is on 'mutually beneficial alliances' which are a necessary feature of competing in the global economy (Anderson, 1997). Development of partnerships could be, for example, crucial to the realization of the entrepreneurial value of mineral resources, particularly in view of high capital and skill intensity requirements which may be lacking in some indigenous communities. In some remote Australian aboriginal communities there are several examples of such partnerships (see, for example, Anonymous, n.d.). Considerations of sustainable development and a meaningful commitment to corporate social responsibility of the non-indigenous partners must, however, be prerequisites here. Tri-sector partnership arrangements and sustainability performance indicators (Warhurst, 2001) could be an approach for ensuring the accrual of positive benefit to the indigenous communities involved. Market-driven economies are very much dependent upon an entrepreneurial class and entrepreneurship is arguably embedded into and mandated by a set of social and moral codes. As indigenous entrepreneurship prospers, these codes will become more apparent in social and economic relationships with others. The issue of socially responsible corporate behaviour in relation to aboriginal relations has also been discussed in Chapter 3, 'Ethical Entrepreneurship'.

An 'assertively pragmatic approach' (Shatz, 1987) within a bargaining framework and a project participation agreement that assures preservation of the essential cultural values and principles of importance to the indigenous stakeholder, appears to be a successful model for participation in the global economy (Anderson, 1997). Assurances on non-irreparable environmental damage, non-compromising of indigenous rights claims, more positive than negative social impact, the widest possible development of education and employment-related training, and business development opportunities for Tahltans and their substantial equity participation, are among the principles specified by the Tahltan Tribal Council of Tahltan people of British Columbia for project participation and are representative of the requirements of First Nations and Tribal Councils across Canada, who acknowledge partnerships as a vital component of their successful participation in the global economy (Anderson, 1997). This pragmatic perspective and its tie-ins to historical events in terms of Treaty-partnerships, agreements or promises made between indigenous peoples and colonial settlers, is a model that can be followed by other indigenous groups as well.

Government incentives, agencies and programmes play an important role in the facilitation and fostering of both tribal and indigenous small business. As mentioned earlier, United States tax incentives have been skillfully used by Choctaw of Mississippi to attract corporate partnerships. An integral part of New Zealand's state support of community employment initiatives and programmes largely involves the activities of the Community Employment Group (CEG), of the governmental Department of Labour. The CEG is central government's major funder of community based employment initiatives. It works through field workers – Community Employment Advisors (CEA), with local communities and groups to facilitate job opportunities (de Bruin and Power, 1999; de Bruin *et al.*, 2001). As determinant (v) of the Mataira (2000) schema set out earlier, noted as well, there is a need for advisors and mentors in small enterprise development. A brief example of the empowering role of a CEA (Shayne Toko of Tanui and Ngati Whatua, Maori tribal – iwi descent), in the development of a Maori enterprise that reaped entrepreneurial value from an unused resource – a radio license, follows:

> ...Shayne Toko was conscious that it would not be appropriate to try and push through new ideas concerning the development opportunities for Ngati Whatua without being able to demonstrate the capacity to generate positive outcomes for the tribe. At the time Ngati Whatua had a number of opportunities that were not being taken up. ...The first such opportunity identified concerned an unused radio license. This gave Ngati Whatua the right to broadcast on an FM frequency. Drawing upon close family links with the then chairman of the Runanga O Ngati Whatua, in 1992, Shayne was involved in a development process that would eventually lead to the establishment of the radio station Mai FM. In his CEA (Community Employment Advisor) role he facilitated a three-year funding programme to Ngati Whatua Runanga. He worked closely with radio station management during the set up phase and assisted with advice concerning challenges to the utilisation of the licence by Brierley Investments Ltd. (BIL). The outcomes were the establishment of Mai FM, employment creation and enhancement of awareness of Maori language amongst Maori (and other ethnic groups) youth. The initiative also demonstrated that Ngati Whatua could manage a commercial enterprise and confirmed their capability to manage competitive issues raised by BIL (as owners of competing radio stations). ...Importantly, this project served to raise awareness amongst the wider iwi of the existence of CEG as an organisation providing practical community focused assistance (de Bruin *et al.*, 2001).

Today, the success of Mai FM as well as the importance of changing demographics in this global age – in this instance, the growth of Auckland's young, Maori and Pacific Island Group population, has been demonstrated by the station's rise in 2002 to be Auckland's most preferred radio station (Corbett, 2002).

The Mai FM example also illustrates that for indigenous business, outcomes are not merely commercial ones. The achievement of cultural goals, such as strengthening ethnic identity, improving self respect and confidence and the provision of positive role models, in addition to the usual commercial goals of running a profitable business and providing employment and training, are considerations. Environmental goals may be another consideration. Since commercial viability is not the only aim, a social audit should form an integral part of any evaluation of success. Additionally, in assessing the commercial viability, particularly of micro businesses, the opportunity cost of capital and labour considerations are more appropriate in some contexts (Fuller *et al.*, 2001). In welfare dependent indigenous communities, the opportunity cost of labour will be the welfare benefit/social security payment.

Indigenous Self-Employment, Small Enterprises

Labour market disadvantage of indigenous people is significant. For example Maori have much lower labour force participation rates, on average around three times higher unemployment rates,[7] higher underemployment and significantly higher long-term and youth unemployment and joblessness rates, than non-Maori (de Bruin and Dupuis, 1995; Te Puni Kokiri, 2000: 21-25). Fostering self-employment and indigenous owned and operated small enterprises, is viewed as an integral part of any package to provide employment opportunities, as well as reduce the high levels of welfare dependency among indigenous people.

Before proceeding with any further discussion, it is useful to point out that the moot question is: 'what is an indigenous business?' French (1998) identified the parameters that could potentially be used to define a Maori business to include ownership, aims and goals, culture, management practices, product, and numbers of Maori managers and employees. His study of Maori business people's perceptions on defining a Maori business, while not being able to come up with a single definition, showed that ownership, culture, organizational aims and goals and management methods and structures were extremely important for a definition. The study also highlighted the paucity of information and statistics on Maori business, which in turn creates barriers for implementing effective policies and programmes for advancing Maori business.

Despite a paucity of research on indigenous business, it can generally be asserted that obstacles to self-employment among indigenous people are broadly similar to those faced by other groups (for instance youth – see Chapter 12). These are chiefly, a lack of human capital – skills and experience, financial capital and other resources. The policies and processes by which these obstacles are addressed, however, need special awareness and sensitivity to the cultural and other unique needs of indigenous people. Thus, for example, in New Zealand the concept of whanaungatanga (kinship) was recognized as an important principle informing the fieldwork operations and operating style and culture of the Alternative Employment Programme (de Bruin et al., 2001). Furthermore, racist attitudes and opposition is also put forward as an additional barrier that has to be overcome in self-employment and for small business ventures of indigenous people. Thus for Maori:

> A Maori business can expect to encounter more opposition than would be expected from normal business competition, especially if it is starting to become successful (Boswell et al., 1994: 90).

Lack of human capital is a major barrier to increased indigenous employment and self-employment. A World Bank study of indigenous people and poverty (Psacharopoulos and Patrinos, 1993), for example, shows that education and experience is an important factor in explaining the overall earnings differential between indigenous and non-indigenous workers. While broadening the definition of human capital to recognize cultural capital (de Bruin, 1999; see also Chapter 7, 'Community Entrepreneurship') could, however, be a useful short-term solution to overcoming some educational deficiencies among indigenous people. Raising overall education and skill levels of indigenous peoples is undoubtedly crucial to indigenous economic development.

The lack of capital and access to finance constrained by land tenure of multiple ownership rather than individual title and problems arising out of indigenous institutional structures, are often suggested as barriers to small enterprise development. Increasingly, however, the banking industry sees the opportunities presented by active indigenous relationships and this augurs well for indigenous entrepreneurship. For instance, the Bank of Montreal, a major financial intermediary in Canada, actively pursues an aboriginal relations strategy which focuses on improving products and services to aboriginal people and communities in a culturally appropriate fashion and this in itself demonstrates the entrepreneurialism of the Bank. An Aboriginal Banking Unit with aboriginal regional managers has been established and the Managers of Aboriginal banking:

> ...Provide the bank with counsel and training in matters of Aboriginal community protocol, tradition and culture. Aboriginal business is a significant and growing business opportunity, which a major Canadian financial institution would be foolish to neglect. We need to listen and understand, if we are to earn the right to bank Aboriginal business (Bank of Montreal, 1993:6).

Similarly, the Business Development Bank of Canada has an Aboriginal Banking Unit which is active in developing customized products and services for Aboriginal entrepreneurs (see: http://www.bdc.ca/bdc/home/) and in New Zealand, Westpac Trust, a major registered bank, has established Aotearoa Financial Services to target Maori banking opportunities (Sullivan and Margaritis, 2000). For the financial sector, namely the commercial and development banking system, to make a worthwhile contribution to the development of the indigenous entrepreneur, however, it should also be innovative and 'supply-leading'[8] (de Bruin, 1977). In this connection, the financial institutions 'may supply initiative and enterprise, as well as finance, for the creation, transformation, and expansion of industrial and other ventures' (Cameron and Patrick, 1967: 8). With micro businesses and particularly those in more remote communities, there is nevertheless often risk averse behaviour or prejudice against indigenous customers (Hunter, 1999). While government funding (for example CEG funding in New Zealand), can mitigate this market failure, there is also scope for institutional innovations, such as Grameen-style banks and Rotating Savings and Credit Associations. The effectiveness of the Grameen model, which originated in Bangladesh, in mitigating risk through local community assessment, monitoring and trust, is another alternative that may be applied in indigenous communities (McDonnell, 1999).

Support networks are an important consideration. As the embeddedness theme of this book highlights, entrepreneurship is not solely an economic activity, as its context is a complex array of social interplays and interactions. These interactions are built upon notions of trust and loyalty, and much of what this is, is predetermined by support mechanisms. For indigenous entrepreneurs, support is often found within the familiarity of cultural networks which are deeply connected to the characteristics of family, extended families, community and tribal relationships. In the fieldwork findings on Maori entrepreneurship, whanau (family) featured prominently as support givers, confidantes and investors and gave respondents endorsement and consolation (Mataira, 2000).

There is, in general, a difference in the business related values of indigenous people and non-indigenous people that operate within the standard western business model. Schaper (1999) points to key differences in Aboriginal Australians and non-Aboriginal Australians. Aboriginal attitudes toward possessions are utilize and share, in contrast to the accumulate and acquire disposition of non-Aboriginals; Aboriginals have a relationship with the land and interaction is co-operative compared with the non-Aboriginal focus on land ownership and competitive interaction; for Aboriginals, rights are kinship based compared with individual rights of non-Aboriginals and finally, the operating unit is society for Aboriginals and the individual for non-Aboriginals (Schaper, 1999: 89). These value differences pose tensions and difficulties for entrepreneurial activity. There is possibly a need for indigenous entrepreneurship to develop a hybrid values model to operate successfully in the global society. As Mataira points out, entrepreneurs are, for Maori, 'the modern day "bicultural navigators", indigenous capitalists who weave, craft and sow their skills against adversity. They walk precariously between two worlds to make a difference' (2000: v).

It is evident that indigenous peoples are beginning to learn how to develop their knowledge base and expertise in modern areas of sustainable resource management and resource utilization, in marketing and sales and by drawing on their competitive advantage as can be seen in industries like cultural tourism. This has already led to an increase in self-employment and augurs well for continued growth of private indigenous enterprises. Increasingly, Maori businesses for example, are diversifying away from traditional agriculture and fisheries based business and taking advantage of new opportunities offered by the globally integrated service sector. For instance, Team Logistics New Zealand Ltd is a young and growing company in international freight forwarding and logistics. It operates from Christchurch, in the South Island of New Zealand. The company manages the flow of goods and information across a customer's global supply chain, arranging, for instance, all the necessary export or import documentation and clearances, and other attendant services, such as setting up letters of credit, which facilitate delivery from one destination to the next. Moving of penguin regurgitate and export of the spoils of game hunting are among the recent customer services provided. Hopefully, the future will see the continued growth of self-employment and examples of globally integrated indigenous businesses such as Team Logistics will become commonplace.

Concluding Comments

Historical factors, such as the negative impact of European settlement on many indigenous groups, together with land and resource dispossession and a long policy environment of neglect and acculturation, have strongly contributed to high levels of indigenous disadvantage. Fortunately, the tide has turned and assertive action and national and international support for the indigenous economic development cause is becoming more apparent. Particularly as the global economy spreads into developing countries, culture and cultural heritage as a key determinant in economic development is also acknowledged.

As highlighted in the case of Maori, '...Entrepreneurship offers the leverage for Maori development and the delivery of opportunities to Maori' (Mataira, 2000: 277). We contend that this is true for all indigenous groups. Entrepreneurship at multi levels – individual/family, tribal, and the overarching macro cultural level in terms of what is envisaged as heritage entrepreneurship, will be a key driver of indigenous development in the Global Age. Integral to unlocking indigenous development through the entrepreneurial process, however, is the need for leadership that can not only harness the entrepreneurial value of existing tribally owned resources but also grow this resource base through the exercise of heritage and tribal entrepreneurship. A vital element of this leadership will also be the ability to effectively incorporate the cultural values and ethical principles of indigenous people into a viable framework of commercial practice and governance, that can not only operate at the more localized community level, but is also capable of being extended to the internationally competitive global arena. Indigenous economic development ultimately occurs within the reality of a global economy and mutually beneficial alliances play a key role in tapping into global opportunities. Supportive government policies to enhance opportunity, at all levels of entrepreneurship, and including human capital development, will also be crucial to indigenous economic development.

We conclude this chapter by signalling the need for more research into indigenous business, entrepreneurship and entrepreneurial leadership, adding the caveat, however, that full consideration must be given to the conduct of this research within the boundaries, albeit dynamic boundaries, of indigenous research methods.

Notes

1. In its initial conceptualization Anne de Bruin termed the concept underpinning this chapter 'cultural entrepreneurship', but on further reflection, realized that the use of the

term cultural was problematic. Culture, has a multitude of meanings, such as the culture of an organization, and does not immediately convey the notion of entitlement that heritage does.

2. Supporting this assertion is the significant rise in tribal organizations involved in the fishing industry following Maori fisheries settlements. There were 50 tribal fishing operations in 1996 compared with none in 1989 (Durie, 1998: 170).
3. We include here two elements from the Cornell and Kalt (1992) category of 'external opportunity'. Firstly, '*Market opportunity*: unique niches or opportunities in local, regional, or national markets. These opportunities can come from particular assets or attributes (mineral, tourist attractions, distinctive artistic or craft traditions), or from supportive federal policies (as in gaming, wildlife, and favourable tax treatment)'. We widen this, however, to include also opportunities in international markets. Secondly, '*Access to financial capital*: the tribe's ability to obtain investment dollars from private, governmental or philanthropic sources. Access depends on such factors as federal tax policy, tribal reputation, private sector knowledge and experience, and public funding'.
4. tikanga – truth, correct principles.
5. matauranga – secular knowledge; hinengaro – emotional intellect.
6. American Indians have received on average less than 20 per cent of market royalty rates (i.e. rates paid to non-Indians), for mineral extraction from their land (Jaimes, 1992: 128).
7. The latest quarterly figures show that in December 2001, the European/Pakeha unemployment rate was 3.7 per cent compared with the Maori rate of 12.9 per cent (Statistics New Zealand, 2002). Non-Maori are more than twice as likely as Maori to be self-employed, even though as a per centage of all employed, Maori self-employment has doubled over the 1981-1996 period (Te Puni Kokiri, 1999).
8. This 'supply-leading' concept was developed in Patrick where 'Supply-leading has two functions: to transfer resources from traditional (non-growth) sectors to modern sectors, and to promote and stimulate an entrepreneurial response in these modern sectors' (1966: 175, 176). Patrick also points to the expectational and psychological effect brought about by the availability of 'supply-leading funds'. 'It opens new horizons as to possible alternatives, enabling the entrepreneur to "think big"' (1966: 176).

References

Altman, J. (2000), 'The Economic Status of Indigenous Australians', *CAEPR Discussion Paper No 193*, Centre for Aboriginal Economic Policy Research (CAEPR), Australian National University, Canberra.

Altman, J. (2001) 'Indigenous Communities and Business: Three Perspectives, 1998-2000', *CAEPR Working Paper No 9/2001*, Centre for Aboriginal Economic Policy Research (CAEPR), Australian National University, Canberra.

Anderson, R. (1997), 'Corporate/Indigenous Partnerships in Economic Development: The First Nations in Canada', *World Development*, Vol. 25(9), pp. 1483-1503.

Anonymous (2001), 'Breaking Tribal Tradition: Life on the Reservation is an Affluent One for Mississippi's Choctaw', *New Zealand Weekend Herald*, August 25-26, 2001, C7.

Anonymous (n.d.), 'Indigenous Partnerships: Mining: Case Studies Working in Partnership: The Mining Industry and Indigenous Communities', http://www.industry.gov.au/resources/indigenouspartnerships/CaseStudies/ (accessed 4 January, 2002).

ATSIC – Aboriginal and Torres Strait Islander Commission (2002), 'Issues: Disadvantage', http://www.atsic.gov.au/ (accessed 22 April, 2002).

Bank of Montreal (1993), *Aboriginal Banking Review*, Bank of Montreal, Toronto.

Boswell, K., Brown, D., Maniopoto, J. and Kruger, T. (1994), *Grassroots II: Community Development Initiatives at the Grassroots*, MAF Policy Technical Paper 94/10, Ministry of Agriculture and Fisheries, Wellington.

Cameron, R. and Patrick, H. (1967) 'Introduction', *Banking in the Early Stages of Industrialisation*, Oxford University Press, New York.

Collins, S. (2002), 'Multi-million-dollar Volcano Threatening to Blow', *The New Zealand Herald*, 2 May, pp. A10-11.

Corbett, J. (2002), 'Talkin' about Mai Generation', *The New Zealand Weekend Herald*, May 4-5, pp. B5.

Cornell, S. and Kalt, J. (1992), 'Reloading the Dice: Improving the Chances for Economic Development on American Indian Reservations', in S. Cornell, and J. Kalt (eds), *What Can Tribes Do? Strategies and Institutions in American Indian Development*, American Indian Study Centre, University of California, *Harvard Project on American Indian Economic Development Project Report Series*, http://www.ksg.harvard.edu/hpaied/publ. htm (accessed 1 May, 2002).

de Bruin, A. (1977), 'The Financial Sector and Indigenous Entrepreneurial Development in Papua New Guinea', unpublished dissertation, University of New England, Armidale.

de Bruin, A. (1999), 'Towards Extending the Concept of Human Capital: A Note on Cultural Capital', *The Journal of Interdisciplinary Economics*, Vol. 10, pp. 59-70.

de Bruin, A. and Dupuis, A. (1995), 'A Closer Look at New Zealand's Superior Economic Performance: Ethnic Employment Issues', *British Review of New Zealand Studies (BRONZS)*, No. 8, pp. 85-98.

de Bruin, A. and Power, G. (1999), *The Partnership Approach to Local Employment Generation*, in P. Morrison (ed.), *Labour Employment and Work in New Zealand: Proceedings of the Eight Conference*, Victoria University of Wellington, Wellington, pp. 156-163.

de Bruin, A., Power, G. and Toko, S. (2001), 'The Role of Community Employment Creation: Lessons and Challenges for a New Era', in P.Morrison (ed.), *Labour Employment and Work in New Zealand: Proceedings of the Ninth Conference*, Victoria University of Wellington, Wellington, pp. 156-162.

Duffy, D. and Stubben, J. (1998), 'An Assessment of Native American Economic Development: Putting Culture and Sovereignty Back in the Models', *Studies in Comparative International Development*, Vol. 32(4), pp. 52-82.

Durie, M. (1998), *Te Mana, Te Kawanatanga: The Politics of Self-Determination*, Oxford University Press, Auckland.

Firkin, P. (2001), *Entrepreneurial Capital: A Resources-Based Conceptualisation of the Entrepreneurial Process*, Working Paper No. 7, Labour Market Dynamics Research Programme, Massey University, Albany and Palmerston North.

French, A.J. (1998), *What is a Maori Business: A Survey of Maori Business Peoples Perceptions?*, unpublished research report, Massey University, Palmerston North.

Fuller, D., Howard, M. and Cummins, E. (2001), 'Indigenous Small Enterprise Development: The Case of Ngukurr, South East Arnhem Land', in C. Massey, C. Cardow and C. Ingley (eds), *SEAANZ, Creating Innovative Growth Companies*, Proceedings of the 14th Conference of the Small Enterprise Association of Australia and New Zealand, 13-15 September, Wellington, New Zealand, pp. 160-170.

Hunter, B. (1999), 'Indigenous Self-employment: Miracle Cure or Risky Business?', *CAEPR Discussion Paper No. 176*, Centre for Aboriginal Economic Policy Research (CAEPR), Australian National University, Canberra.

Jaimes, M. (ed.) (1992), *The State of Native America*, South End Press, Boston.

Janke, T. (1998), *Our Culture: Our Future*, Michael Frankel and Company, http://www.icip.lawnet.com.au/frontpage.html (accessed 24 January, 2002).

Mataira, P. (2000), *Nga kai arahi tuitui Maori: Maori Entrepreneurship: The Articulation of Leadership and the Dual Constituency Arrangements Associated with Maori Enterprise in a Capitalist Economy*, unpublished PhD thesis, Massey University, Albany, New Zealand.

MBCI (2002), http://www.choctaw.org/index/economics/ (accessed 28 January, 2002).

McDonell, S. (1999), 'The Grameen Bank Micro-credit Model: Lessons of Australian Indigenous Policy', *CAEPR Discussion Paper No. 178*, Centre for Aboriginal Economic Policy Research, Australian National University, Canberra.

Merrill, R. (1954), 'Some Social and Cultural Influences on Economic Growth: A Case of the Maori', *Journal of Economic History*, Vol. 14. pp 401-408.

Milne, J. (2002), '$1million to Develop Maori Trademark', *The Dominion*, January 24, p.1.

Oinas, P. (2001), 'Entrepreneurship as Mobilization of Resources: The Case of e-Commerce', in *Conference Proceedings, RENT XV, Research in Entrepreneurship and Small Business, 15th Workshop, November 22-23*, Vol. 2, pp. 127-138, Small Business Institute, Turku School of Economics and Business Administration, Turku, Finland.

O'Sullivan, F. and Collins, S. (2002), 'Biggest Claim to Get Urgent Hearing', *The New Zealand Herald*, May 2, pp. A1, A3.

Parata, R. (1995), 'Maori Investment for the Future', *Proceedings of the Hui Whakapumau, Maori Development Conference*, August 1994, Department of Maori Studies, Massey University, Palmerston North, pp. 149-160.

Patrick, H. (1966), 'Financial Development and Economic Growth in Underdeveloped Countries', *Economic Development and Cultural Change*, Vol. 14(2), pp. 174-189.

Psacharopoulos, G. and Patrinos, H. (eds) (1993), *Indigenous People and Poverty in Latin America: An Empirical Analysis*, Latin American Technical Department, Regional Studies Program, World Bank, August.

Riley, M. and Moran, K. (2001), 'Protecting Indigenous Property Rights: Tools that Work', in M. Riley and K. Moran (eds), 'Intellectual Property Rights: Culture as Commodity', *Cultural Survival Quarterly*, Vol. 24(4), http://www.cs.org/publications/CSQ/244/introduction.htm (accessed 22 April, 2002).

Rose, D., Sanderson, K., Morgan, P., Stuart, G., and Andrews, G. (1997), *Factors Inhibiting or Impeding Maori Economic Development*, Business and Economic Research Limited, Wellington.

Schaper, M. (1999), *Journal of Small Business Management*, Vol. 37(3), pp. 88-93.

Shatz, S. (1987), 'Assertive Pragmatism and the Multi-national Enterprise', in D. Becker and R. Sklar (eds), *Postimperialism: International Capitalism and Development in the Late Twentieth Century*, Lynne Reinner, Boulder, CO, pp. 93-105.

Solomon, M. and Watson, L. (2001), 'The Waitangi Tribunal and the Maori Claim to their Cultural and Intellectual Heritage Rights Property' in M. Riley and K. Moran (eds), 'Intellectual Property Rights: Culture as Commodity', *Cultural Survival Quarterly*, Vol. 24(4), http://www.cs.org/publications/CSQ/244/solomonwatson.htm (accessed 22 April, 2002).

Statistics New Zealand (2001), 'Census Snapshot', http://www.stats.govt.nz/ (accessed 26 March, 2002).

Statistics New Zealand (2002), *Household Labour Force Survey December 2001 Quarter*, Statistics New Zealand, Wellington.

Sullivan, A. and Margaritis. D. (2000), 'Public Sector Reform and Indigenous Entrepreneurship', *International Journal of Entrepreneurial Behaviour and Research*, Vol. 6(5), pp. 265-275.

Taylor, J. and Hunter, B. (1998), 'The Job Still Ahead: Economic Costs of Continuing Indigenous Employment Disparity', ATSIC, http://www.atsic.gov.au/ (accessed 22 March, 2002).

Te Puni Kokiri – Ministry of Maori Development (1999), *Maori Self Employment*, http://www.tpk.govt.nz/maori/work/self.htm (accessed 19 April, 2002).

Te Puni Kokiri – Ministry of Maori Development (2000), *Progress Towards Closing Social and Economic Gaps between Maori and non-Maori: A Report to the Minister of Maori Affairs*, Te Puni Kokiri, Wellington.

USM – University of Southern Mississippi Center for Community and Economic Development, (1999), *The Economic Impact of the Mississippi Band of Choctaw Indians on the State of Mississippi:* Executive Summary, http://www.choctaw.org/index/economics/ec/ec1/ec1.html (accessed 28 April, 2002),

Waitangi Tribunal (1988), *Muriwheua Report*, Government Printing Office, Wellington.

Waitangi Tribunal (1996), *The Taranaki Report: Kaupapa Tuatahi*, WAI 143, Government Printing Office, New Zealand.

Warhurst, A. (2001) 'Corporate Citizenship and Corporate Social Investment: Drivers of Tri-Sector Partnerships', *The Journal of Corporate Citizenship*, Vol. 1, Spring, pp. 57-73.

Chapter 11

Elder Entrepreneurship

Anne de Bruin and Patrick Firkin

Introduction

A range of social and economic factors is changing the relationship between older people and paid employment. Of significance is the contemporary challenge to the view of ageing as a time of withdrawal and decline. Consequently, use of a particular age, hitherto often taken as the age of 65, as an indicator of automatic transition out of the paid workforce is increasingly being questioned. Indeed the whole concept of retirement has become problematic. One aspect of this changing age-work relationship, and one which has garnered some attention in the media but less so in the academic literature, is the phenomenon of the older worker in self-employment, or the elder entrepreneur.

Despite the lack of comprehensive data, as early as 1986, *Venture* magazine was signalling the growth of entrepreneurship among older people (Aspaklaria, 1986). This was, as Marsh noted in her *Wall Street Journal* article a few years later, counter to conventional wisdom that views older people as risk averse and therefore less inclined to take chances associated with starting a business (Marsh, 1989). Several other journalists have drawn attention to the phenomenon of older entrepreneurs (see, for example Bacon, 1989; Shaver, 1991; Stern, 1991; Moore and Neuman, 1992; Murphy, 1992; Weissman, 1992; Norris, 1993; Minerd, 1999; *The Economist*, 1999).

As part of the trend towards acknowledging the differentiated experiences of particular sub-groups of entrepreneurs, initially conducted in terms of ethnicity or gender, there is emerging an interest in the older entrepreneur. Recent research into this phenomenon reported that 10 per cent of people starting new businesses were 50 years of age or older, and in the European Union the proportion of self-employed is very high in the 60 plus age groups (Peters *et al.*, 1999). Interestingly, this research found that businesses started by people around the age of 50 years have a rate of survival up to three times higher than those begun by people in their teens and early twenties (ibid). However, the growth level of these businesses was lower than those run by younger entrepreneurs. Peters *et al.* (1999) conclude that the numbers of elder entrepreneurs is likely to increase and continue to grow. This view is supported by Blackburn *et al.* (1998) who, in their targeted study of entrepreneurship in the 50 to 74 year age group, forecast an upsurge in entrepreneurship among those over 50 years. They cite a number of reasons that are explored in subsequent sections.

Although the media spotlight is often on large-scale enterprises of an entrepreneurial nature (see, for example *The Economist*, 1999), as with other groups, the entrepreneurial activities of older people are likely to centre on a diverse range of smaller, more mundane businesses, run on a full or part time basis. While many entrepreneurs have become self-employed at some point in their working lives and continue this activity as they get older, this chapter highlights the need for scrutiny of businesses that are begun when the entrepreneur is older. We are interested, therefore, in novice elder entrepreneurs and serial entrepreneurs who have started a further business when in the older age group.

The chapter initially outlines the available, though limited, literature on the participation of older people in entrepreneurial activity. Some possible drivers and motives that might explain why these entrepreneurs opt for self-employment at this stage of their life cycle are then canvassed. Woven into this discussion, in order to both supplement the existing literature and provide some supporting empirical material, are interview data from a major New Zealand research project – 'Labour Market Dynamics' (LMD).[1] Also incorporated is the work of Blackburn *et al.* (2000), which is one of the few available pieces of larger scale research to specifically target the elder entrepreneur. It explores the individual and business profiles of 669 people from the United Kingdom who were aged 45 years and older when starting a business. Given their very relevant focus, two pieces of much smaller scale qualitative research targeted at older female entrepreneurs are additionally drawn on (Kean *et al.*, 1993; McKay, 2001).

Interestingly, as a counter to the media's portrayal and scholarly views of this phenomenon, research in the United Kingdom suggests that there is a low enthusiasm for entrepreneurship among those in the Third Age (Curran and Blackburn, 2001). The authors explain this in terms of the low incomes of a large proportion of this age group, the high risk of self-employment itself and finally, the exaggerated views about the wishes of a longer living, healthier, Third Age cohort, to engage in the formal economy. We conclude the chapter, therefore, by emphasizing the need for more research on elder entrepreneurship, signalling some directions for future investigation in this area.

Before proceeding, however, it is necessary to clarify two issues. The first addresses the age at which the term 'elder' applies. A possible demarcation is the retirement age of 65 years, which is often used in relation to older workers (Statistics New Zealand, 1998). However, the following discussion shows that this is a problematic marker. As well, many of the issues that confront older people in the workforce apply to people in their 50s. The International Labour Organization uses the age of 55 years as their benchmark, though they acknowledge that some countries employ the much younger age of 45 years (ILO, 1995). Given the variations in age parameters in the literature and data on older workers, we opt for a mid-point between the extremes and adopt 50 years as the dividing line. This matches the eligibility for certain services and products and demarcates the start of the 'Third Age' (50 to 75 years) (Blackburn *et al.*, 1998).

The second issue concerns the meaning of entrepreneurship and its related terms. In the context of this discussion we see entrepreneurship as a multi-faceted phenomenon, made up of two forms – opportunity and necessity entrepreneurship (Reynolds *et al.*, 2001: 4-5). The former occurs when businesses are started and grown to take an advantage of a unique market opportunity, while the latter covers instances when businesses are started because it is the best option available, for instance following redundancy or job loss. Illustrating this is the case of one of the LMD research participants who, after being laid off from a farm management position and being unable to get further work in this area, started his own fencing business. Regardless of the form it takes, we also define entrepreneurship quite broadly to encompass a range of activities from self-employment to the creation of substantial organizations (Reynolds, 1991).

Ageing and Entrepreneurship: The Literature

As Peters *et al.* (1999) note, there is mixed evidence on the relationship between self-employment status and age. It is generally accepted, however, that self-employment demonstrates lifecycle effects (Fuchs, 1982; Leung and Robinson, 1998) with participation rising by age (Fuchs, 1982; Evans and Leighton, 1989; Quinn and Kozy, 1996; Blanchflower, 1998; Leung and Robinson, 1998). This has also been confirmed in the course of detailed research into specific groups of self-employed, such as studies among ethnic minorities (Clark and Drinkwater, 1998). Evans and Leighton (1989) observe that this age related trend into self-employment increases until the early 40s and then remains constant until retirement. More commonly, a pattern is described of gradual build up which peaks during a middle period and then declines (Blackburn *et al.*, 1998; Peters *et al.*, 1999; Reynolds *et al.*, 2001). Reviewing three data sets from the United Kingdom, Blackburn *et al.* (1998) report that those over 45 years contribute much more to self-employment and business ownership than younger age groups. This confirms, for them, the idea of an 'age launch window'. Based on a number of other commentators, they suggest this window exists from the early 30s to mid 40s. Peters *et al.* (1999) set these parameters at 30 to 40 years. Alternatively, Reynolds *et al.* (2001) find the years between ages 25 and 44 to be the most active, with 55 per cent of activity occurring during this period and the balance evenly distributed either side. Those aged 45 years and older make up 22 per cent of entrepreneurs in the countries surveyed in the Global Entrepreneurship Monitor (GEM) report.

Participation rates, both in general and more specifically in relation to older age groups, vary between countries (Peters *et al.*, 1999; Reynolds *et al.*, 2001). In reviewing European Union states, Peters *et al.* (1999) observe that Denmark, Sweden, Portugal and Greece have a somewhat older self-employed population than other countries, such as Belgium and Italy, where younger age groups are over-represented. Despite the absence of any analysis of entrepreneurship in people aged over 65 years, the GEM Report in New Zealand shows a 'significant degree of participation [in entrepreneurial activity] by people older than 35 years' (Frederick and Carswell, 2001: 20). This runs against the international trend described above, and gives New Zealand the highest proportion of older entrepreneurs among all the countries reported on in the literature.

Another important trend noted internationally (Fuchs, 1982; Quinn and Kozy, 1996), and in New Zealand (Haines, 1991; Bururu, 1998), is for the participation rates in self-employment to markedly increase for those over 65 years. Labour market statistics from New Zealand, illustrate this well. Although the 1996 New Zealand Census (Statistics New Zealand, 1998) indicates that labour force participation declines gradually from about the age of 55 years, and more sharply after age 60, of all those over the age of 65 years engaged in full-time work, over half (51.1 per cent) were self-employed.[2] While those in this group who were working part time were less likely to be self-employed, still more than a third (34.7 per cent) of those over 65 worked this way.[3] This may be explained, according to Blackburn *et al.* (1998: 22), by the fact that 'although many in the Third Age become economically inactive in this period (mainly through retirement), those who remain economically active are often self-employed'. Thus, compared with employees, the self-employed have more control over their ongoing involvement in work, and may be able to more easily vary their hours and conditions to suit their personal circumstances so as to continue working or develop a staged or partial retirement (Fuchs, 1982; Quinn and Kozy, 1996).

Although on a smaller scale, two other pieces of data can be added from New Zealand. Gilbertson *et al.* (1994) were surprised to find 14 per cent of new entrepreneurs attending a course with the Small Business Unit of the Capital Development Agency in Wellington, were in the 50 years and older category. In terms of the LMD study referred to earlier, just under a quarter of the 46 entrepreneurial individuals or couples who were interviewed qualified as older entrepreneurs. Another six (13 per cent) had commenced businesses in their late 40s. Of the former group, most had started businesses when they were younger and maintained them into their senior years. Only one would meet the criteria for a novice elder entrepreneur and his experiences are presented in the next section, as the case of Tom. Another three were serial entrepreneurs who commenced their second enterprises when over the age of 50 years. Those who began their businesses while in their 40s were evenly split between novice and serial entrepreneurs.

While various indications of the participation rates of older people in self-employment can be determined, there are severe limits on these data. Little specific information exists on the size and make-up of those who engage in self-employment after the age of 50 years, either as a novice or serial entrepreneur. Compounding this international problem are methodological decisions to exclude entrepreneurs over 65 years from an analysis. Lin *et al.* (1998) do this in order to generate a 'typical workforce sample'. Similarly, the GEM (Frederick and

Carswell, 2001; Reynolds *et al.*, 2001) surveys the 'working age population' of numerous countries. Rather than this population being made up of all those engaged in paid work, however, it is set between 18 and 64 years, thereby offering no information beyond what is now seen as an arbitrary cut-off point.

Not only is there very limited data available on the group that Fuchs (1982) identifies as 'switching' to self-employment later in life – as opposed to the self-employed who, over time, age with their businesses – but determining the role of age in influencing such a switch appears mixed. This may be because, as Peters *et al.* (1999) demonstrate, the effects of age need to be considered in light of their inter-relationship with other determinants – such as opportunity, attitudes and qualities, class, gender, education, financial resources, experience and background (general, industry-specific and self-employment) and employment status. Other factors such as research time-frames, sample sizes and constitution, and levels of analysis also need to be considered.

The uncertain relationship between participation rates and the influence of age-related factors is well illustrated by Blanchflower *et al.* (2001: 680 – emphasis in original) who found that while the probability of self-employment increases with age, 'the probability of *preferring to be self-employed* is strongly decreasing with age'. The latter part of their finding seems to be supported by research with a group of 463 people in the United Kingdom aged between 50 and 75 years (Curran and Blackburn, 2001) who were surveyed regarding their attitudes to self-employment, and proved to have limited enthusiasm for such as option. Prominent among the reasons[4] for people not considering self-employment were the absence of income guarantees (64.8 per cent) and the feeling that it was too late or they were too old (60.8 per cent). A lack of job security and the high risk associated with this form of work were equally important considerations for some (50.4 per cent), while stress (43.2 per cent), long hours (40 per cent), a lack of knowledge (39.2 per cent) and other commitments (30.4 per cent), were significant issues for a number of people. Between a quarter and a fifth of people rated cashflow (24.8 per cent), pensions (24 per cent), record keeping (22.4 per cent), finding customers (20 per cent) and getting finance (19.2 per cent) as issues. Curran and Blackburn (ibid) conclude, 'it is difficult to argue that this explanatory study found more than a moderate level of interest among the 50 to 75 age group for self-employment'.

It is against this background of uncertainty and limited specific data that we now explore a range of factors that may be implicated in the transition to self-employment late in a person's working life. Many of these factors are seen by Blackburn *et al.* (1998) as contributing to, or as possible influences on, the upwards movement of the 'age launch window'. This movement opens up the possibility that many more older people will become self-employed.

Causal Factors of Elder Entrepreneurship

The decision to enter self-employment is often the result of a mix of push and pull factors (Bururu, 1998; Clark and Drinkwater 1998; McGregor and Tweed, 1998; Morris, 1998) and later life entrepreneurship is no exception. In this section we highlight and discuss some broad, and other more individual-specific influences, that might drive, encourage, or attract people into self-employment. While many of these factors will be similar to those that operate with entrepreneurs of any age, we have attempted to isolate those that might impact especially on older people, and to identify the aspects of others that have particular relevance to this group. Given that many factors have the potential to impact positively or negatively on the self-employment decision, in some cases we consider both possibilities. As well, we give examples of how factors that lie behind one person's drive to become self-employed, can have an opposite effect in another case.

As a result of low birth rates and stable, or declining populations, the proportion of older people in developed countries is rising (Turner *et al.*, 1998). Larger numbers of any particular group are likely to increase the proportion of that group in an activity. The media often credits this as a principle reason for the growing numbers of older entrepreneurs (Minerd, 1999; *The Economist*, 1999). Although the demographic bulge that is the baby boomer generation offers an explanation based on larger numbers of people passing through various life stages, it cannot be the whole story. While this would account for higher numbers of self-employed people at all ages within this group, including the older sub-groups, it does not explain the sense that is gained from media reports that a growing proportion of older people are choosing to work this way later in life.

Alongside demographic patterns, advances in medicine and improvements in public health and social well-being have seen older people live longer and previously debilitating conditions are now able to be treated, or their worst effects often postponed till later in life (Moody, 1994). Therefore early old age no longer signals a period of rapid decline. Improvements in health status are an important factor that allows the older person more opportunities. Consequently, we see more older people engaged in a range of activities and settings. Certainly, only 8.8 per cent of those surveyed by Curran and Blackburn (2001) considered health problems as reasons for not considering self-employment. In a kind of circular pattern the experiences of the elderly reinforce that pre-existing, stereotypical views of this group may be faulty. However, modification to accommodate the new reality could open up further opportunities for the elderly, previously circumscribed by attitudes.

This virtuous circle is well illustrated in the work of Kean *et al.* (1993). Using the cases of five older women who started businesses late in life, these authors were able to demonstrate some correspondence between key features of successful ageing and the move into self-employment. In conclusion, they call for more effort to be made in promoting self-employment among older people since 'entrepreneurship among seniors encourages vitality and leads to a more productive and satisfying ageing process' (Kean *et al.*, 1993: 40). In a similar vein, some of those interviewed by McKay (2001) indicated that their entrepreneurial activities contributed to their self esteem, keeping them active, and countering ageism.

Another reason for changing views of ageing comes from a greater realization that, although we often tend to treat the elderly as a homogenous group, this is erroneous. Not only do individuals of the same age display wide heterogeneity in their experiences of ageing across all spheres, there is also clear diversity across groups.[5] Research by Blackburn *et al.* (2000) illustrates this by highlighting various age and gender related differences between the experiences of younger (45 to 55 years) and older (55 years and over) Third Age entrepreneurs, and men and women. For instance, in relation to gender, men were much more likely than women to cite push factors as the reason for setting up a business. In an example of age based differences, those in the older category were more likely to see finance as the solution to set up difficulties, while younger entrepreneurs were more likely to want to undergo formal training and seek professional advice. Research by McKay (2001) reinforces both gender and age issues by pointing not only to the differences between male and female entrepreneurs, but also to the effects of generational and life cycle factors.

Cohorts represent an important distinction to consider, since members share similar opportunities and experiences (Uhlenberg and Miner, 1996). Leung and Robinson (1998) suggest that cohort differences might help explain variations in areas such as education, willingness to take risks, and desire for independence, and the effects these have on self-employment rates. As well, given the positive relationship between education and entrepreneurship, Blackburn *et al.* (1998) acknowledge that the lower overall educational profile of current Third Agers may mean a lower rate of entrepreneurial activity. However, they suggest that newer age cohorts may be educationally better equipped to exploit knowledge- and technology-based opportunities which will likely characterize a great deal of future entrepreneurial activity. While agreeing that older cohorts of women may have been educationally disadvantaged, McKay (2001) is more cautious about this positive future scenario, noting that women may still face certain obstacles in terms of education. Outside of training and education, Blackburn *et al.* (1998) note that younger cohorts may be healthier and better financially prepared as they age.

Against the positive shifts that are occurring in terms of attitudes and perceptions of the elderly, discrimination based on age still operates within society and has been shown to negatively affect older people's job tenure and employment status (Encel, 1997; Johnson and Neumark, 1997). This is despite age discrimination being illegal in many jurisdictions. Many of those interviewed as part of the LMD study perceived and experienced this type of discrimination and its effects. Peters *et al.* (1999: 72) neatly summarize the connection between this sort of discrimination and movements by older people into self-employment: 'It may also be that so-called "active ageist policies" in companies with respect to hiring, training and lay-offs may increase the number of older workers seeking work but not as employees'. Another aspect of discrimination is the ageism experienced by older people when they are trying to start a business. This was significant enough in the United Kingdom to warrant a special government initiative to try to 'overcome gaps in services, advice and opportunities to counter [such] discrimination' (*Professional Engineering*, 1999).

Policy and legislative changes could be a further influence on the decision to engage in self-employment later in life. In general terms, the removal of the compulsory retirement age, and legislation that outlaws discrimination based on age, are likely to impact on people's engagement with paid work. Retirement is thus becoming a far more fluid phenomenon. It should be noted, however, that the problematizing of traditional views of retirement, while perhaps novel for men, is less so for women who frequently bridge paid and unpaid spheres and whose lives are not so rigidly demarcated by rhythms of paid work (Onyx and Benton, 1996). Given this fluidity, there is increasing attention to the notion of partial or staged retirement (Quinn and Kozy, 1996; Moody, 2000). Self-employment in later life may offer ways to facilitate this partial approach to retirement by offering a graduated exit from paid work and/or providing more flexible working hours (Fuchs, 1982; Quinn and Kozy, 1996).

Changes to the eligibility age for government social security payments (in New Zealand the National Superannuation eligibility age moved from 60 to 65 years) are also likely to have a substantial impact on older people's considerations of paid work (Statistics New Zealand, 1998). Peters *et al.* (1999: 73) rate access to state pensions as a significant issue in influencing the willingness of older people to become, or continue as, self-employed.

Specific measures to try and address the ageing workforce may also have an influence on older people's participation in self-employment. For example, Reynolds *et al.* (2001) suggest that in those countries with low proportions of people in the 25-44 years age group, which the GEM Report finds as the years of highest entrepreneurial participation, governments might want to encourage people in other age groups, especially the elderly, to be more active in entrepreneurial activity to make up this shortfall and increase their overall self-employment rate. Peters *et al.* (1999) acknowledge this policy approach as a possible driver, while Blackburn *et al.* (1998) note the individual and collective benefits that might be gained from greater entrepreneurial activity by older people.

A significant affect of age on entrepreneurial involvement is, quite simply, that people gradually make the shift into self-employment over a working life (Evans and Leighton, 1989; Blanchflower *et al.*, 2001). Such a shift might be prompted by it becoming easier with age to break into entrepreneurship (Blanchflower *et al.*, 2001), or by people gathering the necessary resources and being exposed to numerous opportunities across time (Evans and Leighton, 1989). Blackburn *et al.* (1998: 21) suggest that 'the over-50's, ... have had more chance to acquire the correct characteristics, especially occupational experience, capital and a stable domestic environment' necessary to embark on some form of entrepreneurial activity. These and other related factors are now considered in more detail.

Throughout their personal and working lives, older people will have built up a range of skills, knowledge, expertise, experience and contacts. These human and social capital factors are valuable and necessary resources for any entrepreneur (Morris, 1998). Such capital may be specific to the industry or sector that the person has largely been involved in, but also incorporates more general skills and experiences in the workforce. One participant interviewed in the LMD study shifted from farming to developing a wool insulation business based in large part on the knowledge, skills and contacts he had built up over many years. However, lengthy service, especially in one area or industry, or with one employer, can reduce the more general applicability of skills, thereby limiting possibilities in self-employment. When he was made redundant after 30 years as an electrician with a single company, another participant in the LMD study briefly considered, and then rejected, setting up his own business. He believed that working for so long with one employer in a restricted area had narrowed his skill base. Consequently, though he had worked for 30 years in his field, his role had been so specific that he now talked of having to 'get back into his trade'.

Of course, the accumulation of capital need not be confined to paid work and employment. As the studies by Kean *et al.* (1993) and McKay (2001) point out, this is especially true for women. Life experiences can be just as important (McKay, 2001) and, as Kean *et al.* (1993:39) put it, the choice of some form of self-employment in later life can draw on the wide range of experience and skills that people have refined over a lifetime. In this way, such entrepreneurial activity comes to represent an extension of their life history.

In his study of older white urban males Fuchs found that the type of work people did was a highly influential factor, such that those who switched late in life to self-employment were in 'wage and salary jobs that are similar in many respects to self-employment' (1982: 347), giving examples of managers, professionals and salesmen. Interestingly, Quinn and Kozy (1996) argue that some might opt for self-employment late in life in order to try a completely different type of work. This was the case for one of the LMD interviewees, whose experiences are briefly outlined later. Prior experience in self-employment was also an important factor identified by Fuchs (1982), and it proved to be influential for the serial entrepreneurs interviewed as part of the LMD study who had started subsequent businesses as they got older. Equally important is the match between skills and experience, and the types of entrepreneurial ventures on offer, or most in demand (Blackburn *et al.*, 2000).

Access to finance is recognized as important in a business start-up and lack of capital is a frequently noted obstacle (see for example Evans and Leighton, 1989; Blanchflower, 1998; Blanchflower and Oswald, 1998; Peters *et al.*, 1999; Blanchflower *et al.*, 2001). Consequently, Blanchflower and Oswald (1998: 28) contend that with 'all else equal, people with greater family assets are more likely to switch to self-employment from employment'. The elder entrepreneur might be advantaged by having a stronger economic base on which to draw, for example, redundancy payments, private pension monies, savings built up over the life cycle and equity in property (Blackburn *et al.*, 1998). Against this there might be difficulties faced by older entrepreneurs in securing loans and finance – perhaps the result of ageist attitudes, as well as the additional dangers inherent in risking money earmarked for retirement. Indeed in their study of Third Age entrepreneurs, Blackburn *et al.* (2000) found that problems obtaining finance were the most common and major difficulty facing this group, and these were most pronounced among the older categories. Improving access to finance was seen as a primary way of overcoming a significant obstacle to starting a business by many in this study, and just over one quarter of participants saw help with finding appropriate finance as the most important element of the business support they needed. Problems accessing finance were a reason for a fifth of respondents preferring not to be self-employed in a survey of those over 50 years (Curran and Blackburn, 2001).

Financial factors may operate in other diverse ways to promote self-employment. Statistics New Zealand (1998) note that elderly people who work are better off financially. This creates an incentive to engage in some form of paid work, even if the person is retired from a full time job. As the age of entry to government pension schemes rises, or the level of payment decreases, older people may have to consider remaining in some form of paid work to offset these changes. Any ongoing engagement with paid work might take the form of self-employment in some manner, a motivation Kean *et al.* (1993) observe in their American study. Similarly, some of the older women interviewed by McKay (2001) were motivated to engage in self-employment by a desire to augment their income. The experiences of a farming couple, interviewed as part of the LMD study, illustrate different aspects of this discussion on financial factors. Having sold their farm they decided to invest much of the capital in an innovative, but risky, orchard venture, with the intention of augmenting their retirement fund. Unfortunately, a range of problems saw the project fail and swallow up the equity from the farm sale that they had used in the development.

Other factors that could be implicated in the decision to embark on self-employment later in life emerge over the lifecycle. One that was mentioned by some of the LMD study interviewees was the opportunity that arose once a person or couple's family grew up and left home. This is the stable domestic environment that Blackburn *et al.* (1998) talk of. Given the negative impact on families that self-employment can have, an issue frequently mentioned in the LMD interviews and noted by Gilbertson *et al.* (1994), some people felt much more comfortable embarking on a business knowing it would not affect their children or family life. McKay (2001) found family and flexibility to be two key differences between the motivations and considerations of younger and older women entrepreneurs. While younger women might be influenced by family responsibilities and issues – either not to engage in self-employment because of these or to structure any self-employment around them – older women were not so constrained or motivated. Such a view is echoed by the Carnegie, UK Trust who see those aged 50 years and older as being freer from the constraints of work and a family, but not so old as to be infirm (cited in Peters *et al.*, 1999: 20). Similarly, Morris (1998) views semi-retirement as a time when people might feel better able to experiment socially and professionally. The influence of family in entrepreneurial decisions is captured in the comments from one of the LMD interviewees. He and his wife had been contract and sharemilkers for much of their working lives but, up until recently, had made their family the key consideration when choosing farms.

> We could have been bigger than we are now but we started when we were 29 and I already had children then and so we took each one of our steps and we probably weighed it up more because I didn't want the kids to suffer either. So we probably took less of a risk than we could have to be a bit more secure for the kids. ...But now we don't have to worry about them. ...The next place that we go to we only have to worry about us two. For me it's always been I've got to look at this and see if the kids would fit in. And all of sudden I think we've only got to worry about us.

While the desire to be self-employed is strongest amongst the young (Blanchflower *et al.*, 2001), this need not preclude some older people possessing the various personal characteristics necessary to start their own business and seeking the higher levels of life and job satisfaction that self-employment can bring (Blanchflower, 1998). Older workers may keenly feel such desires after many years as an employee, however Blackburn *et al.* (1998) find contradictory evidence on the relationship between age and job satisfaction. Though the 'desire to become my own boss' was found by Peters *et al.* (1999: 44) to be high with younger people, but fall and reach a minimum around middle age, it rose again with older groups. Older people need not always seek to avoid the challenges that self-employment can bring. This is illustrated by the experiences of one couple, aged in their 50s and interviewed as part of the LMD study, who had started a speciality meat processing venture.

> It was either [this] or just stay in the comfort zone and get bored and frustrated and probably be dead by the time we were sixty when we may as well be alive when we're 75 or 80.

Quite simply, as the wife of the farmer-turned-orchardist couple put it, entrepreneurship is in people's blood, so age serves as no obstacle if such a desire is there.

Older people doing particularly physical work, can face limitations which make them consider changing the type of work they do, as highlighted by the comments of this sheetmetal worker, interviewed in the LMD study.

> I don't want to be doing it till I'm 65. ...The factory is freezing cold [in winter], because that's the nature, it's an all steel installation. You've got about three rollers out all the time so it gets fairly hot in the summer.

Though he was not in physically demanding work, this next interviewee welcomed the change from the stress and demands of business that buying and running a second-hand bookshop brought him.

> It's fabulous, relaxed, no stress. I open at 9.00am, I close at 5.00pm, I come home and that's it. And I've got into a nice routine. I like swimming so I go down to [the] pool every morning about 7.30am and swim and get down to the shop round about 8.30am. Go and have a coffee at the café and open the shop about quarter to nine.

In this vein, the possibility that self-employment brings for modifying hours of work as a person gets older, can be an important factor in deciding to become self-employed (Fuchs, 1982; Quinn and Fozy, 1996).

Of course, major changes, or the prospect of them late in one's life, can bring significant challenges. This was evident in a study of older people's attitudes to self-employment and the reasons given by respondents for not starting a business (Curran and Blackburn, 2001). These included worries over income, job security, risk, stress, feeling too old or that it was too late, and coping with the long hours. For all manner of reasons, the thought of embarking on a new direction also drew out a very negative response in some of those interviewed in the LMD study, and they expressed little hope that they could make such changes. Age, again, was sometimes the reason. The electrician mentioned earlier saw this as another key factor against his becoming self-employed.

> [It's] too competitive. [I'm] too old to compete with the young guys. There are a lot of young contractors in this city. Maybe 30 years ago I should have had a crack at it but now. ...I know myself that my age is against me.

Alongside these various factors are the context in which self-employment takes place. Somewhat against the OECD trend (Blanchflower, 1998), self-employment is a growing feature of the New Zealand economy and a prominent facet of its labour market. New Zealand was one of five countries with the highest prevalence of entrepreneurial activity in the GEM research (Reynolds *et al.*, 2001). Also to be considered at the broader level are the impacts of the radical economic transformation of the New Zealand economy since the mid 1980s and the effects of the shifting economic climate. As Davidson (1995) observes, the fundamental restructuring that the New Zealand economy has undergone over recent years has had significant implications for the nature of work and the structure of the labour force. The impact of these changes, large scale private and public organization restructurings, wider responses to economic recessions, labour market deregulation and the influence of technological changes, have been cited as drivers behind the marked growth in self-employment (Haines, 1991; Bururu, 1998). As evidence of the effect of these influences there was a significant increase in self-employment and the number of small business over the 1980s, a time of major structural change in the economy (Davidson, 1995).

In terms of the relationship of older workers to such a changing labour market there are, however, contradictory views. Thus the impact on their decision-making is uncertain. As Quadagno and Hardy (1996: 336-7) point out, some evidence:

> Implies that older workers are a privileged group, because they have relatively low rates of unemployment, are the least likely of all groups to be employed part-time for economic reasons as opposed to voluntary reasons, and least likely to be fully employed but not earning enough to raise family income above the poverty line.

Yet, they also note that research has found that older workers have been 'especially vulnerable to downsizing resulting from manufacturing declines and have benefited little from the expansion of services'. This negative impact of downsizing more generally has been acknowledged by the International Labour Organization (ILO) (Encel, 1997), and Henretta (2001) observes that the vulnerability of older workers may be increasing. Those falling into the younger bracket of the older category, that is below the age of eligibility for social security benefits, are the most susceptible to job loss, often with an inability to get further employment after this loss (Quadagno and Hardy, 1996; Chan and Stevens, 2001). Hence our interest in the groups under traditional retirement age. Encel (1997: 138) notes that the ILO has identified the concentration of older people among the long-term, chronically unemployed in all industrialized countries, as an issue of major concern. Noting a particular gender bias, Blackburn *et al.* (2000) report the general trend towards each successive generation of men being less likely to be employed at the age of 50 years than the preceding one.

In some cases, therefore, labour market factors may exert some pressure to become self-employed. For instance, Felstead *et al.* (1999: 8) found that 'non-standard' workers from Canada and the United Kingdom, which in their terms included the self-employed and a range of other alternative working arrangements, were more likely to be from one end or other of the age spectrum, and older workers 'may be in this status involuntarily, perhaps pushed out of full time and permanent jobs because of labour market restructuring and corporate downsizing'. Interview data from the LMD study revealed many older people worried about their job security and ability to get further jobs if laid off. Some experienced this vulnerability first hand. Though none of the older people who were interviewed and had such experiences turned to self-employment, this is a group who could take such an option. In their study of Third Age entrepreneurs Blackburn *et al.* (2000) found that an inability to find a job was the second most significant reason for moving into business ownership (11 per cent of their sample). A slightly different perspective on the impact of labour market factors comes from some of the women McKay (2001:159) interviewed. After many years out of or on the periphery of the workforce they 'believed that their age, work experience and gender would prevent them from finding meaningful and challenging jobs' and so they chose to become self-employed.

Public and private sector restructuring could be implicated in various ways in promoting self-employment amongst older workers. Though they did not consider its affect on self-employment, in a recent study of mature job seekers in New Zealand, McGregor and Gray (2001) found that around 18 per cent of men had become unemployed after being made redundant. This climbed to 33 per cent in the 51-55 years age group. Peters *et al.* (1999: 42-43) found that redundancy as a motivation for self-employment increases with proprietor age. Necessity entrepreneurship also featured prominently in the Blackburn *et al.* (2000) study, with redundancy being the most prominent reason for starting a business among those surveyed (22 per cent of their sample).

Restructuring often involves the contracting out of roles previously performed in a company, thereby reducing company workforces but increasing opportunities for self-employment. Thus, private contracting and consultancy work may result in internal job losses, but open up self-employment opportunities for displaced workers (Haines, 1991). One couple interviewed in the LMD study, and who managed a processing plant for a large company, saw both risks and opportunities when the company decided to sell off the plant and contract out the work. Ultimately, given the area they lived in and their age they felt they had few options, other than to buy the plant themselves. This proved to be a sound decision for a few years, until the couple experienced the reverse process when the company elected to once again undertake the operation themselves, forcing the business to close. They were then left with having to find other employment. Even if people were not victims of these ongoing and significant changes, as will be seen in the case discussed next, having to continually live with such uncertainty might still prompt a move into self-employment.

The experiences of Tom,[6] a novice elder entrepreneur in the LMD study, illustrate well the impact of New Zealand's economic restructuring, privatization and labour market change. Tom had worked for the same state enterprise in the banking sector, since he left school in the late 1950s, progressing to managerial level. From the mid-1980s he experienced and survived several waves of rationalization, reorganization and downsizing of the organization. Privatization in 1990 also saw him retaining his employment. However, when word of another major restructuring became known in 1996, he decided that he had had enough and took early retirement. Tom started his own business, interestingly in a field completely different from the banking industry. He bought a catering business with the proceeds from early retirement. Despite enjoying this business, he realized after about a year that he could utilize his specialist skills and knowledge to better advantage. Consequently, he had put the catering company on the market and was looking for new opportunities in the finance industry, by moving into his own mortgage broking business. At the close of the interview Tom summed up the course his working life had taken by considering how things had changed. In doing so he illustrates typical push factors and labour market changes that might prompt, or even force, some older people into self-employment later in life:

I guess people, or most people, get in a comfort zone. And they, not so much these days, but it used to happen – you used to leave school, start a career and expect to be in that job when you retire in 40 years time. That's gone. It's not necessarily a bad thing, but I guess sometimes changes are forced on you.

Many of the opportunities for self-employment arising from organization restructuring fall into the broad categories of corporate management and associated professionals (Bururu, 1998). After agricultural/fishery and trades groups, these two are the next biggest sources of self-employment in New Zealand (ibid). They would broadly fit into Cohany's (1996) definition of independent contractors, the largest category of workers with alternative employment arrangements in the United States. Cohany goes on to note that, as a group, men who are 65 years and older are over represented amongst independent contractors. This may be explained by the nature of contract jobs that emerge from restructuring and who is likely to fill them. However, Cohany also points out that the proportion of independent contractors who work part time exceeds that of traditional workers and suggests that this is the result of the older age profile. Independent contracting may thus offer older people bridging employment, or greater working flexibility more generally, two motives for self-employment already canvassed.

In terms of the relationship between unemployment and self-employment rates, Peters *et al.* (1999) raise the importance of distinguishing between individual and aggregate unemployment, though contrasting arguments can be made in both cases. Unemployment can prompt individuals to seek other work alternatives, but can also negatively affect people so as to diminish their drive and resources for seeking employment. High levels of aggregate unemployment reduce the chances of people finding work as employees, but also limit business opportunities. Importantly, however, experiences and circumstances differ between groups. It is possible for instance, as Blackburn *et al.* (2000) note, to have high levels of unemployment among older people, even at times of economic stability. In the New Zealand context, Bradford claims that 'because so many people have had to face the despair of long-term unemployment, there have been increasing moves into profit making self or group employment' (cited in Davidson, 1995: 109). While their research does not draw the implication that being a beneficiary drove people into self-employment, McGregor and Tweed (1998) found that 5.2 per cent of a group of 1,514 small and medium enterprise (SME) owners they surveyed, had been in receipt of a welfare benefit at some time in the preceding three years. Peters *et al.* (1999: 42) found that avoiding unemployment was a significant motivation for both young and older people to start a business.

The range of choices available to people might offer another possible incentive for moving into 'non-standard' forms of work, of which different types of self-employment provide an array of options (Felstead *et al.*, 1999). Product market reforms may have stimulated greater opportunities (Bururu, 1998) and a host of alternatives outside the traditional, or typical types of businesses, have also emerged – franchise holders, independent contractors, pyramid sellers, cooperatives and 'community businesses' (Haines, 1991). Some of these may be well suited to the elder entrepreneur as Stern (1991) illustrates in respect of franchising in her piece on 'Late Blooming Entrepreneurs'.

Technology, too, may add to these new work forms and create other opportunities (Haines, 1991). Even if it has been fraught with uncertainty and is yet to realize the promised rewards, the dot.com revolution has undoubtedly signalled the possibilities that the internet offers. However, Kirkwood (2001) makes the important point that despite holding huge potential for older people, technology is geared much more towards the young. While one view of ageing might locate older people outside of the world of technology, the success of programmes such as SeniorNet seems to indicate that the elderly as a group cannot be so easily classified (Moody, 2000). Technology has allowed different forms of working, such as home or tele-working (Mangan, 2000), and will also transform other forms of work. As such, the nature and pace of technological change has implications for how older people work and the employment they engage in. As has already been noted, newer cohorts of older people will likely be better prepared to engage with new technology- and information-based opportunities.

Conclusion: Future Research

As McKay (2001) argues in respect of women, there is a need to recognize the diverse and heterogeneous nature of entrepreneurs and the groups they belong to, and to design and carry out research accordingly. Elder entrepreneurs are one such group and in exploring the phenomenon of Third Age entrepreneurship this chapter has highlighted the paucity of research in this area. To conclude we point to the need for future research to address these deficits and suggest some directions that might be fruitfully pursued. As Peters *et al.* (1999) note in respect of Europe, the importance of SMEs is being increasingly recognized. These are an integral part of the New Zealand economy (Cameron and Massey, 1999). It becomes important, therefore, to determine what the implications and effects of population ageing will be for entrepreneurship and the SME sector (Peters *et al.*, 1999: 8), making the exploration of elder entrepreneurship an area of growing interest and significance in social, economic, political and policy terms.

In a wider context, it would be valuable to expand the work of Blackburn and Curran (cited in Blackburn *et al.*, 2000) to assess the attitudes of older people toward entrepreneurship. This type of inquiry could also investigate the match between the education, skills, experience and interests of those in the Third Age, as compared to likely growth areas of entrepreneurial opportunity. As to entrepreneurial activity by this group, a number of areas of significant interest can be identified, many of which replicate more general entrepreneurial research. These include but need not be limited to:

- *The entrepreneurs*: their make up and backgrounds (traits, skills, qualifications, experience and prior entrepreneurial experience). An examination of in-group characteristics could be made, based on factors such as gender, ethnicity and the like, and age sub-groups could also be investigated. (Blackburn *et al.* (2000) and McKay (2001) have established the importance of such comparisons.) Some differentiation could be made between those entrepreneurs who started younger and have kept the business as they age, and those who start businesses when older (with this second group being classified into novice, serial and parallel entrepreneurs).
- *The businesses*: types, size, matches with entrepreneurs backgrounds, and longitudinal data (to explore viability and growth for instance).
- *The transitions*: timing (age of entrepreneur), reasons and process. The context also needs to be carefully considered on a number of levels, from factors such as economic climate, through to prevailing attitudes to older people. The effects of wider labour market trends and changes also need to be considered in this regard. Identifying the obstacles that are most difficult to overcome, and the most useful types of support and services would be valuable in policy terms.

Additionally, information on the networks, including web-based networks, of elder entrepreneurs would be of much interest. Other research could examine the changing relationship between older people and technology and explore the implications of this for elder entrepreneurship. Research could also canvas older entrepreneurs whose ventures did not survive. McGregor and Gray (2001), for instance, found that a small proportion, mostly male, of the mature job seekers they surveyed (16 per cent) had been forced to sell, or close, their own businesses. Though not often researched in detail, the nature of business failures among older entrepreneurs would provide interesting insights. Given Peters *et al.* (1999) finding that while more successful, businesses started by those over 50 years exhibited lower rates of growth, it seems important that comparisons are undertaken between the activities of elder entrepreneurs and those in other age groups. This could include the types of businesses, profiling the people and examining the processes involved. At a higher level, country studies could compare participation rates as well as identify and contrast social and economic factors that have a bearing on older people's entrepreneurial activities.

While additional information could be obtained by extending age parameters in other, more general, research and data sets, it is clear that dedicated research on self-employment among older workers is warranted. This could be conducted in a similar fashion to research that has been carried out on other groups, for instance self-employment among ethnic minorities. As well as statistical information and analysis, the interview data of the LMD study highlights the importance of qualitative data, such as work histories, in obtaining fine grain detail of, and important insights into, the entrepreneurial experiences of older workers.

Notes

1. The Labour Market Dynamics and Economic Participation (*LMD*) Programme, funded by the New Zealand Foundation for Research, Science and Technology, is an interdisciplinary research project that was initially designed to explain the dynamics of economic participation by exploring the interface between households and the labour market in three regional labour markets in New Zealand. The first phase of the *LMD* programme sought to explain how individuals made decisions about access and participation in the labour market, with emphasis on the life cycle of the household. The interview data we use here are from this first phase. See Shirley *et al.* (2001a, 2001b, 2001c, 2001d, 2001e), for further details.
2. This includes those who were self-employed, with employees and without employees.
3. Given that these figures are based on categories that include those unemployed and looking for work and those involved in unpaid work in a family business, the proportions would be much higher for those in some form of paid work alone.
4. These figures indicate the numbers of people who identified these reasons.
5. Calastani (1996) highlights this useful distinction between individual-level variation as heterogeneity, and group-based differences as diversity.
6. Not his real name.

References

Aspaklaria, S. (1986), 'Startups After Sixty', *Venture*, Vol. 8(9), pp. 30-33.

Bacon, D. (1989), 'Entrepreneurial Bug Biting More Older Americans', *Nation's Business*, Vol. 77(5), p. 6.

Blackburn, R., Hart, M. and O'Reilly, M. (2000), *Entrepreneurship in the Third Age: New Dawn or Misplaced Expectations?*, paper presented at 23rd ISBA National Small Firms Policy and Research Conference – 'Small Firms: Adding the Spark', Aberdeen University, 15-17 November, 2000.

Blackburn, R., Mackintosh, L. and North, J. (1998), *Entrepreneurship in the Third Age*, Small Business Research Centre (SBRC), Kingston University, Surrey.

Blanchflower, D. (1998), *Self-employment in OECD Countries*, paper presented at the International Conference on Self-Employment, Burlington, Ontario, Canada, September 24-26, http://cerf.mcmaster.ca/papers/seconf/oecd.pdf (accessed 2 July, 2000).

Blanchflower, D. and Oswald, A. (1998), 'What Makes an Entrepreneur?', *Journal of Labour Economics*, Vol. 16, pp. 26-60.

Blanchflower, D., Oswald, A. and Stutzer, A. (2001), '"Latent" Entrepreneurship Across Nations', *European Economic Review*, Vol. 45, pp. 680-691.

Bururu, R. (1998), 'Self-Employment in New Zealand', in *Labour, Employment and Work in New Zealand* – Proceedings of the 8th Annual Conference, Department of Geography, Victoria University of Wellington, Wellington.

Calastani, T. (1996), 'Incorporating Diversity: Meaning, Levels of Research, and Implications for Theory', *The Gerontologist*, Vol. 36(2), pp. 147-156.

Cameron, A. and Massey, C. (1999), *Small and Medium-Sized Enterprises: A New Zealand Perspective*, Longman, Auckland.

Chan, S. and Stevens, A. (2001), 'Job Loss and Employment Patterns of Older Workers', *Journal of Labour Economics*, Vol. 19(2), pp. 484-521.

Clark, K. and Drinkwater, S. (1998), *Pushed Out or Pulled In? Self-Employment Among Ethnic Minorities in England and Wales*, paper presented at the International

Conference on Self-Employment, Burlington, Ontario, Canada, September 24-26, http://cerf.mcmaster.ca/papers/seconf/pushed.pdf (accessed 16 July, 2001).

Cohany, S. (1996), 'Workers in Alternative Employment Arrangements', *Monthly Labor Review*, Vol. 119(10), pp. 31-45.

Curran, J. and Balckburn, R. (2001), 'Older People and the Enterprise Society: Age and Self-Employment Propensities', *Work, Employment and Society*, Vol. 15(4), pp. 889-902.

Davidson, C. (1995), 'Employment in New Zealand After the "Revolution": The Outcome of Restructuring in the 1980s', *British Review of New Zealand Studies (BRONZS)*, Vol. 8, pp. 99-115.

Encel, S. (1997), 'Work in Later Life', in A. Borowski, S. Encel and E. Ozanne (eds), *Ageing and Social Policy in Australia*, Cambridge University Press, Melbourne.

Evans, D. and Leighton, L. (1989), 'Some Empirical Aspects of Entrepreneurship', *American Economic Review*, Vol. 79(3), pp. 519-535.

Felstead, A., Krahn, H. and Powell, M. (1999), 'Young and Old at Risk: Comparative Trends in "Non-Standard" Patterns of Employment in Canada and the United Kingdom', *International Journal of Manpower*, Vol. 20(5), pp. 277-297.

Frederick, H. and Carswell, P. (2001), *Global Entrepreneurship Monitor: New Zealand 2001*, New Zealand Centre for Innovation and Entrepreneurship (UNITEC), Auckland.

Fuchs, V. (1982), 'Self-Employment and Labour Market Participation of Older Males', *Journal of Human Resources*, Vol. 17(3), pp. 339-357.

Gilberston, D., Wright, H., Yska, G., Gilbertson, D, and Students, (1994), *Kiwi Entrepreneurs: A Study*, The Graduate School of Business and Government Management, Working Paper Series, 1/95, January 1995, Victoria University of Wellington, Wellington.

Haines, L. (1991), *Small Business is Big Business: A Review of Trends and Policies*, New Zealand Planning Council, Wellington.

Henretta, J. (2001), 'Work and Retirement', in R. Binstock and L. George (eds), *Handbook of Ageing and the Social Sciences* (4th Edition), Academic Press, CA.

International Labour Office (1995), *World Labour Report 1995*, International Labour Organization (ILO), Geneva.

Johnson, R. and Neumark, D. (1997), 'Age Discrimination, Job Separations, and Employment Status of Older Workers', *The Journal of Human Resources*, Vol. 32(4), pp. 779-811.

Kean, R., Van Zandt, S. and Maupin, W. (1993), 'Successful Ageing: The Older Entrepreneur', *Journal of Women and Ageing*, Vol. 5(1), pp. 25-42.

Kirkwood, T. (2001), *The End of Age: New Directions*, Reith Lectures 2001 – Lecture 5, http://www.bbc.co.uk/radio4/reith2001/lecture5/shtml (accessed 2 April, 2002).

Leung, D. and Robinson, C. (1998), *Explaining the Recent Rise in Self-employment: Lifecycle, Cohort, and Aggregate Economy Effects*, paper presented at the International Conference on Self-Employment, Burlington, Ontario, Canada, September 24-26, http://cerf.mcmaster.ca/papers/seconf/rise.pdf (accessed 2 July, 2000).

Lin, Z., Yates, J. and Picot, G. (1998), *The Entry and Exit Dynamics of Self-Employment in Canada*, paper presented at the International Conference on Self-Employment, Burlington, Ontario, Canada, September 24-26, http://cerf.mcmaster.ca/papers/seconf/dynamics.pdf (accessed 2 July, 2000).

McGregor, J and Gray, L. (2001), *Mature Job-seekers in New Zealand*, Report of a Project from Massey University funded by the Public Good Science Fund, Massey University, Palmerston North.

McGregor, J. and Tweed, D. (1998), 'Unemployment to Self-Employment: The Long and Winding Road?', *Social Policy Journal of New Zealand*, Vol. 10, pp. 190-202.

McKay, R. (2001), 'Women Entrepreneurs: Moving Beyond Family and Flexibility', *International Journal of Entrepreneurial Behaviour and Research*, Vol. 7(4), pp. 148-165.

Mangan, J. (2000), *Workers Without Traditional Employment: An International Study of Non-standard Work*, Edward Elgar Publishing, Cheltenham, Gloucester.

Marsh, B. (1989), 'Baby Boomers to Continue the Fast Pace of Start-Ups in '90s: "Healthy, Wealthy Elderly Boom" in Entrepreneurial Activity is Forecast', *Wall Street Journal*, June 19, p.1.

Minerd, J. (1999), 'A "Gray Wave" of Entrepreneurs', *The Futurist*, Vol. 33(6), p. 10.

Moody, H. (1994), 'Four Scenarios for an Ageing Society', *The Hastings Center Report*, Vol. 24(5), pp. 32-35.

Moody, H. (2000), *Ageing: Concepts and Controversies* (3rd Edition), Pine Forge Press, CA.

Moore, L. and Newman, R. (1992), 'Great Businesses for Retirees Still Working', *U.S. News and World Report*, Vol. 112(20), pp. 80-83.

Morris, M. (1998), *Entrepreneurial Intensity: Sustainable Advantages for Individuals, Organisations, and Societies*, Quorum Books, Westport, CT.

Murphy, A. (1992), 'The Start-Up of the '90s', *Inc*, Vol. 14(3), p. 32.

Norris, M. (1993), 'Life Begins at 60 For a Change', *Nation's Business*, Vol. 81(9), p. 8.

Onyx, J. and Benton, P. (1996), 'Retirement: A Problematic Concept for Older Women', *Journal of Women and Aging*, Vol. 8(2), pp. 19-34.

Peters, M., Cressey, R. and Storey, P. (1999), *The Economic Impact of Ageing on Entrepreneurship and SMEs*, The Netherlands/United Kingdom, EIM Small Business Research and Consultancy and Warwick University.

Professional Engineering (Anonymous) (1999), 'Older Entrepreneurs Get Help to Fight Ageism', *Professional Engineering*, Vol. 12(10), p. 8.

Quadagno, J. and Hardy, M. (1996), 'Work and Retirement', in R. Binstock and L. George (eds), *Handbook of Ageing and the Social Sciences* (3rd Edition), Academic Press, CA.

Quinn, J. and Kozy, M. (1996), 'The Role of Bridge Jobs in the Retirement Transition: Gender, Race and Ethnicity', *The Gerontologist*, Vol. 36(3), pp. 363-372.

Reynolds, P. (1991), 'Sociology and Entrepreneurship: Concepts and Contributions', *Entrepreneurship: Theory and Practice*, Vol. 16(2), pp. 47-70.

Reynolds, P., Hay, M. Bygrave, W., Camp, S., and Autio, E. (2001), *Global Entrepreneurship Monitor: 2000 Executive Report*, Babson College, Babson, MA.

Shaver, K. (1991), 'Retirees Decide to Mind Their Own Businesses', *Wall Street Journal*, July 18, p. B1.

Shirley, I., Firkin, P., Cremer, R., Eichbaum, C., de Bruin, A., Dewe, P., Dupuis, A. and Spoonley, P. (2001a), *Transitions in the Hawkes Bay Labour Market: Education and Training*, Labour Market Dynamics Research Programme Research Report, Massey University, Albany and Palmerston North.

Shirley, I., Firkin, P., Cremer, R., Eichbaum, C., de Bruin, A., Dewe, P., Dupuis, A. and Spoonley, P. (2001b), *Transitions in the Hawkes Bay Labour Market: Welfare and Unemployment*, Labour Market Dynamics Participation Research Programme Research Report, Massey University, Albany and Palmerston North.

Shirley, I., Firkin, P., Cremer, R., Eichbaum, C., de Bruin, A., Dewe, P., Dupuis, A. and Spoonley, P. (2001c), *Transitions in the Hawkes Bay Labour Market: Unpaid Work and Paid Work*, Labour Market Dynamics Research Programme Research Report, Massey University, Albany and Palmerston North.

Shirley, I., Firkin, P., Cremer, R., Eichbaum, C., de Bruin, A., Dewe, P., Dupuis, A. and Spoonley, P. (2001d), *Transitions in the South Waikato Labour Market: An*

Ethnographic Study, Labour Market Dynamics Research Programme Research Report, Massey University, Albany and Palmerston North.

Shirley, I., Firkin, P., Cremer, R., Eichbaum, C., de Bruin, A., Dewe, P., Dupuis, A. and Spoonley, P. (2001e), *Transitions in the Waitakere Labour Market: An Ethnographic Study*, Labour Market Dynamics Participation Research Programme Research Report, Massey University, Albany and Palmerston North.

Statistics New Zealand (1998), *New Zealand Now: 65 Plus*, Statistics New Zealand, Wellington.

Stern, L. (1991), 'Late Blooming Entrepreneurs', *Home-Office Computing*, Vol. 9(11), pp. 28-32.

The Economist (Anonymous) (1999), 'Face Value: The Pygmy Problem', *The Economist*, Vol. 353, p. 68.

Turner, D., Giorno, C., De Serres, A., Vourc'h, A. and Richardson, P. (1998), *The Macroeconomic Implications of Ageing in a Global Context*, OECD Economics Department Working Papers No. 193, OECD, Paris.

Uhlenberg, P. and Miner, S. (1996), 'Life Course and Ageing: A Cohort Perspective', in R. Binstock and L. George (eds), *Handbook of Ageing and the Social Sciences* (3rd Edition), Academic Press, CA.

Weissman, M. (1992), 'Thinking Outside the Box', *World*, Vol. 26(3), pp. 24-31.

Chapter 12

Youth Entrepreneurship

Kate Lewis and Claire Massey

Introduction

If, as Krueger and Brazeal (1994) suggest, it is possible to speak of a single group as being entrepreneurial, or having the potential to be so, then the youth of today possess far more entrepreneurial potential than previous generations. They are forming their attitudes to employment and work in an age where there is an unprecedented focus on entrepreneurship and its stimulation: a global push for a culture of enterprise and the development of entrepreneurial individuals, groups and organizations. Given the amount of media attention that focuses on entrepreneurship and high profile entrepreneurs, it is almost impossible to believe that this environment will not play a major part in influencing an individual's perceptions about employment options. The consequence may well be an increase in the supply of individuals who are self-employed or who regard themselves as 'entrepreneurs' (Bruno and Tyebjee, 1982).

However, it is not easy to confirm whether this increase is occurring or not. While many different countries present anecdotal evidence to suggest the presence of an increasing number of young entrepreneurs (this term is used here to refer to those who establish businesses and those who are self-employed), there is a dearth of hard evidence. There are few countries where the official statistics record the age of the business owner, and in the past, age has not been a variable of great interest to those interested in labour market analysis. Even now, where researchers do examine age, they tend to focus on older workers rather than those who are young.

An equally significant gap in the literature on youth entrepreneurship is in the development of theories that apply specifically to this group. While much of the research implies that 'young entrepreneurs' are different from other entrepreneurs, there is an absence of theories that enable us to more clearly identify these differences and develop appropriate responses from the perspective of a policy-maker. For example, an understanding of the characteristics of young entrepreneurs compared to 'all entrepreneurs', would enable support measures and assistance programmes to be designed and delivered more effectively. However, while some researchers imply that young entrepreneurs are in some way special, they appear to be happy to apply general theories of entrepreneurship to the young.

Having said this, there are still gaps in our understanding of the way in which existing theories of entrepreneurship apply to this particular group. For example, although there is a substantial literature on the motivations of entrepreneurs in general, there has been little focus on the reasons why young people consider entering into entrepreneurial activities such as self-employment. There is also a lack of understanding of the decision-making processes young people engage in when considering entrepreneurship and self-employment. The consequence is that there is a lack of research on how to influence the decisions made by these individuals. There is also an ongoing debate within the literature on the best way to support young people both before and after start-up.

The first section of this chapter examines the literature on entrepreneurship and young people, with a particular focus on research relating to the barriers to business start-up for young entrepreneurs, and the types of support they require. This is followed by an examination of young entrepreneurs in New Zealand, a country in which government policy has recently been focused on the development of an innovative culture. The chapter concludes with a framework for understanding the needs of youth within the context of a policy-making setting. Within the chapter the term 'young' is used to refer broadly to those under 30 years, although some of the research discussed uses much narrower age bands (for example 15-24 years). Entrepreneurship is also used as a proxy in this instance for self-employment.

The Literature

Within the literature few researchers have focused on age as a predicating demographic characteristic of entrepreneurship. Even fewer have considered it as potentially influential in terms of entrepreneurial entry. Consequently there is minimal material dealing with the young as a separate group; this contrasts with the specific focus that has been directed at other groups such as women and ethnic minorities. What research has been done primarily focuses on the phenomenon of youth entrepreneurship (often in the context of analysing the labour market as a whole), barriers to start-up, and support measures (including programmes that seek to promote the concept of enterprise with school age students).

The Increase in Youth Entrepreneurship

An individual's entry into entrepreneurship is largely driven by freedom of choice[1] and as such individuals are not precluded from entry by gender, ethnicity, scholastic ability, socioeconomic background or age (Morris, 1998). However, despite the presence of diversity in the self-employed population this suggests, aggregated statistics often effectively disguise the presence of subsets, such as the young, within the total population of entrepreneurs (Staber and Bogenhold, 1993; Cameron and Massey, 1999).

A number of factors have contributed to the increasing presence of youth entrepreneurship throughout the world. These include the decline in traditional paths to employment, high global levels of youth unemployment, and the changing nature of work (Henderson and Robertson, 2000). In a substantial investigation into youth self-employment in an economically depressed region of England, MacDonald and Coffield (1990) described youth enterprise as part of a changing culture of work in late 20th century capitalist economies, which involves a move away from employment in large-scale manufacturing industries towards small flexible craft and service based firms.

Another perspective on youth entrepreneurship is offered by researchers who attempt to draw a parallel between an individual's age and the probability that he or she will enter entrepreneurship. Most agree that this likelihood increases with age (Cromie, 1987; Burrows and Curran, 1991; OECD, 1992; Blanchflower and Meyer, 1994; Carr, 1996; Shane, 1996; Blanchflower, 1998; Feldman and Bolino, 2000). This does not mean, however that alertness to business opportunities is relative to age or experience, rather that age leads to the accumulation of resources to enable the execution of entry activities.

Fain (1999) monitored American self-employment during the 1972-1979 period and noted that the average age of the self-employed had dropped, and that although self-employed individuals were still older than their traditionally employed counterparts the difference was less noticeable. Payne (1984), Blackburn and Curran (1993) and Birley and Westhead (1993) all suggested the likelihood of being self-employed increased through an individual's twenties. A different perspective is added by Kenyon and White's (1996) study. Here 40 per cent of respondents believed other people's perceptions about their age had no impact on their ability to run their business, 45 per cent believed there was some impact, and 15 per cent said it impacted on all aspects of their business.

Similarly, Lorrain and Raymond (1990), Birley and Westhead (1993) and Alsos and Kolvereid (1998) stressed that the suggestion that experienced, or older, founders are at an advantage to novice founders is overemphasized, and that empirical investigation has revealed no such positive relationship. Although previous experience is acknowledged as providing credibility in terms of securing finance, on the whole, novice business founders (which the majority of young entrepreneurs will be) have been found to go through the start-up phase in the same way as the more experienced individual (Alsos and Kolvereid, 1998). They also experience barriers to start-up in much the same way as other entrepreneurs.

Barriers to Start-up

One of the dominant facets of start-up that appears to significantly impact on young entrepreneurs is capital constraints (Blanchflower and Oswald, 1998). However, work by Evans and Leighton (1989) that observed that the likelihood of switching into self-employment was independent of age, stressed that all entrepreneurs face liquidity constraints (younger no more than older). The young may face difficulties in raising capital because their age makes it harder to establish credibility, but older entrepreneurs may face difficulties because of other responsibilities they already have, for example dependents and home ownership.

The message seems to be that while it is *age* itself that affects the young, it is *circumstances* that affect the older entrepreneur. The distinction points to the fact that individuals can modify their circumstances but not their age: Blanchflower and Oswald's (1998) assertion that capital constraints have a greater negative impact on the young seems plausible.

With regard to self-employment in Australia, Chapman *et al.* (1998) concurred with the international observations regarding age and asserted, along with Blanchflower and Meyer (1994), that the most probable explanation of the lack of youth participation in self-employment was related to the greater potential for liquidity constraints among the group. Aronson (1991, cited in Carr, 1996) also considered liquidity an issue, as well as age being a surrogate for work experience and the ability to establish a professional reputation. Lorrain *et al.* (1992) noted that young Canadian entrepreneurs (a sample of 606 <30 at start-up) were not that different from their older counterparts. This research concluded that if those studied did have work experience it was probably in the same industry in which they started their business, and had role models. They also noted that familial networks played a more significant role for the younger set. The role of family, in the context of youth entrepreneurship, is a common theme in the literature, however, increasingly countries are establishing specific measures – either for supporting young entrepreneurs (through business support schemes) or for encouraging the development of the notion of 'enterprise' (usually through educational programmes).

Support Initiatives

A not inconsiderable number of youth entrepreneurship initiatives have been devised in response to rising levels of youth unemployment (OECD, 2000, 2001). These types of initiatives represent the broad approach to encouraging youth enterprise, i.e. an approach where 'business start-ups' are not the desired primary outcome of an initiative, nor the measure for a programme's success. Rouse (1998) concludes that this type of programme assists young unemployed people to develop their ideas about themselves and work, consequently moving out of unemployment and into work, or self-employment.

The focus in this type of literature (towards a closer examination of the entrepreneur's environment) appears to confirm the view that entrepreneurship is not so much a finite behaviour as an ongoing process. As such, the sources of assistance within the environment, and the assistance an entrepreneur receives, are both crucial parts of that process. The focus also acknowledges that entrepreneurship can be a context-dependent process. Recognizing then that entrepreneurial potential can be a function of the environment, a focus on the sources of assistance available to the young entrepreneurs in their environment is relevant.

Environmental factors that stimulate entrepreneurship have been the focus of considerable research. Bruno and Tyebjee (1982) specifically identified the importance of having supporting services available. Krueger and Brazeal (1994) concurred, and underlined the importance of the *visibility* of such services, as well as their availability. Indeed perceptions of the level of support within the environment are considered to be as important as the actual availability of those services (Naffziger *et al.*, 1994). While the way in which young entrepreneurs perceive their environment has not been examined, it can be argued that if young entrepreneurs do not see evidence of support for their aspirations, then their perception of the feasibility of entrepreneurship entry will diminish (Learned, 1992, cited in Naffziger *et al.*, 1994).

The heterogeneous nature of entrepreneurs as a group implies the inherent difficulty in designing assistance programmes that are effective for all within the group (OECD, 1992). Therefore, broad (i.e. generic) policy solutions may be largely ineffective (Curran, 1993, cited in North *et al.*, 1997). Many countries appear to have recognized this with specific policy initiatives targeted at women and ethnic groups. In some countries youth are now also specifically targeted – either as entrepreneurs (i.e. business start-ups) or for their potential to establish a business. Clearly identifying a target population and accurately assessing the type of support they require would be critical. This type of targeting is what Stevenson and Lundström (2001) described as 'niche' entrepreneurship policy (targeted at specific groups of the population where opportunities to increase business ownership rates are deemed desirable). These niches can be devised on either demographic grounds, or the level of potential inherent in a group (for example youth). However, the OECD (2001) observed recently that no single policy model exists for the promotion of entrepreneurial activity among the young, and that as new programmes develop in different cultural and national settings, they tend to show more, rather than less variety in their content and delivery mechanisms.

According to a study of the policy environment in ten countries, (Stevenson and Lundström, 2001), a number of countries have targeted youth policies. These include Australia, Canada, Spain, Sweden, Taiwan and the United Kingdom. In Australia there is the national programme 'Enterprise Education in Schools' as well as the federal initiative 'Promoting Young Entrepreneurs'. There are also state initiatives. Support for this area is increasing, at least partly because an evaluation of the impact of enterprise education in Australia (2000) was favourable enough to result in the announcement of A$25million funding over four years. In Canada the focus on entrepreneurship in the youth population is part of the government's Youth Employment Strategy. In Spain high youth unemployment has seen the pursuit of youth entrepreneurship as a solution, with initiatives at a national and regional level. For example, the 'Young Enterprise Scheme' supports the creation and development of enterprises by people under 35, with help including subsidies and support. In Sweden, according to research published in 2001, 26 per cent of new business starters are under thirty. 'Open for Business' sites in four locations provide learning and advisory support for people under 30 who want to start their own business. Incubators for young entrepreneurs also exist in some Swedish cities. In Taiwan the National Youth Commission was established in 1966 to explore the best ways to encourage the development of young entrepreneurs. This led to the establishment of 'Youth Industrial Parks' and the 'Youth Enterprise Loan Scheme'. More recently (1998), the Commission established a network of business Start-Up Coordinators to strengthen local counseling support for young entrepreneurs. In the United Kingdom there are several national initiatives that aim to develop young entrepreneurs, including 'Shell Livewire' (a start-up support programme for those between 16 and 30) and the 'Prince's Youth Business Trust' (which helps unemployed and disadvantaged youth into self-employment by providing business advice, mentoring, loans and bursaries).

Italy is also a country that has made significant advances in terms of targeted assistance for young entrepreneurs. Regional development policy targeted young entrepreneurs with its 'Legge 44' (or Legge De Vito) policy that was initiated in 1986 (Arzeni, 1998). It also provided for the establishment of a new agency for youth entrepreneurship in Southern Italy. The programme is designed to sustain businesses set up by young people resident in Southern Italy. Typically, participants are 18-29 years of age and are assigned a 'tutor' for about 18 months (implying no less than 120-130 days of consulting assistance and training). The law offers other forms of assistance including financial and other incentives, technical assistance and basic and vocational training during the start-up phase. Follow-up studies have yielded encouraging results, finding that more than half the enterprises formed have survived longer than three years (OECD, 2000). However, an evaluation study that used a control group of non-subsidized enterprises found that the survival of the subsidized firms depends on the existence of the subsidies, rather than on the ability of the screener to select good potential firms (Battistin, Gavosto and Rettore, 1998 cited in OECD, 2000).

The linkages between entrepreneurs and the support measures they use is a crucial part of the complex set of interrelationships that make up the entrepreneurship process (Aldrich and Zimmer, 1986, cited in Stearns and Hills, 1996). The entrepreneur's ability to connect to appropriate assistance was seen by Cromie (1992) as more important that actually identifying their problem. This emphasis on the choice of assistance is also consistent with Alsos and Kolvereid's description of entrepreneurship as a 'chain of multiple options' (1998: 101). The choices entrepreneurs make about what assistance to use appears to have a direct bearing on their ability to function effectively. Young and Welsch (1983) suggested that the relationships between the entrepreneur and the information source have the potential to be modified by a number of variables not considered in their work; age could logically be one such variable.

In terms of accessing or initiating a 'support relationship', Chapman et al., (1998) noted the impact of the Internet in facilitating access to a greater range of assistance and information sources. Considering this in terms of Young and

Welsch's (1983) point regarding the influence of personal characteristics on assistance choices, the methods of access selected by the young self-employed may be influenced by the technological expertise they may possess. Such expertise may have also created parallel expectations regarding ease, speed, and efficiency of access.

The timing and duration of the support offered to young entrepreneurs also needs further investigation. A study of youth self-employment in an English area of virtual work collapse revealed that the young entrepreneurs felt they could access sufficient assistance during the start-up phase, but that ongoing support and help in developing their venture was lacking (MacDonald and Coffield, 1991). Kenyon and White (1996) made a similar point in an Australian context, describing how support programmes focus on establishing a business rather than providing continual support to a business in its formative stages. The OECD (2001) suggest that gaps in terms of ongoing assistance provision reflect the bias in some official programmes towards addressing short term labour policy issues. Moran and Sear (1999) argued that business support for young people needs to be more responsive, and occur past the period of start-up and initial survival. Tangible support mechanisms need to parallel the shift in policy that Fraser and Greene (2001) identified: namely that enterprise support policy has moved from a focus on enhancing the quantity of entrepreneurs in the 1980s, to attempts to improve the quality of businesses in the 1990s.

In Southern Italy, Capaldo (1997) observed that the creation of firms by young people with limited initial experience was on the increase. The study found that more investigation was needed into how the young facilitate contacts with external advisors, which again places emphasis on how the young self-employed establish assistance relationships. While acknowledging the exploratory nature of the work Capaldo (1997) asserted that the phenomenon was present in other areas of Italy and Europe, and stressed that it is the research attention that is recent, not the phenomenon of youth entrepreneurship itself.

The positive impact of networks and role models, as forms of assistance for entrepreneurs is well established in the literature (Shapero, 1984, cited in Naffziger *et al.*, 1994; Lorrain *et al.*, 1992; Schiller and Crewson, 1995; Matthews and Moser, 1996; Tay, 1996; Walstad and Kourilsky, 1998; Handy, 1999; Moran and Sear, 1999). The number of contacts available to an entrepreneur has a direct bearing on their ability to solve business problems according to Cromie (1992). Blackburn (1997) signalled a movement by young entrepreneurs away from 'mass counseling' and attendance on courses towards searching for specific advice on an ad-hoc basis when problems or particular thresholds in the development of the business occurred. Moran and Sear (1999) describe mechanisms for 'experience exchange networks' as essential for enabling young people to learn from each other.

The importance of family within an entrepreneur's informal networks was also noted, particularly for younger entrepreneurs (OECD, 1992; Rosa, 1993; Kenyon and White, 1996; North *et al.*, 1997; Moran and Sear, 1999). Payne (1984) suggested that this assistance would consist of advice, support, and direct financial assistance, whereas Moran and Sear (1999) argued that it would typically not involve direct financial help. However, Matthews and Moser (1996) suggested that role models from outside the family structure might be more critical. Field *et al.*, (1994) expanded on the importance of formal and informal networks, suggesting that an entrepreneur's ability to use them effectively was directly related to their personal characteristics. The characteristic of age could have an impact, however whether age inhibits or encourages networking is not clear. Age could potentially influence an individual's ability to both construct a network and use it effectively. In Australia, Kenyon and White (1996) found that networks for young self-employed were critical, but that their ability to establish such networks, formal or informal, was considered weak and diminished by their age. The availability of appropriate role models for the young self-employed as a group was also gauged as poor.

Typologies of Entrepreneurs

The literature also includes some attempts to develop a typology of young entrepreneurs. While these are often based on those that have been developed in relation to entrepreneurs in general, there are some where age as an individual characteristic is a factor.

Rouse (1998) characterized the start-up experience as an identity project and proposed worker identities (i.e. the artist's identity, the worker's identity). At the business level MacDonald and Coffield (1991) described the businesses of young entrepreneurs as either 'running', 'plodding' or 'falling'. Blackburn (1997) also devised 'types' of young entrepreneurs based on characteristics of the business. His categories were: 'high flyers' (displaying past growth and are actively seeking expansion), 'stable businesses' (experiencing some growth, but owner/managers are content with business size and are not seeking major expansion), 'transition businesses' (businesses that could expand or close in the near future, but are vulnerable to changes in market conditions and/or face resource constraints which render their future uncertain) and 'drifter businesses' (the firm's existence is precarious, and the owner has no real commitment to the business).

The Kauffman Center for Entrepreneurial Leadership (Slaughter, 1996) devised three categories of entrepreneurs: 'aspiring' (an individual who desires and plans to create new ventures who have not yet made the leap from employment), 'lifestyle' (the motivation for becoming self-employed is to earn an income for themselves and their family) and 'high growth' (those who enter self-employment with the intention of growing as large as possible as quickly as possible). Shutt *et al.* (2001) typology of successful young people in business consists of 'the graduates' (highly qualified in terms of educational background who possess an inclination towards entrepreneurialism), 'the replicators' (those who immediately prior to commencing self-employment, or some time before that, were employed in a related sector), 'the excluded' (these individuals come from a highly disadvantaged background) and 'the lifestylers' (those in the study who did not typically have common paths into self-employment, and perhaps could be described as opportunity driven).

The incomplete nature of the research on typologies serves to underline the situation that is true of the field of youth entrepreneurship as a whole. It is still relatively under-served in terms of empirical research and undeveloped in terms of theories. In the second half of the chapter the 'case of New Zealand' is used to provide the context for the framework for developing enterprise that is presented in the final section of the chapter.

The Case of New Zealand

In New Zealand there is currently high interest in the development of a 'culture of enterprise'. The media regularly reports on examples of entrepreneurial behaviour (generally in the context of successful business start-ups) and a number of government policies are designed to develop a strong small and medium enterprise (SME) sector and an entrepreneurial workforce.

This interest is relatively recent. When a Labour government was elected in 1984 it set about restructuring the economy in an effort to revitalize a state that had grown used to protectionism as the most appropriate ideology for a country of New Zealand's size. In a series of far-reaching policy decisions that fundamentally affected New Zealand society as well as the economy, a number of interventionist policies and programmes were dismantled. Non-core activities were sold off to the private sector, and redundancies climbed. While for some, redundancy offered the opportunity to invest in a new business, the ideological fervor for dismantling state agencies and leaving it 'to the market' to provide appropriate services, was also extended to the Small Business Agency. The SBA was disestablished in the mid 1980s, leaving a gap that was not wholly filled by the employment resource centres and enterprise agencies that became a common sight in most New Zealand towns.

This situation (where the New Zealand environment was characterized by few elements of support for the new or small business) continued until 1994 when the annual budget statement reintroduced small and medium enterprises as a particular target. The shift away from a traditional 'industry policy' to a policy that explicitly recognized the contributions of the SME sector was almost complete. It was some time before policy makers addressed the broader themes of 'enterprise', innovation, and entrepreneurial behaviour, but in 1999 an important policy statement was made.

After consulting with communities and business groups throughout the country, the Bright Future policy document was released (Ministry of Commerce, 1999). Focusing on five 'steps ahead' ('lifting our skills and our intellectual base; better focusing the Government's efforts in research and development; improving access to capital; getting rid of the red tape stifling innovation; promoting success, and supporting creative and innovative New Zealanders'), it presented quite a different set of objectives from that of the business development policy which existed at that time (which focused on SMEs). In fact, Bright Future is consistent with Stevenson and Lundström's (2001) definition of an *entrepreneurship* policy. The report by the Science and Innovation Advisory Council (SIAC, 2001) outlined a series of strategies for increasing innovative and entrepreneurial behaviours in New Zealand businesses. More recently, the Innovation Framework (SIAC, 2002) again emphasized the commitment of the government to policies and programmes that address the development of 'enterprise' in a broad sense (with an expectation that high levels of enterprise will have a positive impact on innovation and also lead to entrepreneurial behaviours – often defined as businesses start-ups).

However, despite these policy statements, little has yet been done to operationalize their objectives. Progress has been particularly slow in relation to the establishment of programmes that develop enterprise (and entrepreneurial behaviours) in youth. Stevenson and Lundström argue that an effective policy framework has to have a set of programmes that directly address a number of interrelated themes. These include: promoting entrepreneurship as a career objective; providing entrepreneurship education; reducing barriers to entrepreneurial behaviour; providing start-up finance; offering support to start-up businesses; and identifying appropriate target groups. If one compares the situation in New Zealand to these, one would have to conclude that while the policy framework does exist in New Zealand there is an absence of a set of programmes or measures that are integrated with each other.

This absence of specific measures that seek to develop enterprise and encourage entrepreneurial behaviours is even more obvious if one uses the framework developed by Reynolds *et al.* (1999) in one of their earlier reports on the Global Entrepreneurship Monitor (GEM) study. They recommend that governments focus on creating an entrepreneurial culture; develop specific policies and programmes that impact on entrepreneurship; target women and those in particular age brackets and increase the overall education level of the population.

While in New Zealand at present there are some moves that are consistent with these recommendations, and some positive indicators, such as the growth in opportunities for accessing entrepreneurship education (Cameron and Frost, 2001), there is no coordinated programme for integrating these measures. Given the anti-interventionist stance of both conservative (National) and Labour governments since 1984, this is not entirely surprising. The consequence of almost twenty years of government, where restructuring and privatization have been high on the agenda, is that the whole apparatus of support (long-running programmes, institutions and people whose career is business development) is missing. New Zealanders have also grown accustomed to a lack of government support, and a cultural identity is emerging where New Zealand is seen as the 'David who takes on Goliath' (as in the recent challenges to the USA's protectionist policies for their beef farmers). The popular myth that New Zealanders have of themselves, as being innovative and able to take on the world with a piece of 'number 8 fencing wire' is also alive and well.

This perception was underlined in 2001 with the release of the first GEM study to include New Zealand. The research identified the country as one of the world's top five most entrepreneurial countries: with New Zealand having the highest rate (15 per cent) of 'opportunity entrepreneurship' and only a moderate amount (2.8 per cent) of 'necessity entrepreneurship' (Frederick and Carswell, 2001). On a certain level it appears that New Zealanders are doing quite well without government help. But there is a strong argument that this is merely good luck and that if New Zealanders are to continue to be entrepreneurial and innovative, then more active means needs to be found to encourage this to occur. The country as a whole has to plan how to develop a 'stock' of future entrepreneurs, and make a commitment to addressing the challenges of ensuring that young people are assisted to become more enterprising. The most commonly accepted method for ensuring this occurs is through improving the number of programmes that provide enterprise education. Overseas research postulates that such experience in entrepreneurial activity through schools or other organizations does have an impact upon individual's entrepreneurship aspirations (Gibb, 1993; Kourilsky and Walstad, 1998; Lethbridge *et al.*, 2000).

One of the schemes that does exist is run by a private organization. The Enterprise New Zealand Trust (ENZT) provides young New Zealanders with exposure to enterprise and entrepreneurship through a range of schemes for students of different ages. The ENZT is part of what the OECD (2001) has described as a growing movement that challenges the orthodox view that enterprise creation is the domain of venture capitalists and seasoned risk-takers. As a charitable trust the ENZT provides numerous enterprise education courses to school students of varying ages. The ENZT's flagship programme is the Young Enterprise Scheme (YES). The YES was established in the early 1980s and is a programme that gives students the opportunity to run their own company within the school environment. At some schools the YES is run as an in-class activity, while in others it is an extracurricular option. YES teams are supported by a teacher, a regional coordinator from the ENZT, and generally a mentor sourced from the business community.

The Trust's programme may soon be joined by others. In April 2002 the Enterprise Culture and Skills Activities Fund was announced, with the objective of promoting attitudes, values and skills that support entrepreneurial activity and business success in New Zealand. Run by Industry New Zealand (the government agency charged with industry and regional development) the NZ$1.7 million fund has yet to announce the successful recipients of its first funding round. However, it is probably safe to say that the prospect of funding will have drawn some new organizations into the delivery of enterprise education. Whether this fund will be successful (in terms of the overall policy objectives) is not yet clear: the absence of any reliable information on enterprise, entrepreneurship and innovation in relation to youth, may mean that the first efforts offer more in the way of steep learning curves than results.

Young New Zealand Entrepreneurs

The problem is that too little is known about New Zealand youth and their attitudes to enterprise and entrepreneurship. Even if one accepts self-employment as a proxy for enterprising behaviour, it is not easy to identify the number of self-employed young people. Nor do the figures that are available necessarily reflect the reality of the situation. In a 1999 evaluation of BIZ (the government's flagship business development programme that offers a range of services to those already in business, including free training), a phone survey of 800 businesses which had BIZ input, asked respondents whether a woman was a key decision-maker in the business. An incredibly high 64 per cent answered yes (Andrews *et al.*, 2000) although only approximately 33 per cent of firms are usually regarded as being owned by women according to the annual business survey conducted by Statistics New Zealand. It is possible that the place of young people is similarly underestimated, and that the aggregated figures conceal their role in existing businesses, such as those owned by parents or other family members.

Although there is no clear statistical representation of the young's growing participation in self-employment in New Zealand (only 16.3 per cent of those self-employed were recorded as being in the 20-29 age bracket at the 1996 Census, according to Statistics New Zealand, 1998), there is sufficient anecdotal evidence to make it clear that young people are increasingly seeing self-employment as an option. It may also be related to changes in the labour market that have occurred as New Zealand has shifted from a manufacturing to a service based economy. This has resulted in a decline in traditional avenues of entry into the labour market for young people (Lane, 1999). Formerly able to enter the labour market as apprentices and in other trainee roles, many more are opting for further education instead. Some are opting for self-employment. The glimpse of New Zealand offered by the case below seems to be different from the one described by Haines in 1991, where young workers were unlikely to be self-employed. In New Zealand today, young people are aware of self-employment as an option, and those taking it up appear to be well informed of the places they can go to for advice and assistance.

Young Maori woman Christall Rata started her business in her early twenties. Aria Design manufactures, markets, and sells Hapene (an innovative product Christall created from flax). Christall is quick to acknowledge the support she has received from her family and the benefits of sharing workspace with another company run by young entrepreneurs. In terms of business assistance Christall is concerned that outsiders are unaware of the real needs of young business people and the different levels of support they often need: "People talk about 'production' – but it is really flax supplies, where to get them, how to get them, where to store them, how to transport ... people talked about how hard it must have been to find a patent attorney but really finding a good courier company was just as hard" (Lewis, 2002a, in Cameron and Massey, 2002: 135).

In research conducted by one of the authors (Lewis, 2000), nine young entrepreneurs described their 'business support networks'. While these networks included sources that could have been predicted according to the literature (e.g. family), there were a number of unexpected findings within the experiences captured. For example, while parents were often involved in the ventures, the typical power relationship expected within a 'family business' had been inverted. In a number of these cases the young person held the position of authority rather than the adult assuming that position upon entry to the venture.

The support networks described were predominantly informally based. While these informal connections were perceived as more useful than formal networks, they were also the most difficult to facilitate. In response to this difficulty many of the young entrepreneurs had elected to enact more formal memberships (of organizations such as the Chamber of Commerce) to compensate for the lack of opportunities to exchange information with other young entrepreneurs or access targeted assistance. Indeed while numerous professionals comprised part of the networks of young entrepreneurs, their involvement was described as a perceived necessity (in terms of compliance), rather than as an 'assistance choice'. Both these points indicate an inherent misalignment between what young entrepreneurs need and what is provided for them.

The respondents also described networks that were quite diverse. However, all were rich in terms of the expertise that was made available to the young entrepreneur. The difference in the networks described by individuals, indicates that youth in itself does not guarantee that the networks described by a group of young people will be no more similar than those described by any other groups of people of a similar age. However, where the individuals who made up this group were similar was in the needs that motivated them to seek assistance.

This research offers important insights into how assistance to the young can best be delivered, and points to an important gap in the New Zealand context: very little is known about how entrepreneurs and the owners and operators of businesses relate to the organizations that offer them assistance and support. Devlin (1977, 1984) is one of the few researchers who has attempted to assess the relationship of businesses to their support networks. His research revealed that owners at this time sought advice infrequently, and had poor knowledge and use of potential sources of advice. Palanysamy (1985) investigated the usefulness of assistance sources to businesses in the Palmerston North area, where sources of assistance were described as various but under-used, with the majority of respondents considering advisory services to be useful overall. The study also revealed that the perceived level of usefulness affected the frequency of use.

In one of the few studies to specifically identify the age of the respondents (20 per cent of the sample was 29 or younger), Gilbertson *et al.* (1995) conducted an investigation into the enabling and disabling factors affecting entrepreneurs in the

Wellington area. The interview-based study noted finance as the major impediment to venture creation, but did not specifically consider the potential links between age and the assistance source data obtained. Bollard (1988: 17) acknowledged the young as part of a rising breed of new entrepreneurs, stressing that it was 'extremely difficult for a young person to start a small business successfully without an industry background, business experience, or finance'. He argued that New Zealand's education system does not develop young business operators and the lack of young business operators (at this time) was due to this deficiency.

More recently, Cameron and Massey (1999) have described the nature of assistance available to the New Zealand SME sector in their work on the sector in New Zealand, including government and community assistance and the role of external advisors. The same authors have also compiled a directory of the assistance available to entrepreneurs. This book, published in conjunction with Industry New Zealand, is into its third edition (Massey and Cameron, 2002) and has evolved in response to the needs of New Zealand's entrepreneurs. It records a comprehensive conglomeration of assistance providers, as well as specific information regarding the target group of each advisory service.

A policy-maker's perspective is provided by Lane (1999), who identifies information gaps in New Zealand regarding youth enterprise and self-employment policy. These gaps were considered even more crucial given current economic changes, the decline in employment options for those under 25 and the consequent impact on the traditional transition from formal education to the labour market. Lane (1999) suggested that self-employment was an unrealistic option for the majority of youth as they lack both skills and capital.

Although this may be true, it is in some ways irrelevant. Despite the absence of statistics on youth entrepreneurship, one thing is clear: some young New Zealanders are entering self-employment and their needs have to be catered for if their experience is going to be satisfying (in whatever way this is defined by the individual involved). While generic assistance for young entrepreneurs is available in New Zealand through existing services such as BIZ, whether the available assistance matches the specific needs of young entrepreneurs is less clear. More importantly (given the commitment to youth and enterprise), will there be any more attention paid to the needs of this group in the future? As already shown by Lewis (2000), young New Zealanders are willing to use the services offered by support agencies. But in order to be successful, support agencies need to pay close attention to what these individuals are saying. They also need to be listening to the opinions of their *future* customers.

In a recent evaluation of the Young Enterprise Scheme (Lewis, 2002b), all of the respondents were asked to explain what they understood the word 'enterprising' to mean. The significance of the responses lay not in the descriptors themselves but in the perceptual gaps between adult and student stakeholder groups. While both groups tended to focus on the tangible outcomes (i.e. measurable behaviours) rather than intangible outcomes (i.e. beliefs), it was the students who took a 'broader' approach to defining 'being enterprising'. Given the current heightened awareness in New Zealand of the role of entrepreneurship and innovation, it is interesting to note that the descriptors most frequently used by students were 'being innovative' and 'turning an idea into a business' (demonstrating a perceived link between the concepts of innovation and enterprise). Both these descriptors ranked more highly than 'running your own business', indicating that students felt 'being enterprising' was far more diverse than just self-employment.

This research also indicates an inherent misalignment similar to that noted in the research on young entrepreneurs already in business (Lewis, 2000). Here the misalignment is between the 'clients' of enterprise education and the providers of the service. If New Zealand is to increase its 'stock' of entrepreneurs by improving the quality and reach of enterprise education and developing programmes that help create a culture of entrepreneurship), then these sorts of misalignment must be overcome and an agreed strategy for increasing enterprise and entrepreneurial skills must be acted upon. However, one of the barriers to this situation occurring is that there is no widely accepted framework to use to address this objective.

Conclusion

Internationally there is increased attention being paid to the potential for traditionally 'hard to reach groups' (such as women, ethnic minorities and young people) to contribute to a nation's economy. Arguing that this approach is in direct contrast to an orthodox view of new venture creation (i.e. an approach which is driven by venture capitalists and seasoned risk-takers), the OECD identifies three premises of what it describes as the 'anti-orthodox movement' in relation to young people and entrepreneurship. Firstly, it argues, younger people can indeed found new businesses and succeed. Secondly, this activity can contribute handsomely to economic dynamism and growth and thirdly, for these reasons the encouragement of youth entrepreneurship should have a place in national, regional and local labour market and education policies (OECD, 2001).

The same report goes on to recommend that: the field must become more institutionalized (i.e. with agencies that cooperate with each other in terms of scarce resources, best practice, funding); more programme evaluation is needed; more cooperative connections with others need to be established, and more networks and support groups are needed for young entrepreneurs. However, if the case of New Zealand is used as an example, this ideal situation will not occur until there is a greater understanding of the needs of this group.

As the New Zealand experience shows, it is clear that young people are engaging in entrepreneurial activities and are ready to consider self-employment as an option for the future. It is also clear that this intention is articulated, not out of necessity, but in response to the opportunities present. However, the level of activity within the 'group' is not being matched by a parallel emphasis on the provision of assistance that is specific rather than generic. The emphasis on fostering young entrepreneurs in New Zealand needs to move beyond assistance for business start-up to ongoing support that will enable the solidification and expansion of youth enterprise. The current emphasis fails to acknowledge that business start-up is not the only manifestation of youth entrepreneurship, or indeed entrepreneurship in general. Enterprising behaviour in young people can span multiple dimensions of citizenship; entrepreneurship is not confined only to the context of business. There can be, and are, social entrepreneurs, sporting entrepreneurs, technology entrepreneurs and design entrepreneurs in New Zealand. The lack of awareness of these differing dimensions indicates the need to establish a positive paradigm of successful experience through the media and other channels.

The dearth of instruments to facilitate youth entrepreneurship in New Zealand is in part due to this narrowness of perception regarding the nature of entrepreneurship, but also due to the lack of empirical knowledge of the young entrepreneur's experience and their assistance needs. As David Storey emphasized in his influential book on the small firm sector in the United Kingdom, understanding people who exhibit entrepreneurial behaviour (for example through the establishment of businesses) is critical if good policy is to be developed (Storey, 1994). In New Zealand (as in other counties), activities to address this knowledge gap are a necessary precursor to effective policy developments in the field. This would help prevent policy becoming fragmented and focused on addressing short-term rather than long-term youth employment issues. It would also ensure that 'young entrepreneurs' are viewed in their own right – with the potential for different behaviours from that of other entrepreneurs. The different typologies of entrepreneurs (as introduced in the first section of this chapter) are not all necessarily relevant to young people.

While these help us to understand variations that exist among entrepreneurs in general (including those who enter entrepreneurship for different reasons, who act in different ways and who run businesses of different sizes), they do not assist in improving the way in which support services are more effectively matched to the needs of young entrepreneurs.

It was in this context that the framework presented on the next page was developed: to contribute to the emerging field of enterprise education in New Zealand by providing a framework for those seeking to devise particular programmes for the various groups of young people with the potential to become engaged in enterprise and/or entrepreneurship.

The framework will assist those who are seeking to develop programmes for the young, who are currently trapped by the prevailing assumption that the models and methods of explaining entrepreneurship in general will not vary if applied to the young as a group. This assumption provides stakeholders who aim to support youth entrepreneurship with little guidance. Entrepreneurship and enterprise are both worthy objectives, and different programmes must be developed to acknowledge the different needs of those who have the potential to become more enterprising as well as those for whom entrepreneurship is the goal. If Alsos and

Figure 12.1   A Framework for Developing Enterprise

Readiness (level of skill and/or exposure to enterprise)

High

Group A: Ready	Group B: Ready & Able
Behaviour – be a successful employee or student.	Behaviour – be ready to be self-employed, or already be self-employed.
Characteristics – likely to have been exposed to enterprising role models and/or had an enterprise education experience.	Characteristics – likely to have self-employed parents, prior work experience and had an enterprise education experience.
Services – likely to require information and advice about business start up.	Services – likely to require complex information and business advice and/or mentoring, and the opportunity to network with other enterprising young people.
Group C: Pre-enterprising	**Group D: Interested**
Behaviour – be a successful employee or student.	Behaviour – interested in being self-employed or already be self-employed.
Characteristics – unlikely to have been exposed to enterprising role models and/or had an enterprise education experience.	Characteristics – likely to have self-employed parents, prior work experience and/or had an enterprise education experience. May already have a business idea.
Services – likely to require exposure to information about being enterprising and what it takes to start a business.	Services – likely to require skill development and information and advice about business start-up or management.

Low

Low   High

Intention (to be enterprising)

Kolvereid's (1998) argument that 'entrepreneurship can be conceived of as a chain of multiple options' is to be taken seriously, then those supporting the chain must pay attention to *every* link.

Note

1. An alternative view is presented by the most recent iteration of the GEM study (Reynolds *et al.*, 2001), which identifies both 'opportunity-based' entrepreneurship and 'necessity-based' entrepreneurship.

References

Alsos, G. and Kolvereid, L. (1998), 'The Business Gestation Process of Novice, Serial and Parallel Business Founders', *Entrepreneurship: Theory and Practice*, Vol. 22, pp. 101-114.

Andrews, G., Heinemann, A., Massey, C., Tweed, D., and Whyte, S. (2000), *Evaluation of the BIZ Programme*, BERL, Wellington.

Arzeni, S. (1998), 'Entrepreneurship and Job Creation', *OECD Observer*, February/March, pp. 18-20.

Birley, S. and Westhead, P. (1993), 'A Comparison of New Businesses Established by "Novice" and "Habitual" Founders in Great Britain', *International Small Business Journal*, Vol. 12, pp. 38-60.

Blackburn, R. (1997), *Enterprise Support for Young People: A Study of Young Business Owners*, Small Business Research Centre, Kingston University, Surrey.

Blackburn, R. and Curran, J. (1993), 'The Future of the Small Firm: Attitudes of Young People to Entrepreneurship', in R. Atkin, E. Chell, and C. Mason (eds), *New Directions in Small Business Research*, Avebury, Aldershot, pp. 1-17.

Blanchflower, D. (1998), *Self-employment in OECD Countries*, paper presented at the Canadian International Labour Network Conference, Burlington, Ontario, http://cerf.mcmaster.ca/papers/seconf/oecd.pdf (accessed September 7, 2000).

Blanchflower, D. and Meyer, B. (1994), 'A Longitudinal Analysis of the Young Self-Employed in Australia and the United States', *Small Business Economics*, Vol. 6, pp. 1-19.

Blanchflower, D. and Oswald, A. (1998), 'What Makes an Entrepreneur?', *Journal of Labour Economics*, Vol. 16, pp. 26-60.

Bollard, A. (1988), *Small Business in New Zealand*, Allen and Unwin/Port Nicholson Press, Wellington.

Bruno, A. and Tyebjee T. (1982), 'The Environment for Entrepreneurship', in C. Kent, D. Sexton and K. Vesper (eds), *Encyclopaedia of Entrepreneurship*, Prentice Hall, NJ, pp. 288-307.

Burrows, R. and Curran, J. (1991), 'Not Such a Small Business: Reflections on the Rhetoric, the Reality, and the Future of the Enterprise Culture', in M. Cross and G. Payne (eds), *Work and the Enterprise Culture*, Falmer Press, London, pp. 9-29.

Cameron, A. and Frost, A. (2001), 'Enterprise Education in New Zealand Tertiary Institutions: An Exploratory Survey', in *Creating Innovative Growth Companies: Proceedings of the 14th Annual Conference of the Small Enterprise Association of Australia and New Zealand*, NZ Centre for SME Research, Wellington, pp. 40-51.

Cameron, A. and Massey, C. (1999), *Small and Medium Sized Enterprises: A New Zealand Perspective*, Addison Longman Wesley, Auckland.

Capaldo, G. (1997), 'Entrepreneurship in Southern Italy: Empirical Evidence of Business Creation by Young Founders', *Journal of Small Business Management*, Vol. 35, pp. 86-92.

Carr, D. (1996), 'The Paths to Self-employment? Women's and Men's Self-employment in the United States 1980', *Work and Occupations*, Vol. 23, pp. 26-53.

Chapman, B. Gregory, B. and Klugman, J. (1998), *Self-employment in Australia: Description, Analysis and Policy Issues,* paper presented at the OECD Conference on Self-employment, Burlington, Canada, http://cerf/mcmaster.ca/papers/seconf/Australia. pdf (accessed September 7, 2000).

Cromie, S. (1987), 'The Attitudes of Aspiring Male and Female Entrepreneurs', in K. O'Neill, R. Bhambri, T. Faulkner, and T. Cannon (eds), *Small Business Development: Some Current Issues*, Avebury, Aldershot, pp. 25-41.

Cromie, S. (1992), 'The Problems Experienced by Young Firms', *International Small Business Journal*, Vol. 9, pp. 43-61.

Devlin, M. (1977), *Needs and Problems of Small Businesses: Some Research Findings*, Occasional Paper No.15, Massey University, Palmerston North.

Devlin, M. (1984), *The Status of Small Business Research in New Zealand*, Development Finance Corporation, Wellington.

Evans, D. and Leighton, L. (1989), 'Some Empirical Aspects of Entrepreneurship', *American Economic Review*, Vol. 79, pp. 519-535.

Fain, J. (1999), 'Ranking the Factors that Affect Occupational Outcomes', *Industrial Relations*, Vol. 38, pp. 92-105.

Feldman, D. and Bolino, M. (2000), 'Career Patterns of the Self-employed: Career Motivations and Career Outcomes', *Journal of Small Business Management*, Vol. 38, pp. 53-67.

Field, A., Goldfinch, S. and Perry M. (1994), *Promoting Small Business Networking: An Agency Comparison*, New Zealand Institute for Social Research and Development, Wellington.

Fraser, S. and Greene, F. (2001), 'Enterprise Regained? Enterprise Support and Self-employment', in *Proceedings of the 24th ISBA National Small Firms Policy and Research Conference*, ISBA, Leeds, pp. 507-530.

Frederick, H. and Carswell, P. (2001), *Global Entrepreneurship Monitor: New Zealand 2001*, New Zealand Centre for Innovation and Entrepreneurship, Auckland.

Gibb, A. (1993), 'The Enterprise Culture and Education and its Links with Small Business, Entrepreneurship and Wider Education Goals', *International Small Business Journal*, Vol. 11, pp. 1-34.

Gilbertson, D., Wright, H., Yska, G. and Gilbertson, D. (1995), *Kiwi Entrepreneurs: A Study*, Graduate School of Business and Management, Victoria University, Wellington.

Handy, C. (1999), *The New Alchemists*, Hutchinson, London.

Henderson, R. and Robertson, M. (2000), 'Who Wants to be an Entrepreneur? Young Adult Attitudes to Entrepreneurship as a Career', *Career Development International*, Vol. 5/6, pp. 279-287.

Kenyon, P. and White, S. (1996), *Young People and Self-employment in Australia*, National Clearinghouse, Hobart.

Kourilsky, M. and Walstad, W. (1998), 'Entrepreneurship and Female Youth: Knowledge, Attitudes, Gender Differences, and Educational Practices', *Journal of Business Venturing*, Vol. 13, pp. 77-88.

Krueger, N. Jr., and Brazeal, D. (1994), 'Entrepreneurial Potential and Potential Entrepreneurs', *Entrepreneurship: Theory and Practice*, Vol. 18, pp. 91-104.

Lane, R. (1999), *Youth Entrepreneurship and Self-employment Options*, Ministry of Youth Affairs, Wellington.

Lethbridge, S., Mortlock, M., Gibson-Sweet, M. and Ringwald, K. (2000), 'Realising the Potential of Young Women Entrepreneurs in South Wales', in *Proceedings of the 23rd*

ISBA National Small Firms Policy and Research Conference, Aberdeen, November 2000, pp. 649-663.

Lewis, K. (2000), *Assistance and the Young Self-employed in New Zealand*, unpublished research report, Massey University, Palmerston North.

Lewis, K. (2002a), 'Christall Rata: Aria Design', in A. Cameron and C. Massey (2002), *Entrepreneurs at Work: Successful New Zealand Business Ventures*, Pearson Education, Auckland, pp. 133-135.

Lewis, K. (2002b), *Building an Enterprising Generation: An Evaluation of the Young Enterprise Scheme*, unpublished Masters thesis, Massey University, Palmerston North.

Lorrain, J., Belley, A. and Dussault L. (1992), 'Young Entrepreneurs: Beliefs and Reality', in Babson College of Entrepreneurial Research Conference, *Frontiers of Entrepreneurial Research*, Babson College, Babson, MA, pp. 103-105.

Lorrain, J., and Raymond, L. (1990), 'Young Entrepreneurs: Beliefs and Reality', in Babson College of Entrepreneurial Research Conference, *Frontiers of Entrepreneurial Research*, Babson College, Babson, MA, pp. 221-222.

Lundström, A., and Stevenson, L. (2001), *Entrepreneurship Policy for the Future,* Swedish Foundation for Small Business Research, Sweden.

MacDonald, R. and Coffield F. (1991), *Risky Business? Youth and the Enterprise Culture,* Falmer Press, London.

Massey, C., and Cameron, A. (2002), *Small Business Assistance Directory: 2002*, Industry New Zealand, Wellington.

Matthews, C. and Moser, S. (1996), 'A Longitudinal Investigation of the Impact of Family Background and Gender on Interest in Small Firm Ownership', *Journal of Small Business Management*, Vol. 34, pp. 29-43.

Ministry of Commerce (1999), *Bright Future*, Ministry of Commerce, Wellington.

Moran, P. and Sear, L. (1999), 'Young People's Views of Business Support: The Case of PSYBT', *Journal of Small Business and Enterprise Development*, Vol. 6, pp. 166-177.

Morris, M. (1998), *Entrepreneurial Intensity: Sustainable Advantages for Individuals, Organisations and Societies,* Quorum Books, Westport, CT.

Naffziger, D., Hornsby, J. and Kuratko, D. (1994), 'A Proposed Research Model of Entrepreneurial Motivation', *Entrepreneurship: Theory and Practice*, Vol. 18, pp. 29-42.

North, J., Blackburn, R. and Curran, J. (1997), 'Reaching Small Business? Delivering Advice and Support to Small Businesses through Trade Bodies', in M. Ram, D. Deakins, and D. Smallbone (eds), *Small Firms: Enterprising Futures*, Paul Chapman, London, pp. 121-135.

OECD (1992), *Employment Outlook,* OECD, Paris.

OECD (2000), *Preparing Youth For the 21st Century: The Transition from Education to the Labour Market,* OECD, Paris.

OECD (2001), *Putting the Young in Business: Policy Challenges for Youth Entrepreneurship*, OECD, Paris.

Palanysamy, M. (1985), *The Range, Relevance and Perceived Effectiveness of the Sources of Information and Advice Available to Small Business*, Massey University, Palmerston North.

Payne, J. (1984), 'Young Self-employed Workers', *UK Employment Gazette*, November, pp. 497-503.

Reynolds, P., Camp, S., Bygrave, W., Autio, E. and Hay, M. (2001), *Global Entrepreneurship Monitor: 2001 Executive Report,* Babson College, Babson, MA.

Reynolds, P., Hay, M. and Camp, S. (1999), *Global Entrepreneurship Monitor: 1999 Executive Report*, Babson College, Kauffman Foundation and London Business School, Babson, MA.

Rosa, P. (1993), 'Family Background and Entrepreneurial Attitudes and Activity in British Graduates', in R. Atkin, E. Chell and C. Mason (eds), *New Directions in Small Business Research*, Avebury, Aldershot, pp. 36-54.

Rouse, J. (1998), *Business Start-Ups as 'Identity Projects': A Longitudinal and Qualitative Study of Youth Enterprise Scheme Participants*, paper presented at 21st ISBA National Conference, Durham, November.

Schiller, B. and Crewson P. (1995), *Entrepreneurial Origins: A Longitudinal Inquiry*, Capitol Research Inc, Washington D.C.

Science and Innovation Advisory Council (2001), *New Zealanders: Innovators to the World: Turning Great Ideas into Great Ventures*, SIAC, Wellington.

Science and Innovation Advisory Council (2002), *Final Report from the Science and Innovation Advisory Council*, SIAC, Wellington.

Shane, S. (1996), 'Explaining Variation in Rates of Entrepreneurship in the Unites States: 1899-1988', *Journal of Management*, Vol. 22, pp. 747-781.

Shutt, J., Sutherland, J. and Koutsoukus, S. (2001), 'Evaluating the Prince's Trust Young People's Business Start-up Programme 1994-1999: Learning Lessons', in *Exploring the Frontiers of Small Business: Proceedings of the 24th ISBA National Small Firms Policy and Research Conference*, Institute for Small Business Affairs, Leeds, England, pp. 385-412.

Slaughter, M. (1996), *Entrepreneurship: Economic Impact and Public Policy Implications: An Overview of the Field*, Kauffman Center for Entrepreneurial Leadership, Babson, MA.

Staber, U. and Bogenhold, D. (1993), 'Self-employment: A Study of Seventeen OECD Countries', *Industrial Relations Journal*, Vol. 24, pp. 126-137.

Stearns, T. M., and Hills, G. E. (1996), 'Entrepreneurship and New Firm Development: A Definitional Introduction', *Journal of Business Research*, Vol. 36, pp. 1-4.

Stevenson, L. and Lundström, A. (2001), *Patterns and Trends in Entrepreneurship/Sme Policy and Practice in Ten Economies*, Swedish Foundation for Small Business, Sweden.

Storey, D. (1994), *Understanding the Small Business Sector*, Routledge, London.

Tay, R. (1996), *Degree of Entrepreneurship: An Econometric Analysis Using the Ordinal Probit Model*, Lincoln University, Lincoln, New Zealand.

Walstad, W. and Kourilsky, M. (1998), Entrepreneurial Attitudes and Knowledge of Black Youth, *Entrepreneurshi:p Theory and Practice*, Vol. 23, pp. 5-18.

Young, E. and Welsch, H. (1983), 'Information Source Selection Patterns as Determined by Small Business Problems', *American Journal of Small Business*, Vol. 7, pp. 42-49.

Index

For Product Safety Concerns and Information please contact our EU
representative GPSR@taylorandfrancis.com Taylor & Francis Verlag GmbH,
Kaufingerstraße 24, 80331 München, Germany

Printed and bound by CPI Group (UK) Ltd, Croydon, CR0 4YY
08/05/2025
01864406-0004